A CHEERFUL NIHILISM

Richard Boyd Hauck

A CHEERFUL

NIHILISM

Confidence and "The Absurd" in

American Humorous Fiction

Indiana University Press

BLOOMINGTON / LONDON

8-1971
am. Let.

Library of Congress catalog card number: 79-135007
ISBN: 253-31345-7
Published in Canada by Fitzhenry & Whiteside Limited,
Don Mills, Ontario
Manufactured in the United States of America

ACKNOWLEDGMENT IS MADE to Random House, Inc., for permission to
quote from *Lion in the Garden,* edited by James B. Meriwether
and Michael Millgate, and from the following copyrighted works of
William Faulkner: *The Hamlet, The Town, The Mansion, As I
Lay Dying,* and "A Bear Hunt" from *Collected Stories of William Faulkner.*

PERMISSION TO QUOTE from *Faulkner in the University,*
edited by Frederick L. Gwynn and Joseph L. Blotner, was given
by the University Press of Virginia. Quotations from "Night-Sea Journey,"
Copyright © 1966 by John Barth (first published in *Esquire Magazine*),
in *Lost in the Funhouse,* from other stories in
Lost in the Funhouse by John Barth, and from *The Floating
Opera,* Copyright © 1956, 1967 by John Barth, *The End of the
Road,* Copyright © 1958, 1967 by John Barth, *The Sot-Weed
Factor,* Copyright © 1960 by John Barth, and *Giles Goat-Boy,*
Copyright © 1966 by John Barth, are reprinted by permission
of Doubleday & Company, Inc. Permission to quote from
John Enck, "John Barth: An Interview," *Wisconsin Studies
in Contemporary Literature,* VI, Winter-Spring, 1965,
© 1965 by the Regents of the University of Wisconsin,
pp. 3-14, was granted by the University of Wisconsin Press.

FOR MARGARET

whose first sentence

was "I know."

I be dog if hit don't look like sometimes
that when a fellow sets out to play a joke,
hit ain't another fellow he's playing that
joke on; hit's a kind of big power laying
still somewhere in the dark that he sets
out to prank with without knowing hit, and
hit all depends on whether that ere power
is in the notion to take a joke or not,
whether or not hit blows up right in his
face like this one did in mine.

V. K. RATLIFF

CONTENTS

(ix

Contents

Preface

"For God's sake, get you confidence."
THE CONFIDENCE-MAN

IT IS CONVENIENT to refer to Camus's essay on Sisyphus in any study of the absurd, but it is not necessary to do so to study American absurd humor. I refer to the essay because it concisely defines in modern terms the absurd sense as the sense of meaninglessness experienced by the man who has no abstract faith. Camus also offers absurd creation as the only tenable answer to this sense of meaninglessness. He does not say where a man gets the confidence to believe that his act of absurd creation does create meaning. The American authors studied here have made the problem of confidence and absurd creation their primary humorous subject. Their reaction to meaninglessness is both nihilistic and cheerful. The cheerfulness offsets but does not always cancel the nihilism. The logical response to nihilism is despair, but there is a power in the American character to organize, to build, to act, and to laugh in spite of a clear recognition that creation may mean nothing. What I am interested in is this ambivalent reaction to the discovery of the absurd as it is displayed by the major American writers of humorous fiction.

(x i

Before discussing the most outstanding American absurd fiction, I study the roots of the problem and two answers to it as expressed by the primary defender of Puritan faith, Jonathan Edwards, and the brightest light of the age of technology, Benjamin Franklin. The first major genre of absurd fiction was the product of the frontier humorists who preceded Melville and Twain; their work represents the early development of dark realistic humor in America. Herman Melville is the American author who defined confidence and the absurd most completely and accurately; therefore all of his novels are central to my concern. In his best books, Mark Twain achieved a perfect balance between nihilism and the kind of humor that elicits outright laughter. William Faulkner was a moralist and a humorist whose view grew from a perfectly lucid relativism. John Barth is the one modern American fiction writer (among many who are absurdists) who best displays a sense of the problem of confidence and the absurd and most consistently makes it the subject of his books as well as the source of their comic technique.

A novelist's decision to create laughter out of the absurdity of everything appears to me to be an astonishing phenomenon and an apparently arbitrary choice. A Camus elects seriousness; a Twain elects humor. It is possible that the choice depends on a man's health, his wife's temperament, or what he had for lunch. But as I read these books with my students, who are in a way the true authors of this book, I discovered that that laughter is often the automatic American response. These students have been quick to point out that Americans do not worry about meaning: we just go ahead and do things. We do worry about whether America is an idea or a place, but somehow we also recognize the interdependence of fact and idea, and as a result the idea maintains the fact and the fact maintains the idea. America is an absurd creation.

This book is not about existentialism in American fiction; it is about the humor of the absurd in American fiction. Corollary to that, it is a theory of grim humor in American fiction. The problems of the absurd in fiction are also slightly different from the problems of the theater of the absurd, in which severe distortions are used to throw light on unnoticed real absurdities.

Preface

The distortions are what make this theater startling. What is startling in absurd American fiction is that straight reality is presented as being absurdly humorous.

Clearly, humorous absurd fiction is not the exclusive property of Americans. *Don Quixote* and Gogol's *Dead Souls* are funny absurd books, and G. K. Chesterton's *The Man Who Was Thursday* is absolutely definitive. Nor is humor of the absurd confined to the literary arts; the cinema has become as appropriate a medium for it as fiction. I have hoped to demonstrate that the humor of the absurd is a major strain in American literature and is often directly linked to the question of faith or confidence.

During the time I wrote this book, Americans landed on the moon. The reasons for going there are exactly canceled by the reasons for not going. It costs a lot of money, and a lot of Americans have no money. On the other hand, if men do not reach out, why should men bother to make money, pay taxes, or even to eat? Thus our going or not going would be an arbitrary matter except that we genuinely want to go. When asked to defend the space program, those involved in it answer with the usual platitudes: "It's good for the country"; "The moon might be a new source of minerals"; "There are military advantages"; "It's good for our prestige abroad"; and "We've got to beat the Russians." What everyone seems reluctant to say is that we are going because it is beautiful to go and because we love doing absurd things. (Americans are commonly embarrassed to talk aesthetically.) What is most striking about moon exploration is that what men find there is as ambiguous as their reasons for going: a world divided perfectly into darkness and light, a landscape both awesomely sublime and grotesquely empty. At the end of every quest lies the universal duality.

My direct indebtedness to other scholars shows in the notes; wherever I discovered clues and insights in secondary materials, I cite the source. I have not preempted the bibliographer's task; the proper bibliography of humor, the absurd, and confidence would require volumes. The University of Washington Graduate School Research Fund provided considerable financial assistance during the writing and typing of the manuscript. Indispensable practical information was given freely by Professors Robert Heilman, Edward Bostetter, James Hall, Andrew Hilen, and Frederick Anderson, and by Mrs. Dorothee Bowie and Miss Dorothy Smiley. Two colleagues whose wisdom has, through dialogue, considerably enhanced this book are Professors Robert Hudspeth and Lawrence Swingle. Paul Zakaras helped discover the real Ben Franklin and Brent Logan the unreal John Barth. At the University of Illinois, John T. Flanagan directed me in considerable research into American humor, and D. Alexander Brown provided a prime example of cheerful nihilist. My students have contributed the unanswerable questions.

Special feelings are reserved for my parents, Helen Hauck and the late Roy Hauck, and my wife's parents, Jean and Vincent Malmstrom, all of whom graciously contributed that rare balance of financial and moral support. My wife, Dean, a scholar in her own right, works with me in partnership, but I am most grateful to her for the affirmation and cheerfulness which have banished nihilism from our house.

A CHEERFUL
NIHILISM

I

The American Sisyphus

"where the hell else but in America could you have a cheerful nihilism . . . ."

JOE MORGAN

I · SISYPHUS AND ABSURD CREATION

TO BE FULLY CONSCIOUS is to have a sense of the absurd. A sense of the absurd follows the recognition that the universe appears to be meaningless. Camus's characterization of the condemned King Sisyphus has provided modern readers with a working definition of the absurd sense and a partial vocabulary for a study of the absurd sense in fiction. The essay does not tell us anything explicit about humor— Camus believed the problem to be only serious—and it would be only pretense to claim that modern American novelists were influenced by it. (It is, in fact, more relevant to remember that Camus studied Melville.) But the myth encapsulates the problem precisely, and Camus elaborated upon it in clear terms. Sisyphus's story does have a well-known American counterpart: Melville's Enceladus (*Pierre*), a statue wrought in American soil by Nature's vigorous hand, an armless Titan forever defying the gods who mutilated and shamed him. Enceladus's defiance

(3

is absurd because he is totally powerless; nonetheless, it is his defiance. In the same way, Camus's Sisyphus is forever alienated from the gods and therefore forever conscious that his labor cannot have an abstract meaning or ultimate purpose. Sisyphus rolls his stone to the top of the slope in pure agony, knowing constantly that when the summit is reached, the rock will roll back to the plain once more. Paradoxically, the consciousness of the absurdity of this effort is what saves Sisyphus. When he descends to get behind the stone again, he is aware of the "whole extent of his wretched condition: it is what he thinks of during his descent. The lucidity that was to constitute his torture at the same time crowns his victory. There is no fate that cannot be surmounted by scorn."[1] The descent can, said Camus, take place in sorrow, or it can take place in joy. When Sisyphus so wills it, the rock is his own thing (a usage which in the modern English vernacular bears remarkable affinity to Camus's *Son rocher est sa chose*). The struggle itself, without the abstract goal of fulfillment, reward, or heaven, is enough to fill a man's heart: "One must imagine Sisyphus happy."[2]

The assignment of meaning to a struggle without intrinsic value is, in turn, no less absurd than the dilemma of meaninglessness itself, because the dilemma automatically cancels all possibilities for a nonabsurd solution. Commonly, *absurd* means something out of the ordinary, abnormal, impossible, and ludicrous. The term is used in this way by a man who assumes that there is a normal world from which absurd acts and events deviate. But another point of view—the awareness of total absurdity—sees everything as absurd. This all-encompassing view is paradoxical: it sees that there is no norm, that everything deviates from a man's inner sense of rightness or his suspicion that there should be ultimate meaning. The man who has a sense of the absurdity of everything can shift his viewpoint at any time to see the impossible as probable and the normal as abnormal.

A man's awareness of total absurdity depends upon the failure of his intellect to discover that rightness and meaning which his inner sense suspects. Camus's explanation of this is not essentially different from that of Biblical myth. In innocence, the world was explainable. Adam—as Milton's God insists in Book III of *Paradise Lost*—had no reason to doubt that there is an ultimate meaning. In Paradise, Adam would have gradually gained a broader and deeper understanding of that meaning as God revealed it to him. Through his right reason, he would have known the logic of the organization of things; through his unclouded sight, he would have seen the data of the world correctly. As he developed in God's grace, he would have shared in the knowledge of the universe's raison d'être. In the fallen world that Adam's children know, however, a man finds himself in one of two states: a seeming innocence which is really ignorance (to Milton one of the worst effects of the fall—a cloistered virtue that is no virtue), or a disturbing awareness characterized by a sense of displacement, an alienation from the source of organized explanation, a detachment from hope, and a lack of confidence that meaning exists at all. Camus described this feeling as an inner longing for happiness and reason. Man intends to find meaning, inwardly suspecting or hoping that meaning does exist, but is able to discover only nonmeaning.[3] This results in the sense of distance between what man desires and what man can have. The effect is the absurd point of view: "To an absurd mind reason is useless and there is nothing beyond reason."[4]

Terms like *absurd mind, absurd view,* and *absurd man* are inherently ambiguous, and their ambiguity recapitulates the dualities of the absurd condition. All men are absurd, although all are not aware of it. The man who perceives the absurdity of all things has both an absurd mind and a mind which perceives the absurd. A man must have the absurd view if he is to be capable of creating the paradoxical alternative to being destroyed by the sense of the absurd.

The sense of the absurd cannot be removed while consciousness is retained, but it does not have to remain an affliction. Camus called the one positive response *absurd creation.* This term is again ambiguous; it means that creation itself is absurd and that the process is one in which a creator creates absurdity. Camus meant both things by it. The same is true of the term *absurd creator:* a creator is absurd in the way any man is, and what he creates is absurd.[5] The absurd creator finds hope in the special faculty of man to "do his thing." Camus wrote, "The absurd man can only drain everything to the bitter end, and deplete himself. The absurd is his extreme tension, which he maintains constantly by solitary effort, for he knows that in that consciousness and in that day-to-day revolt he gives proof of his only truth, which is defiance."[6] This is the key. Out of defiance and determination comes the accomplishment of creating one's own meaning and one's own self. It is a process that allows a man to refuse to be defined by an easy acceptance of what the world mistakenly believes to be ultimate values. This creative process flourishes by exerting itself against the norm. Camus said: "War cannot be negated. One must live it or die of it. So it is with the absurd: it is a question of breathing with it, of recognizing its lessons and recovering their flesh. In this regard the absurd joy par excellence is creation. 'Art and nothing but art,' said Nietzche; 'we have art in order not to die of the truth.' "[7]

The absurd view is relativistic: it depends partly if not wholly on the assumption that any value can be judged arbitrary when seen from a point outside the framework which produced the value in the first place. It is not a view which discredits the power of moral frameworks, however. Camus declared that one does not need to walk on all fours or to maltreat one's mother simply to illustrate his relativism. Admittedly, Camus did not make clear exactly why this should be so, since an awareness of the absurd makes everything equal: "A sub-clerk in the post office is the equal of a conqueror if consciousness is common to them. All experiences are indifferent in this regard. There are some that do either a service or disservice to man." But the argument against moral nihilism can be sensed throughout *The Myth of Sisyphus*. Camus chose as examples of absurd creators men who "aim only to expend themselves. . . ."[8] They may be annihilators and seducers; he discusses as absurd creators conquerors and Don Juan. But common to all absurd creators is artistry, and artistry implies a construction of the self that recognizes the necessity for the preservation of a framework in which to work. The creator does not want to look ludicrous. He will exist partly because he creates himself for the world as well as for himself. By this reasoning, no book can actually be meaningless or nihilistic; an absurd book is a book about the absurd, and the book itself is the absurd creation that was the author's response to the sense of the absurd.

Of course this is heavily ironic. The perceiver of the absurd must assume a mask, playact, elude nothing, but be elusive. This is not mere hypocrisy. The artist in the absurd universe knows that "the work of art is then the sole chance of keeping his consciousness and of fixing its adventures. Creating is living doubly. . . . All try their hands at miming, at repeating, and at re-creating the reality that is theirs. We always end up by having the appearance of our truths. All existence for a man turned away from the eternal is but a vast mime under the mask of the absurd. Creation is the great mime." To play absurdity against absurdity, to test his strength against the eternal rock, is the artist's source of value and joy. "There is thus a metaphysical honor in enduring the world's absurdity. Conquest or play-acting, multiple loves, absurd revolt are tributes that man pays to his dignity in a campaign in which he is defeated in advance."9

What the man who is conscious of absurdity must do if he is not to commit suicide is to convince himself that an acceptance of what he must accept is an act of will. This decision is in itself absurd creation, for it has no rationale. The rational choices are suicide or unthinking resignation, since to be conscious is to risk being afflicted by the sense of meaninglessness, and unconsciousness is an escape from that sense. The third alternative, the act of choosing to accept the fate and to scorn the gods who assigned the fate, is a self-created—and self-creating—absurdity that negates the crippling effects of the original absurdity. Sisyphus can choose despair or happiness; he chooses to defy the Olympians who have negated the abstract meaning of his existence. By creating his own meaning, Sisyphus has accomplished the supreme act of artistry; he has made something out of nothing. In terms of logic, it is ludicrous to make something out of nothing. But Sisyphus's absurd act is life-affirming as well as ludicrous. It is, then, the highest kind of joke.

(7

The comic response to this high joke is what intrigues the writer and the reader of American stories of the absurd. Camus was serious; he did not promulgate a laughing Sisyphus (although he called him happy). The great American literary humorists—among them Franklin, Melville, Twain, Faulkner, and Barth—possess the absurd sense that Camus has described for the modern age. But they also invariably display a knowledge that the response to the absurd sense can be laughter as well as despair or defiance to the bitter end. To the American absurdist, laughter is the creative response, and despair, though logical, the purely nihilistic response. John Barth's Joe Morgan coins a contradiction in his phrase "a cheerful nihilism." He has unwittingly described the American absurdist's achievement. The American absurdist postulates nihilism cheerfully and his cheerfulness automatically counters his nihilism. He knows that laughter is purely arbitrary. Were he to invent a Sisyphus, he would give him a colossal and cosmic sense of humor.

2 · The Absurd View and American Humor

The absurd view with all its ironies lies at the center of the major questions that have always been posed by American writers. The assumption that men guided by faith can counter the absurdity of a fallen world was an assumption that permeated the motives for the Puritans' mission of founding the City of God on earth. Jonathan Edwards perceived that the finite universe is absurd and came to the solution of faith only after long periods of agony during which he saw the absurdity of trying to choose faith. Franklin's view is absurd and so is his highly imaginative solution, a confidence based on a whole-hearted and admittedly ironic faith in appearances. Melville's Confidence-Man has that Franklinian confidence but in his final honesty is not sure how confident he is of his confidence. Twain's heroes often see the absurd and manipulate it but are unable to overcome their own absurdity. Faulkner, the master of the relativistic view, creates characters who by ordinary standards would be categorized as mean or noble and erases moral distinctions between them by forcing his readers to suspend their values and assume drastic new viewpoints. Of the large number of postwar American writers who have displayed some sense of the absurd, John Barth stands out as the one who has not only created absurd characters but has manufactured his prime subject out of the fact that a thoughtful man can be enmeshed in endless circles of absurd perception which yields absurd creation which yields a renewed absurd perception which yields renewed absurd creation ad infinitum, ad absurdum.

A common pattern in American fiction is the exposure of an innocent hero to a series of events which awakens him to a sense of meaninglessness in nature and lack of moral direction in people. Camus described vividly a dilemma which is directly analogous to that of this Yankee, this New Man, this Fallen American Adam: "in a universe suddenly divested of illusions and lights, man feels an alien, a stranger. His exile is without remedy since he is deprived of the memory of a lost home or the hope of a promised land. This divorce between man and his life, the actor and his setting, is properly the feeling of absurdity."[10] The mythical American prototype of this stranger began in confidence by deliberately cutting his European ties and then became lost on his errand in the wilderness when the promised land changed from "here" to "somewhere." His story usually ends in one of two ways. He finds that all possible solutions to his discovery of absurdity are in turn absurd and thus there is nothing he can do, or he elects, Sisyphuslike, to re-create the absurd world into his own absurd forms.

Very little has yet been said about the combination of the absurd view and humor in American books. Camus did not equate the sense of the absurd with a sense of humor. Indeed, he said, "This is no subject for joking. That way of not taking the tragic seriously is not so grievous, but it helps to judge a man."[11] Camus would have been forced to "judge" much American humor, in that case, for it is common to find in American books the absurd view coinciding with a sense of the ludicrousness of everything. The American absurdist has consistently refused to take seriously the absurdity of everything without postulating at the same time that this absurdity is also hilarious. He retains the full ambivalence of his absurd discovery: his humor is serious and his seriousness is humorous. Although he well could be, he never is a tragedian; he nudges his reader towards laughter instead of despair. He takes a cosmic delight in manipulating the absurd; his affirmation arises from his ability to see and re-create the joke of life. His comedy is ambivalent, but it is comedy.

For the American absurdist, there are even two foci for ambivalent comedy in the very process of discovering the absurd. The first is reason itself, which Camus called "ridiculous" in the final analysis: "Cette raison si dérisoire, c'est elle qui m'oppose à toute la creation."[12] *Dérisoire* suggests "laughable," capable of being derided. The American absurdist knows that since acceptance of "truths"—even those called "self-evident" —is an arbitrary and absurd act of faith, it is ludicrous to make extravagant claims for the absoluteness of the end products of reasoning processes, which must necessarily begin from accepted "truths." The American absurdist is perfectly willing to let his comedy fall upon the empirical method, which begins with an axiom he believes to be questionable, that the universe is a collection of data and the direct experiential observation of that data is the same as the direct experiential observation of truth. But again, his position is ambivalent; in spite of his cynicism about reason and empiricism, he knows that his tradition sees these processes as its most creative tools and that his own exposure of the absurd makes use of them. Thus he laughs at reason and empiricism and depends upon them at the same time. He is the absurd man conscious of the full absurdity of his creation.

The second focus is not *dérisoire* to Camus but is certainly nothing if it is not high comic irony: the absurd solution Sisyphus makes, the choice to enjoy eternal rock-rolling, is itself laughable. The American absurdist draws characters deeply involved in such absurd creation. Some of them are not conscious of their paradox and are laughable for this reason; the laughter in this case may be the ordinary laughter which issues from the superior viewpoint of the witnesses. But the character with whom the American absurdist is most deeply involved is the character who is conscious of his own absurdity. The author, the character, and the reader then share the knowledge that absurd creation can be a matter of joy or despair and that the choice is a separate and arbitrary matter for each of the three. Laughter at this point has its nervous edge, its fear that it will not suffice.

Absurd fiction in America has characteristically been realistic, not, to borrow a modern term commonly used to describe it, antirealistic. Even contemporary American novelists who employ nightmarish settings and grotesque events—Hawkes, Vonnegut, Pynchon, Styron and Donleavy, for example—do not create distorted worlds as much as they perceive that the world is distorted. As far as the American absurdist is concerned, the question of realistic technique is irrelevant because if everything is absurd, distortion is impossible. The American absurdist does not feel the need to alter drastically what appears to be normalcy before he transforms it into fiction. His so-called distortion is superficial. He may employ an allegory which, though it has numerous facets, is simple in conception (*Giles Goat-Boy*) or a unique point of view (*Three Thousand Years Among the Microbes*), but the effect of such shifts is an easily perceived revelation of the absurdity of things as they really are. As Bruce Jay Friedman pointed out, one does not need to read modern fiction to find the grotesque, the startling, that which offends one's sense of harmony. "Distortion," "black humor," and "the absurd" can be found on the front page of any newspaper.[13]

A reader's first reaction to George W. Harris's Sut Lovingood is usually incredulity—no one could be that repulsive. But on second thought, lots of people are. No one may ever have thought it a great practical joke to have inadvertently contributed to a woman's death by causing a horse to carry off all her prize quilts, but people have done things equally implausible. Is Sut's trick any less absurd than that of the amateur quick-draw artist who shoots his wife while trying to outdraw a television cowboy? (Such an event makes the news at least once a year.) Sut is simply a metaphor for very real people, and the metaphor is not far removed from its parallel reality. Ken Kesey's Cuckoo's Nest is an asylum. To use an asylum as a metaphor for the world is not a new trick. The supposedly insane inmates are indistinguishable from people on the street. The most withdrawn character, the narrator himself, shares his point of view with the reader, thus making it vividly clear that his apparent insanity is relative. At first sight, Joseph Heller's Milo Minderbinder (*Catch-22*) is unbelievable; he is a manipulator of a fantastic black market and an entrepreneur who makes a contract with the Germans by which American pilots bomb an American airfield, killing and wounding hundreds. Milo is not judged a criminal because he did make a contract and because he shows a profit. What's good for Milo is good for America. Milo's contract is ludicrous—but so were those Japanese Zeroes made out of United States scrap metal. To make the point very broad, Milo's justification-by-contract is no more absurd than the justification-by-treaty of war.

The American absurdist is aware that the absurd sense is dangerous. When a man views morality relativistically, he is capable of justifying any behavior. For Camus, experience and compromise with fixed morality temper and shape absurd creation. The behavior of the absurd creator is not supposed to appear ludicrous; its function is to give the creator a way to live with absurd normalcy. But the American absurdist's interests are much broader. He loves to show that absurd creation can occur anywhere on the endless scale of relative values. He knows that the relativistic view levels all judgments. Faulkner made out of nasty little Mink Snopes a hero who, by the shape of his quest as well as by death, is equal to all the heroes of history. Melville's Confidence-Man is not a common crook but a poser of difficult metaphysical questions. The absurdist also likes to take a course of action which ought to spell trouble for his character and show it to have surprisingly beneficial results. Thus, after a series of lies which fail or even cause misery, Huck tells two men on the river that his "Pap" on the raft has smallpox. This time, his lie saves Jim. This pattern can be reversed; the absurdist may take what appears to be innocent creation and make it have disastrous results. Kittrell J. Warren's Billy Fishback invents a case of smallpox—just as Huck does—and his motives are harmless enough. But Billy's smallpox turns out to be real, and it kills him. By testing the limits of possible action, the American absurdist may seem to be postulating a crippling relativism. In reality, his achievement is positive; he expands the consciousness and increases the tolerance of his reader. He acts affirmatively by writing a funny book.

The humor in American absurd fiction is healthy, and it is sick. It may originate in corrective satire and then proclaim that there are no solutions to any problems at all. It relieves frustrations and frustrates. The American absurdist runs many risks; he knows that an act of absurd creation in the face of a dilemma creates new dilemmas. The ability to see the absurd in all situations may liberate a man from his environment, which would otherwise tailor his conscience and consciousness into conformity with itself. On the other hand, the ability to see all sides to every question may eliminate all motives for action, and a man may find himself in Jake Horner's corner. Barth's character (*End of the Road*) sees all sides so well that he is not able to assume a new, absurd position of his own; he becomes totally immobilized. Benjamin Franklin had a fine sense of the irony of his own solutions but transcended immobility by placing his confidence in his ability to create confidence. Like Franklin, Twain's Connecticut Yankee has confidence along with the absurd view, but his absurd creations take frightening turns. He can, coolly and without remorse, shoot a knight from the saddle and comment on the neatness of the bullet hole. He can machine-gun thousands and be impressed by the efficiency of his machines. Even Franklin—though the epitome of balance and common sense—was capable of cruelty to a wife who died in his absence without his knowing it or seeming to care too much about it. The awareness that the absurd view is both progressive and destructive, serious and hilarious, yet the only possible view, permeates American humor.

The American absurdist takes all of the paradoxes that follow the awakening to the absurdity of everything and plays upon them the way a mathematician plays upon his axioms. He stretches them, applies them in myriad ways, reexamines them, turns them back upon themselves to create paradox compounded by paradox. He plays risky games along the line between the terrible and the hilarious and calls them games without flinching. He ends his stories ambivalently. The reader can laugh if he chooses to do so. He laughs, to be sure, in the full awareness of the possibilities for terror in his laughter. The exploration of meaninglessness is a grim and hilarious game; the explorer wins when he can laugh and loses when he cannot. Whoever the explorer is—writer, reader, or character—he must, to be the American Sisyphus, have a colossal and cosmic sense of humor.

II

Faith and Confidence: American Solutions

"Preach! Write! Act! Do any thing,
save to lie down and die!"

HESTER PRYNNE

I · CONSCIOUS AND UNCONSCIOUS ABSURDITY

THE ABSURD VIEW was an integral part of the motivations behind the problematical questions raised by even those historical personages thought to be totally sober-minded (Jonathan Edwards) or committed exclusively to common sense (Benjamin Franklin). This is not to say that Edwards was a humorist or Ben Franklin incapable of corrective satire. It is to say that both men, familiar to American readers for other reasons, did possess a sense of the absurd and discovered or invented answers to the absurd which were not based in logic or empirical observation. Their solutions can be seen as absurd in turn, since they were created solutions, and it is apparent that both men were aware of the ironies involved in making their solutions.

(15

To illustrate this dilemma in its historical frame, it is illuminating to examine a work by a man whose philosophy was structured to reject the dilemma automatically. Michael Wigglesworth was such a man; he was an unambiguously serious poet who utilized arbitrary values while insisting that they were ultimate. His *The Day of Doom* (1662) is an especially appropriate item to contrast to Edwards's and Franklin's expressions of the absurd dilemma because it was presented as a serious, straightforward promulgation of Calvinistic theory and is read by today's skeptical relativist as the height of Puritan unreasonableness. It is a poem of the absurd written by a man unaware of its absurdity. The doctrine of the poem is actually reasonable as long as the framework of its logic is accepted without question. The poem is laughable to modern readers partly because they view it from a position outside its Calvinistic boundaries, their culture having, for the most part, rejected its assumptions long ago. It is also laughable to the reader who observes that Wigglesworth often violated the frame of his own logic and revealed its absurdity without realizing it. What is not laughable is the probability that most of Wigglesworth's Puritan audience found nothing at all humorous about the poem. The work is also appropriate because it precedes Edwards slightly in time and contains orthodox responses to doctrinal difficulties similar to the ones with which Edwards, not blessed by the ability to accept without question ambivalent points of dogma, constantly struggled.

In stanza 166 of Wigglesworth's poem the infants who died at birth and thus "never had or good or bad / effected pers'nally" come before the Final Judge, the Son of God.[1] The poet did not at this point, as he might have, introduce arguments about the effectiveness of infant baptism; he seemed here to accept as self-evident the principle that those who have not lived long enough to effect their redemption cannot be redeemed. His reasoning slips past the paradox which lies in the doctrine of election: God, who cannot be affected by causation and cannot be forced by any man's works to choose that man, can decide to save those who die at birth as well as those who live and perform deeds. Wigglesworth had, in fact, made just that point in stanza 25, where salvation is awarded to

> an Infant throng
> of Babes, for whom Christ dy'd;
> Whom for his own, by wayes unknown
> to men, he sanctify'd.

The infants' petition to the Judge is simple: why do we, who never had a chance either to sin or obey, stand condemned for Adam's sin?

> Not we, but he, ate of the Tree,
> whose fruit was interdicted:
> Yet on us all of his sad Fall,
> the punishment's inflicted.
>
> (stanza 168)

The answer to this is a masterpiece of rational manipulation, and Wigglesworth did not feel compelled to explain that his Judge only appears arbitrary because He is a finite character in a man-made poem. The answer was simply a matter of widely accepted doctrine. Adam's trespass was "both his and yours" because he was designed to be head of all mankind, a common root; if he had stood, then all would have remained in "Gods true love, never to move, / nor once awry to tread" (stanza 173). You infants, God says, would not be grieving if Adam had remained faithful and you had inherited his good automatically:

> Would you have griev'd to have receiv'd
> through *Adam* so much good,
> As had been your for evermore,
> if he at first had stood?
> Would you have said, we ne'r obey'd,
> nor did thy Laws regard;
> It ill befits with benefits,
> us, Lord, so to reward?
>
> (stanza 174)

Next the Judge says that if the children had been Adam, they would have made the same mistake:

> Had you been made in *Adam's* stead,
> you would like things have wrought,
> And so into the self-same wo,
> your selves and yours have brought.
>
> (stanza 176)

This condemnation by association is not totally illogical given the doctrinal assumptions Wigglesworth accepted. If the parental seed is depraved, there is no way, through inheritance or teaching, that anything but depravity can be passed on to the progeny. Furthermore, since death, according to Scripture, is the direct result of sin, then all men must be sinful since all men die. Sin is simultaneous with wrong reason, and men must have wrong reason (be depraved), or they would know how to overcome death by themselves. Thus the infants, who never had a chance to be redeemed by Christ, cannot logically share heaven with the purified saints. On the other hand, God is not influenced by what men think is logical, and, if He wishes, He may save some infants anyway. Wigglesworth's arguments automatically answer the objection that man must have been made fallible and thus God should be held responsible for defects in manufacture. He apparently accepted the explanation that if Adam had not been left free to fall or obey, no obedience could have occurred and no love for the Creator could have been shown. Wigglesworth's God, like Milton's, knows that in creating a mind capable of choosing to love its Creator, He creates a mind that can also not love its Creator. Again, the explanation does not cover what appear to be motivations and causes operating upon God. None of Wigglesworth's manipulations of logic and inference are original with him; they rest on Biblical statements (cited in marginalia to the poem) and well-known Calvinistic interpretations of them.

Wigglesworth next demolished the embarrassing problem (brought up by the infants earlier) of God's having saved the original sinner—Adam—while extending grace to no more than a few of the progeny who are afflicted with that original sinner's sin. The poet does not give Dante's argument that the Old Testament patriarchs are saved because they foreknew and believed in the coming salvation of Christ or because, in their post-fall state (Adam included), their heroic efforts to overcome sin prefigured Christ's victory. He could have done so; these arguments are suggested by one of the texts (Romans 5) upon which the argument he does use is based. Wigglesworth stresses instead an important Calvinistic interpretation of Romans 5: 15 on the matter of God's free gift and Romans

9: 15 which reads "For he saith to Moses, I will have mercy on whom I will have mercy, and I will have compassion on whom I will have compassion":

> I may deny you once to try,
>   or Grace to you to tender,
> Though he finds Grace before my face,
>   who was the chief offender:
> Else should my Grace cease to be Grace;
>   for it should not be free,
> If to release whom I should please,
>   I have no libertee.

(stanza 177)

Although loaded with potential for being taken as absurd, the doctrine of arbitrary election is (as are all the Puritan tenets of faith) strictly logical inasmuch as it derives directly from the basic assumptions that God is omnipotent and all-knowing, that His will rules the world, and that men cannot, in their fallibility, cause anything or understand the cause of anything. These assumptions are not absurd to the mind that reads Biblical text as Wigglesworth read it. The particular boundaries of his view must be what lie behind the inadvertent and hilarious shift that occurs in stanzas 180 and 181. The Judge does nothing less than concede the babies a point:

> Yet to compare your sin with their,
>   who liv'd a longer time,
> I do confess yours is much less,
>   though every sin's a crime.
>
> A crime it is, therefore in bliss
>   you may not hope to dwell;
> But unto you I shall allow
>   the easiest room in Hell.

But Wigglesworth saw nothing funny, nor did he see any mitigation of the perfection of the logic. In the last part of stanza 181, he closed the door on the matter, the point being orthodox, logical, and clear:

> The glorious King thus answering,
>   they cease, and plead no longer:
> Their Consciences must needs confess
>   his Reasons are the stronger.

Although Wigglesworth's commitment to the orthodox view prevented his having a sense of the absurdity of that view, he did have an awareness of the inadequacy of man's artistic or intellectual attempts to solve problems of ultimate meaning. In short, he knew that his logic was sound, but he also knew that it could only reflect God's knowledge and that ultimately no man could hope to understand more than an infinitesimal fragment of God's plan. There is thus a difficulty for the Puritan even when he accepts without question the structure of Puritan dogma; when he tries to explain God's high knowledge, he will inevitably look foolish. Wigglesworth began his poem with a warning:

> Reader, I am a fool,
> And have adventured
> To play the fool this once for Christ,
> The more his fame to spread.
> If this my foolishness
> Help thee to be more wise,
> I have attained what I seek,
> And what I onely prize.

Wigglesworth's "foolishness" did at least have a purpose; it was not absurd foolishness. It was designed to create in his readers an awareness that ultimate meaning belongs to God.

Although the orthodox Puritan view insists that God knows ultimate meaning and fallen men cannot hope to know this meaning, the Puritan was not without tools to help him know what God wanted him to know. He had Biblical text, God's direct revelation of truth to His prophets, and he had a human conscience, given by God to be an indicator of the difference between abstract right and abstract wrong. In addition, as a man who was willing to use the tools of his own age of reason, he had his intellectual faculties; logic and reason, rightly applied, demonstrated for him the concrete truth of Scripture and illustrated how the abstractions of his conscience could provide solutions to the material problems of the visible world. Theoretically, reason matches intuition in the elect; if one is in God's grace, then what one knows inwardly complements and supports what one observes. The unsaved man, if he is thoughtful, always sees the universe as absurd. The saved man may often see the universe as absurd because he is, after all, finite, but he has moments when a flood of faith reassures him that God is the ultimate meaning. He then transcends absurdity.

The pragmatic mind believes that the act of faith is absurd and still leaves a man in the absurd condition. The pragmatist elects to have confidence that the finite world is knowable and usable and says that the infinite simply cannot be his concern. Some pragmatists may believe that their confidence is empirically based, and these would take Puritan faith to be ludicrous. The thoughtful pragmatist, however, sees that his confidence in finity is arbitrary because finity means the death of confidence itself, the death of meaning-making, and the death of the man. He accepts his confidence as absurd and creates it anyway. He would cheerfully insist that Puritan faith was just as arbitrary and absurd as his pragmatic solution. The Puritan would agree that his faith was given arbitrarily by God but would insist that since God is ultimate meaning, faith is not absurd.

Jonathan Edwards was painfully aware that faith could appear to be absurd, and any moment in which he could escape that awareness was a moment of spiritual joy. Benjamin Franklin's view was that of the thoughtful pragmatist, and it produced the kind of irony and humor that characterizes the absurd sense re-creating itself without a transcendent faith in ultimate meaning. In the Puritan struggle to posit faith can be seen the seeds of the perplexities that delight the American absurdist. In the writings of Benjamin Franklin can be seen the first well-known and fully expressed American humor of the absurd.

2 · PURITAN PERPLEXITY IN ACTION

The Puritan attempt to solve the absurd condition of man by establishing God's city on earth failed, and the doctrine of faith has since been under continual fire. The Great Awakening of the 1730s and 1740s was an attempt to reestablish, not awaken for the first time, the spiritual concerns of a people. It occurred when the most influential thinkers in America were turning to science, to the eighteenth-century style of rationalism, towards the Enlightenment's stress on visible nature as the source of truth.[2] The internal debate in Puritanism about the efficacy of faith versus works was one of the most important factors contributing to a shift in values. Part of the Puritans' perplexity was the problem of discovering who had had experiences that determined whether he was elect and thus fit to join God's body of saints on earth, the church. Where towns had to be built in the woods, farms carved out of the hillsides, and Indians pacified, converted, or killed, works became something more than mere indicators that a man might be in grace. Calvinism had a vision of social good: God's saints, when discovered, would effect God's law in the government of His city. Even Cotton Mather, a defender of orthodoxy, came to the conclusion that a man's wealth and good works must be a sure sign of God's favor. A paradox did exist in the doctrine of faith, and it became manifest very rapidly in the life of New England congregations.

The growing confidence in the efficacy of works in the face of the difficulties of defending the arguments favoring election was neatly reflected by the general acceptance of Solomon Stoddard's revision of the purpose of communion in his interpretation of the Half-Way Covenant. While pastor at Northampton, Stoddard first compromised the doctrine of faith by implementing two communions, one for initiates and another for admitting converts to full membership. In 1677, he swept away all convention and admitted to communion any who would confess to the articles of faith.[3] It was to this revision of the earlier reservation of communion for the purified saints that Edwards (Stoddard's grandson) and the poet Edward Taylor were to react. To Taylor communion was the very act of uniting with the godhead through a Christ made real; the meaning of communion transcended corporeal understanding. To violate this process was to allow the limitations of the world to distort the whole result of faith. But by the time of Taylor's death, Stoddardism was almost universally accepted by New England congregations.[4]

Stoddard's motives and the success of his efforts are directly related to the American sense of the absurd. Stoddard simply pointed out that it was impossible for worldly tests such as a pro-

fession of faith and satisfactory responses to an examination by
the church to show anything about the relationship between the
individual soul and God. The result of Stoddard's success was
that it became possible in the New England churches for any
man to make a try for salvation by following the prescribed steps
without first knowing for sure if inner conversion had taken
place. A sense of loss and meaninglessness or a fear of damna-
tion could now be countered in the personal life by an act of
creation which would be absurd in actuality if it should turn out
to be nothing more than a worldly endeavor. It would now be
possible for an individual to imitate the behavior of one in
grace while no one, including the individual, had any tests for
knowing whether or not he really was saved.

Stoddard's compromise failed to resolve the basic paradox of
faith and emphasized in turn other dilemmas. If the proper de-
terminers of the community's social, political, and religious life
are the elect, and there are no absolute tests for election, what
defense does the community have against eccentric and dangerous decisions from those in power? If the individual's conscience
is the reliable source of moral truth, what happens when one
man's conscience dictates actions contrary to those dictated by
pastor or magistrate? These problems have survived, of course,
in spite of the elect's having been replaced by the elected. Hawthorne probed these paradoxes deeply in *The Scarlet Letter* and
his stories of Puritan character and history. He left his readers
without answers, though he shaped their sympathies towards his
individualists. Hester Prynne admonishes Dimmesdale to be true
to his own nature, to " 'Preach! Write! Act! Do any thing, save
to lie down and die!' " Hers is the creative mind that knows that
no one has " 'exhausted possibility in the failure of . . . one
trial.' "

One of the most startling historical manifestations of the
confusions and dilemmas wrought by this set of contradictions—
the Salem witch trials—has motivated a well-developed literature
in America. What is first fascinating to the literary mind about
the witch trials is the court's absurd standard of differentiation.
If a suspect confessed, he or she was pardoned. If he did not
confess, his refusal was taken as an indication of guilt. Secondly,
the entire case rested on the court's acceptance of what observa-

tion of facts (accusations matched by confessions) seemed to prove: that the afflicted accusers were truly blessed with the guiding light of the Lord. A further attraction of the event is the way in which jealous, vindictive, or self-interested individuals were able, by imitating goodness, to manipulate a court which operated on the assumption that a court can ultimately differentiate moral good and bad. Lastly, the resistance of those who were trying to follow the genuine dictates of their conscience provides the individual heroism and inner conflict required for literary tragedy. The American books which focus on the fascinating paradoxes of the trials include Longfellow's poetic dramas, *The New England Tragedies* (1868), John Neal's novel, *Rachel Dyer* (1828), Mary E. Wilkins Freeman's play, *Giles Corey, Yeoman* (1893), John William DeForest's novel, *Witching Times* (1857), James Kirke Paulding's novel, *The Puritan and His Daughter* (1849), and Arthur Miller's play, *The Crucible* (1953). The last is the definitive modern example.

Miller based his play on a careful examination of historical records and did a masterful job of capturing the dilemmas that plagued the participants. Abigail Williams, the chief accuser, is motivated by a number of dark forces, including her urgent sexual love for John Proctor, her intense contempt for most of the townspeople, and the feeling of power that her initial successes bring her. Once committed, she cannot stop. In a scene cut from the original stage play, Abigail claims that she has a God-given mission to purge the community of hypocrites.[5] It is helpful to know that Miller assigned her this motive, since it deepens our awareness that an insane woman in Salem could be convinced —and could convince others—that she was divinely inspired. But her character is more ambiguous without the scene; the audience then shares with the court the confusions scattered by a fiery psychotic masked as a prophet of God. The emphasis is thrown on the way the court and community (and the audience) can be deceived by the very framework they have constructed for the discovery of truth.

In his portrait of John Proctor, Miller displayed his tremendous respect for a man honest enough to face squarely the question of the reliability of conscience. Proctor is acutely aware of the paradoxes involved in trying to transform inner moral perceptions into actions. He is twice martyred: once, by others, because he stands on principle and once more, by himself, because he is convinced that for him to die for principle is absurd. When at last he goes to the gallows to preserve his name, Elizabeth says with bitter irony, "He have his goodness now." Miller's portrait of John Proctor is a neat condensation of the absurd position of the American hero whose tragedy is planted deep in Puritan perplexity.

3 · JONATHAN EDWARDS: THE SOLUTION OF BEING

In an early sermon, Jonathan Edwards displayed a relativistic view of the universe: "The beauty of trees, Plants, and flowers with which God has bespangled the face of the Earth is Delightsome, the beautiful frame of the body of Man, especially in its Perfection is Astonishing, the beauty of the moon and stars, is wonderfull, the beauty of highest heavens, is transcendent, the Excellency of angels and the saints in light, is very Glorious, but it is all Deformity, and Darkness in Comparison of the higher Glories and beauties of the Creator of all. . . ."[6] A finite viewer disposed to delight naturally views the finite world as beautiful. This world, from plant to angel, is, however, grotesque and deformed in comparison to the infinite beauty of God. When a man is infused with a conviction that there is an ultimate, then his awareness of this world is a sense of the absurd. Since a man is of the world, then, his finite human powers are absurd and incapable of knowing the ultimate, God. A sense of the world as absurd is transcended only when the ultimate comes to the man and God infuses the man's finiteness with faith, which is an assurance that God is ultimate meaning. Edwards spent a lifetime showing by logic and observation that logic and observation would be overwhelmed and left behind in the experience of knowing God as ultimate meaning.

Although Edwards tended to deprecate the visible world when he talked relativistically of the glories of God, it would be a mistake to see him as a mystic who rejected the world to reach the godhead. On the contrary, intellectual manipulation of physics and metaphysics could, in Edwards's view, provide some help in proving God's existence. Moreover, observation properly combined with reasoning could aid him in making metaphors which were at least suggestive of the feeling of the experience of knowing God. In "Of Insects," the young Edwards related that he was at first puzzled as to why "flying spiders" and other insects would spin out their threads or unfold their wings in the autumn and allow themselves to drift towards the sea and certain destruction. Another poetic mind might well have derived a negative reaction; the event could be seen as one more indication that nature is blind, mechanistic, and neutral. The insects and spiders that drift away go in comfortable ignorance to their deaths, and the fact that this makes room for new creatures and prevents the shore from being overrun cannot justify the event to the cynically-minded. But for Edwards, the event was not dire; he recorded his vision of the flights in words of simplicity and beauty and stressed the balance that is achieved in God's nature as a result. The most enlightening aspect of his record of the event is the style of part of the concluding paragraph:

> Therefore when the sun shines pretty warm they leave [the trees], and mount up in the air, and expand their wings to the sun, and flying for nothing but their own ease and comfort, they suffer themselves to go that way, that they find they can go with the greatest ease, and so where the wind pleases; and it being warmth they fly for, they find it cold and laborious flying against the wind. They therefore seem to use their wings, but just so much as to bear them up, and suffer them to go with the wind.[7]

Here his satisfaction, the joy created by witnessing the event, arises from the feeling of the appropriateness of the creatures' desire for warmth being combined with their propensity for allowing themselves to be carried by the wind. They extend their threads or wings and relax. Edwards was attracted to the spiders' and insects' unthinking acquiescence as a natural metaphor for man's surrender to faith in God as Justifier and Balancer.

A similar joy in acquiescence to spiritual feeling and the transcending of intellect is displayed in those intense passages in which Edwards tried directly to describe the experience of knowing God's rightness: "The sweetest joys and delights I have experienced, have not been those that have arisen from a hope of my own good estate; but in a direct view of the glorious things of the gospel. When I enjoy this sweetness, it seems to carry me above the thoughts of my own estate; it seems, at such times, a loss that I cannot bear, to take off my eye from the glorious, pleasant object I behold without me, to turn my eye in upon myself, and my own good estate." Or, to cite the most famous passage, which emphasizes Christ as the link between man's finity and God's infinity:

> Once, as I rode out into the woods for my health, in 1737, having alighted from my horse in a retired place, as my manner commonly has been, to walk for divine contemplation and prayer, I had a view, that for me was extraordinary, of the glory of the Son of God, as Mediator between God and man, and his wonderful, great, full, pure and sweet grace and love, and meek and gentle condescension. This grace that appeared so calm and sweet, appeared also great above the heavens. The person of Christ appeared ineffably excellent, with an excellency great enough to swallow up all thought and conception—which continued, as near as I can judge, about an hour; which kept me the greater part of the time, in a flood of tears, and weeping aloud. I felt an ardency of soul to be, what I know not otherwise how to express, emptied and annihilated; to lie in the dust, and to be full of Christ alone. . . .[8]

These are images of release, of giving up what he elsewhere called his striving, his hoping, his earnest quest for grace. Edwards had his fullest sense of being, of hope, and of certainty when he found himself free of the rational processes that led not to God but to blind corners and frustrations.

Edwards also knew that the experience of knowing God could not be verbalized. He found joy in discovering and re-creating the symbols of the visible world which suggested God's intentions, but he realized that worldly activity, even metaphor-making, could not go beyond the generation of tantalizing figures. These figures may teach a man about God, as he asserted so poetically in "The Images or Shadows of Divine Things," but the meaning of these figures is available only to the purified soul. The question of how to obtain a purified soul was unexaminable, and the unpurified soul would be misled by nature's metaphors. Edwards knew that man's common state of awareness was an absurd position from which any analysis—all understanding except inner illumination provided by God—would have to be absurd.

The very young Edwards was even capable of an antic attitude towards the application of materialistic analysis to matters of the supernatural. His response to the proposition that the soul is corporeal is quite funny:

> I am informed yᵗ you have advan[c]ed a notion yᵗ the Soul is matereal & keeps wᵗʰ yᵉ body till yᵉ resur[e]ction as I am a profes't Lover of Novelty you must allow me to be much entertain'd by this discovery . . . suffer my Curiosity a Littel further I wᵈ know yᵉ manner of yᵉ kingdom before I swear alegance 1ˢᵗ I wᵈ know whether this materiall Soul keeps wᵗʰ in yᵉ Coffin and if so whether it might not be convenient to build a repository for it in order to wᶜʰ I wᵈ know wᵗ Shape it is of whether round triangular or fore square or whethe is it a number of Long fine strings reaching from yᵉ head to yᵉ foot and whether it dus not Live a very discontented Life I am afraid when yᵉ Coffin Gives way yᵉ earth will fall in and Crush it but if it should Chuse to Live above Ground and hover about yᵉ grave how big is it . . . but soppose yᵉ Souls are not so big but yᵗ 10 or a dozen of you may be about one body whether yy will not Quarril for yᵉ highest place . . . .⁹

Edwards often employed such satire as a weapon against those who would reduce God's mysteries to formulae.

His arguments asserting the spiritual source of moral knowledge required that Edwards counter the Arminian notion that a free, self-determining will does exist as part of man's intellect and is capable of formulating by itself an independent moral act. To Edwards, the concept of "free" was total; that is, for an act to be free, it had to be without cause. For a choice to be free, it had to be without motive. Otherwise, the act or choice was determined by cause or motive, and thus not free. He insisted that, except when talking of God's acts, it was ludicrous to conceive of any event that was not caused or motivated. The Arminian position negated God since God was the cause of everything and the only thing in the universe not caused. If God could be caused or motivated, then He was not Prime Mover, and, by definition, God was the Prime Mover. To Edwards, the doctrine of free will left everything in chaotic meaninglessness:

"For by [Arminian] principles, the very notion of virtue or vice implies absurdity and contradiction. For it is absurd in itself, and contrary to common sense, to suppose a virtuous act of mind without any good intention or aim; and by [Arminian] principles, it is absurd to suppose a virtuous act with a good intention or aim; for to act for an end, is to act from a motive. So that if we rely on these principles, there can be no virtuous act with a good design and end; and 'tis self-evident, there can be none without: consequently there can be no virtuous act at all."[10] To say that the human mind can generate virtue is to say that there is no God and no existence, since the universe obviously exists as the result of a cause beyond the mind's comprehension. Existence has to be motivated; there has to be a Motivator.

This was the point Edwards had made earlier in the essay which has been titled "Of Being." Here Edwards tried to hypothesize a Perfect Nothing, testing the conception to see if it could be retained, and found that it would be impossible to demonstrate that Nothing existed. His first argument is a linguistic truism; to say "nothing exists" is to postulate existence automatically. Next, he said that it is obvious that if there were no matter, space would still exist. Edwards implied at this point that the existence of space is another proof of the existence of God: "all the space there is without yᵉ bounds of the Creation, all the Space there was before the Creation, is God himself. . . ." Another crucial argument has to do with the danger of forgetting that the positions of things are relative and that relation proves Being:

> A state of Absolute nothing is a state of Absolute Contradiction absolute nothing is the Aggregate of all the Absurd contradictions in the World, a state wherein there is neither body nor spirit, nor space neither empty space nor full space neither little nor Great, narrow nor broad neither infinitely Great space, nor finite space, nor a mathematical point neither Up nor Down neither north nor south (I dont mean as it is with Respect to the body of the earth or some other Great body but no Contrary Point, nor Positions nor Directions) no such thing as either here Or there or that way or only one way. . . .

It follows that there must be an ultimate relation, one that defines and gives stable meaning to the universe, and that is the relation between God and finity: "there is no such thing as nothing with Respect to Entity or being absolutely Considered we don't know what we say if we say we think it Possible in it self that there should not be Entity."[11] The recognition of relations showed Edwards that absolute value exists in God, whereas, for another mind, a relativistic view could lead to nihilism.

Edwards also believed that when the mind is confined to a worldly view, it makes absurd value judgments because it depends upon the very framework in which finite judgments are made. In *Freedom of the Will* he pointed out that the apparent nature of objects and the circumstances in which objects appeared were large factors in influencing choices. If two apparently equal objects are available and one is nearest, this relative position will determine the choice. What appears to the mind to be deformed or beautiful in an object tailors the way the mind sees the object; in turn, different objects in different circumstances elicit different responses from minds which have been programmed by different experiences. These processes apply equally to moral judgments, and men choose what appears to be future good according to their understanding of the appearances of a situation.

This is not to say that every man is at a loss to know absolutes; it is to say that the partial man—the man relying on what he thinks is his will—cannot make absolute value judgments. But a man can at least share a spiritual knowledge of absolutes when all of his faculties operate together—his vision and other senses, which restore to objects their attributes; his mind, which responds to, organizes, and retains experience; and above all his soul, by which he is fulfilled when through it he is in contact with the Meaning-Maker, God. When in contact with the Meaning-Maker, a man can be a meaning-perceiver. Man cannot generate meaning; God already has done so and is, in fact, meaning itself. God could have a separate existence of His own, but through creation infuses a corporeal universe with meaning, making Himself perceivable. Edwards was perhaps being heretical by implying that God's existence was a dependency of His being perceived, but as far as he was concerned, the argument led only to the axiom that finity has to have been conceived and thus finity proves God.

A man's soul is not activated unless God activates it. God's intermediary Christ made it possible for man's soul to be opened again after the Fall. That God should offer an alternative to the chaos a mind without God's light faces in a relativistic universe is proof that God is infinitely merciful. The Fall was not without its happy result; in rescuing man from his total alienation from meaning, God displays His glory. This Puritan version of the fortunate aspect of the Fall is demonstrated by Edwards in an essay whose title sums up the whole point, "God Glorified in Man's Redemption." Edwards felt his greatest heights of joy when he knew that everything was activated and controlled by God's mind and that God had made it possible for a man in grace to enjoy again the ability to feel, perceive, measure, and act upon a sense of meaning and value in the universe, even though he could never hope to achieve God's absolute knowledge.

Edwards saw the world as a place where man could find himself in an absurd position in which all he perceived was absurdity. Man could not choose to escape the dilemma of relativity. The light that resolves the dilemma is, as the famous Northampton sermon of 1734 calls it, "A Divine and Supernatural Light," and is given by God, not gained by some natural effort. Edwards solved for himself the problems faced by the holder of the absurd view: an act of faith in God as meaning closes the argument. But he could not solve the problem of how to obtain faith. His personal narratives show a man striving not to strive, a man finding sincerity and humility only when he exhausted his efforts to be sincere and humble, a man who loved logic, observation, and metaphor-making but knew that these worldly modes of discovery were left behind in the experience of faith. He believed that it was absurd to think that man could elect to know God. Moreover, God's grace itself must appear "mere and arbitrary" if it is to be totally free. In his moments of joy, Edwards saw that God's choice to give him grace was in itself a high absurdity, a matter of the truly free extension of mercy. When Edwards felt as if he had been chosen, he wept with joy at the sheer surprise of the totally unwarranted and unexpected act from God. That God should bother to choose a fallen man at all appears ludicrous to the saved man just as nonelection appears horrible to the damned. Faith was a way out of absurdity for Edwards, and he knew that the joy of salvation would always have to appear to be absurd from the finite point of view, which is confined to finite understanding.

Of Sarah Pierrepont, a young lady certainly in grace, Edwards observed: "She is of a wonderful sweetness, calmness and universal benevolence of mind; especially after this Great God has manifested himself to her mind. She will sometimes go about from place to place, singing sweetly; and seems to be always full of joy and pleasure; and no one knows for what."[12] Ultimate "joy and pleasure" are beyond the limits of analysis; one is saved when one is saved, and "no one knows for what."

4 · BENJAMIN FRANKLIN: MAN OF CONFIDENCE, CONFIDENCE MAN

To understand the awesome and even heroic comedy of the term "self-made man" as applied to Benjamin Franklin requires a recognition that, in full awareness of all the ironies involved, Franklin first invented his own confidence and then used his confidence to invent himself. His confidence was a creation of the absurd sort because it required leaving facts and logic behind. Edwards's God-given faith was a way to share in God's meaning; it was an essence-permeating feeling that occurred after all tangible proofs and evidences had been argued away. For Franklin, the supernatural was unknowable. Even his religious "faith" was a matter of simple reasoning and research: he subscribed to four or five tenets which appeared to be logical and which were common to all the world's religions. Beyond that, he was not particularly concerned with anything outside the natural world. He was sure that the essential man, if such a spiritual entity did exist, was not determinable. Franklin's confidence was based upon a belief that the world provided sufficient resources in knowledge and material to satisfy all human needs and that the individual mind, using the things of the world as its tools, could create its own sense of value and meaning out of what lay at hand. Franklin knew that his confidence in the natural was just as tenuous as faith in the supernatural. He knew that the world was a world of appearances. The miracle of his life is that he made his confidence work to

create a powerful reality that was his own. His sense of the irony
of having to create this reality out of appearances was deep, but
he carried this awareness lightly. Because Franklin did not take
the absurd game of manipulating appearances to be tragic, he
was able to equate his sense of irony with his sense of humor.
This combination made him the epitome of worldly success and
the first giant of American humor.

Curiously enough, Franklin's mode of thought and the Puritan's perplexity over the doctrine of works are directly linked.
We can believe him when he said that Cotton Mather's *Essays to
Do Good* (mentioned along with Defoe's *Essay on Projects*) gave
him "a Turn of Thinking" and influenced directly "the principal
future Events" of his life.[13] There he found Mather saying: "Sirs,
you cannot but acknowledge that it is the sovereign God who has
bestowed upon you the riches which distinguish you. A devil
himself, when he saw a rich man, could not but make this
acknowledgment to the God of heaven: 'Thou has blessed the
work of his hands, and his substance is increased in the land.' "
The rewards for virtue are measurable in this world as well as
in the next; those who have exercised virtue "have been rewarded
with remarkable success in their affairs, and increase of their
property. . . ." Mather's text was "Cast thy bread upon the
waters—thy grain into the moist ground—and thou shalt find it
after many days."[14] This kind of thinking, startling in contrast
to what seem to be the main spiritual concerns of Puritanism,
was perfectly amenable to Franklin. His point of view called for
an acceptance of the validity of materialistic tests for virtue in
place of abstract uncertainties.

"Imitate Jesus and Socrates." This was Franklin's admonition
to himself; it is the way to acquire humility. Where the Puritan
would have agonized over the possibility of acquiring humility,
recognizing that any attempt would be in itself an absurd act
of pride, Franklin solved the problem by exercising confidence
in himself, his intentions, and the reliability of appearances.
This confidence was the foundation of his famous list of thirteen
virtues, which was an orderly experiment designed to produce a
good man. His method for gaining one of the virtues, chastity, is
a perfect example of how Franklin's practical mind simply did
not fret over moral abstractions: "Rarely use Venery but for

Health or Offspring; Never to Dulness, Weakness, or the Injury of your own or another's Peace or Reputation."[15] The tests of "Reputation" and "another's Peace" imply that morality is relative but nonetheless one does well to remember that the individual is relativistically subject to a moral framework. Things are bad if society punishes a person for doing them. Another test for goodness is pleasure-pain: use venery to feel better, have children, but never to the point of fatigue. The method has its comic touch: what did he mean by "Rarely"? (D. H. Lawrence's famous vitriolic attack on Franklin and the methodology displayed in the thirteen virtues proved, for the most part, that D. H. Lawrence lacked a sense of humor.) As for humility, Franklin did not include it in his list at first because he did not feel the need; he was content with being correct in his beliefs and pronouncements and figured that he was justified in being insolent. But after his Quaker friend convinced him he needed humility, Franklin determined to cure himself of this "vice or folly" along with the others. "I cannot," he said, "boast of much Success in acquiring the *Reality* of this Virtue; but I had a good deal with regard to the *Appearance* of it." Where his friend had said that Franklin could use some humility because he lacked it as a virtue, Franklin saw that he could, indeed, *use* humility. It could be used to make him more persuasive in argument. The humble phrase, "it so appears to me at present," became far more effective in the elucidation and implementation of Franklinian opinions than egotistical openers such as his former favorites, "certainly" and "undoubtedly."[16]

In Franklin's view, there is nothing wrong with imitation. No man can be Jesus except Jesus; none can be Socrates but Socrates. A man can be only Jesuslike, or live in emulation of Socrates. Whereas the Puritan believed that a saved man's soul shared the essence of God through Christ, Franklin did not believe that a man could know any self beneath the apparent self. If a culture admires Christlike behavior or the Socratic method, then a man can advance himself by utilizing Christlike behavior and the Socratic method. Moreover, such imitation inevitably yields good if no one questions the process too closely. Franklin's story of the young Presbyterian minister Samuel Hemphill reflects this view precisely. This young cleric alienated part of his

conservative Philadelphia congregation by stressing the doctrine
of good works over faith. Thus, when it was learned that he had
cribbed some of his sermon material directly from various printed
sources, the conservatives were able to turn the church as a whole
against him. But Franklin retained his admiration for the
preacher: "I stuck by him however, as I rather approv'd his giving us good Sermons compos'd by others, than bad ones of his
own Manufacture; tho' the latter was the Practice of our common
Teachers."[17] Hemphill's plagiarism of better sermons than he
himself might write was hypocrisy, to be sure; Franklin here
condoned it and elsewhere practiced it. But Franklin judged this
kind of hypocrisy to be benevolent and common-sensible. The
plagiarism yielded the specific end of a good sermon, and he did
not feel that the means were harmful. The irony is, of course,
that the means got Hemphill into trouble in spite of the better
ends, but that was only because not everyone was as practical
about it as Franklin.

Other examples of this kind of manipulation abound in *The
Autobiography* and Franklin's other writings. If the Reverend
Mr. Charles Beatty felt bad because his prayer meetings were
virtually unattended by the soldiers, and punishment would
surely result for the troops if attendance did not go up, the
solution was obvious to Franklin's sharp mind: make the preacher
the dispenser of the daily rum ration and give it out after prayers. "Never," he could report, "were Prayers more generally and
punctually attended."[18] The Franklin who created that solution
understood how to use the absurd. The worst vice is not lying,
says Poor Richard; the worst is running into debt, for "Poverty
often deprives a Man of all Spirit and Virtue: *'Tis hard for an
empty Bag to stand upright.*" In short, wealth is not only a result
of virtuous effort but is a source of virtue; fulfill a man's needs
and he will have no motives for misdeeds. The implications of
the aphorism are serious and comic: a man is by nature empty,
and, if he is to have an upright identity, then he must be filled
with something. If that something will also give him a good
appearance in the world, so much the better.

What surprised Franklin about his imitation theory was that
imitation of virtue often yielded something close to true inner
virtue. If he imitated open-mindedness in conversation, he found

that he soon was open-minded. This, in turn, had direct rewards: his stock of knowledge increased and his methodology became more flexible. Imitation of humility puts pride to work; imitation of thrift, temperance, silence, and cleanliness yields thrift, temperance, silence, and cleanliness. As his business and political affairs expanded, Franklin found it easy to give up the conscious and deliberate exercise of his experiment in virtue, but he always carried his little book with him. One virtue, order, proved forever difficult to acquire, however. A constant effort was required to maintain its appearance, but the effort was rewarded to a degree: "I was by the Endeavour a better and a happier Man than I otherwise should have been, if I had not attempted it; As those who aim at perfect Writing by imitating the engraved Copies, tho' they never reach the wish'd for Excellence of those Copies, their Hand is mended by the Endeavour, and is tolerable while it continues fair and legible." With "the Blessing of God," Franklin's experiment in imitation, which he called his "little Artifice," provided him "the constant Felicity of his Life down to his 79th Year in which this is written."[19]

It is difficult to prove that Franklin recognized the irony of his position. If he did not recognize any irony, then he was a malignant, not a benevolent, hypocrite, manipulating appearances for self-gain, changing the rules as he went along, settling for the appearance of virtue instead of virtue, slyly altering his objectives to fit what he perceived to be the accomplishments for which his world would reward him. That is not an accurate view of Franklin, although his glib style and his easy assumption of different masks might leave the reader with that negative impression. His story of the loss of one of his sons to smallpox shows that he did know the irony of having to make choices in a world of deceptive, contradictory, or nondifferentiating appearances. He knew a man has to create decisions that are in actuality absurd because they cannot be based on a sure knowledge of ultimate ends. Franklin's solution was to base his decisions on the appearance of correctness and place his confidence in immediate results. He had to bear additional regret for the loss of his son because he did not pay strict attention to this rule. He had not inoculated the boy because the child was already weakened by an intestinal disorder. Inoculation itself killed many in

Franklin's day, so he thought that he was making a sensible decision. However, the boy caught smallpox and died. Afterwards, Franklin realized that he had not chosen the course of action which would have yielded the smallest amount of pain. He warned parents never to omit inoculation "on the Supposition that they should never forgive themselves if a Child died under it. . . ." His mistake showed, he said, "that the Regret may be the same either way, and that therefore the safer should be chosen."[20] If he had inoculated his son, he would at least have chosen a course of action which would have prevented the sin of omission. Had the inoculation killed the child, the implication is, Franklin would at least have chosen the "safer" course of action. The tragic irony of being unable to forecast all consequences is admittedly great; therefore the only defense against tragedy is to act upon available evidence and accept the results. Decisions should be designed to minimize regret in the event the outcome is fatal. The irony of acceptance is not so difficult to bear as the irony of error.

Franklin also knew that not all appearances were deceptive, dangerous, or tragic. He saw that evidence could be manipulated by logic and the irony of the result could be laughable. The famous codfish story is an irrefutable example of Franklin's sense of irony; in this case, it is also a prime example of his capacities for telling a funny story:

> I believe I have omitted mentioning that in my first Voyage from Boston, being becalm'd off Block Island, our People set about catching Cod and hawl'd up a great many. Hitherto I had stuck to my Resolution of not eating animal Food; and on this Occasion, I consider'd with my Master Tryon, the taking every Fish as a kind of unprovok'd Murder, since none of them had or ever could do us any Injury that might justify the Slaughter. All this seem'd very reasonable. But I had formerly been a great Lover of Fish, and when this came hot out of the Frying Pan, it smelt admirably well. I balanc'd some time between Principle and Inclination: till I recollected, that when the Fish were opened, I saw smaller Fish taken out of their Stomachs: Then thought I, if you eat one another, I don't see why we mayn't eat you. So I din'd upon Cod very heartily and continu'd to eat with other People, returning only now and than [*sic*] occasionally to a vegetable Diet. So convenient a thing it is

(3 7

to be a *reasonable Creature*, since it enables one to find or make a Reason for every thing one has a mind to do.[21]

Franklin here provided a method for solving all problems of value judgment. Nothing has any essential meaning; it has meaning according to the perceptions and manipulations of a creative mind. The relative goodness of things is a function of a man's ability to find or make them beneficial to himself. The creation of values such as "I don't see why we mayn't eat you" depends on an unwavering belief that no abstract force of the kind which insists on absolutes such as vegetarianism can exist. Moreover, the apparently concrete laws of nature are actually ambiguous; one observation dictates vegetarianism while another condones the eating of flesh. An appetizing odor solves the dilemma. Franklin's readiness to change his evaluative point of view to suit situations such as the smallpox question, the codfish incident, and the humility paradox indicates that he did have a firm confidence that values exist only within specific material frameworks and are a product of the mind exercising its own awareness of its relation to its environment. He knew that this confidence does not solve the irony of man's dependency upon appearances, but this confidence did allow him to win in the game of understanding and using those appearances.

Franklin's ability to manipulate and create appearances extended to the very conception and execution of his autobiography. *The Autobiography* was actually the second creation of Franklin by Franklin; the first had been the man himself. He was, he said, the youngest son of the youngest son for five generations back. He had, then, no inheritance to define him with a family name. He cut all family ties and set out not just to make his fortune but to create a self. If the world rewarded rationalism, he would be a rationalist; if money gave a man control over circumstances, he would be wealthy. When the world in the person of Benjamin Vaughan came to him and asked him to relate the rules by which he became scientist, technician, diplomat, humorist, statesman—the best-known figure of his own day—he gave the world Benjamin Franklin in yet another re-creation. His autobiography was an exercise in image-making; he emphasized what had succeeded and played down what had failed. He gave the world some rules but told us that he never allowed them to interfere with the flexibility needed to meet the demands of new situations. Writing *The Autobiography* was a literary recapitulation of what Franklin had always done and was to continue to do; it was one phase of the invention and presentation of Benjamin Franklin. He saw that this act of creation was ironic and sometimes laughable, but his rationale was to be rational—where one perceives absurdity, one would do well to create meaning and smile at the absurdity of creating meaning.

III

From the Absurd Frontier

"Dad cudent see the funny part
frum whar he wer . . . ."
　　　　Sᴜᴛ Lᴏᴠɪɴɢᴏᴏᴅ

I · Tʜᴇ Nᴀᴛɪᴠᴇ Aᴍᴇʀɪᴄᴀɴ Aʙsᴜʀᴅɪsᴛ

THE ABSURD VIEW is the foundation of the comic fiction associated with the period of America's expansion into the frontier. These stories—rough, gory, tall, and grim—reached a large audience during their best years, approximately 1831 (the date of the founding of the New York *Spirit of the Times*) to 1861 (the beginning of the Civil War, the end of the extensive contribution of southerners to northern journals, and the death of the *Spirit*). They appeared in newspapers, sporting journals, and literary magazines and were collected and distributed in highly popular comic anthologies. They came from the pens of writers who lived wherever men confronted the rigors of the wilderness: the old South, Southwest, and far West primarily, but also the woods and wild seashores of the North and

East. The techniques and sometimes the subjects of these stories were readily absorbed into the even taller and more grimly humorous stories of Melville and Twain. In any story of this genre the author revealed his awareness of the absurd view in one of a number of ways. He may have assumed the persona of a storyteller in order to examine directly the dilemmas of men, or (as discussed in the next two sections) he may have drawn a major character who is also an absurdist—the teller of a tall tale or a confidence man who manipulates appearances. These characters may or may not be aware of the absurdity of their creations.

The absurdist in his role as storyteller told comic yarns about hunts, fights, fishing incidents, frolics, courtings, weddings, political events, sermons, camp meetings, practical jokes, games, drinking bouts, and the actions of various backwoods stereotypes and eccentric "originals."[1] These ludicrous stories were close imitations of the real events of frontier and rural life. As a realist in an age of romantic fiction, the native absurdist writing for publication almost always assumed a pseudonym as part of his storytelling mask. (Papers such as the *Spirit,* the St. Louis *Reveille,* and the New Orleans *Picayune* and *Delta* published stories by literally hundreds of pseudonymous writers, most of whom remain unidentified to this day.) The use of a pseudonym was in part a simple imitation of one of the techniques of the eighteenth-century essayists and contemporary British humorists that the authors in this genre knew so well. But more importantly, the writer of comic yarns probably did not want his friends to know that he was afflicted by any lack of seriousness. His stories were always rough or racy, and he was probably a professional man with a genteel reputation to protect—a doctor, lawyer, politician, artist, planter, army officer, actor, or businessman. It may be that he did not want to be identified with the comic characters in his yarns, or perhaps he did not want it known that he was so closely associated with the vernacular-speaking, tobacco-chewing yarnspinners from whom he borrowed some of his best stories. In any case, the assumption of a pseudonym gave him a chance to tell the ludicrous truth about a frontier or rural way of life that had been amply sentimentalized by a host of less critical observers.[2]

Because most of the native absurdists were consciously creating antisentimental stories, their work is often associated with the development of American realism before Mark Twain. All the characteristic techniques of realism are there: the close attention to details unique to the time, place, and people involved in the story, the antiromantic urge to reveal the seamy side of life, the willingness to include raw and vulgar characters, and the careful attempt to re-create dialect. Naturally, the feeling that these stories are realistic is modified by the fact that their writers often stretched and distorted the factual, especially in those yarns intended to be tall tales. But what is going on in these yarns is not so much a matter of exaggeration as it is a recording of the ways in which normal events can be seen as exaggerated from a detached point of view or the ways in which normal people can behave absurdly under the pressures of a strange environment. The humor and the seriousness of these yarns are often based on a recognition that a perceiver can encounter appearances in such a way that real things and mythical things become indistinguishable. The West was tall, and so was the world, when the view was framed in just the right way. The battles in the many southwestern and southern fight stories seem incredible, hilarious, and horrible—all at once—but the absurdist author saw real fights in town on Saturday night that were precisely incredible, hilarious, and horrible. And, in the new country, unbelievable discoveries are constantly being made. What was the reader of the *Spirit of the Times* to do when in one issue he could read about fish-eating Greenland hogs, or the fantastic Gyascutus (a horn-shelled tortoiselike bear-sized animal with great claws and teeth), or the tricky Prock (that famous horse with the short uphill and long downhill legs which enable him to stand upright on a steep mountain slope), and in the next learn about the Ornithorhynchus, which boasts webbed claws, cheek pouches, fur, a duck's beak, a beaver's tail, and a voice like a puppy's?[3] How was he to know that the platypus was real? That *Spirit* writers should make reporting and lying absolutely indistinguishable in style was characteristic of the kind of taletelling that the western traveler knew best. Surely the twin sources of the humorous response from liar and listener alike are the readiness of both to accept a world where myth and reality fall together and the eagerness of both to examine that ambiguous world from the view-point of detached observers who relish the absurd.

The native absurdist characteristically saw the world not only as ambivalently real and mythical but also as both comic and horrible; in other words, he grasped the basic ambivalence of man's condition itself. There were, interestingly enough, some immediate physical motivations behind his selection of the grimly comic mode. As Bernard DeVoto pointed out, frontier and rural settlers were always afflicted by epidemics; the average "well" person living that supposedly idyllic pastoral life must have run a constant fever of one degree.[4] The populace of any newly opened area included numerous embittered men and women who had left the relative comfort of eastern cities or old family farms in Europe to pursue what turned out to be an illusion of easy wealth. The dangers and privations of life at the edge of the wilderness were the most immediate reality for everyone. Why, then, did the literary yarnspinner bother with comedy at all? Possibly the comic turn was always there because this elicited saving laughter, a response which overcame the horror. An even stronger motivation lies in the character of the frontier literary artist himself. The yarnspinner who wrote for the papers did not write stories for a living; actually, he was seldom paid. But he was by nature a creative man, trying daily by his profession—medicine, the law, business—to impose order on chaos. The writing of comic stories was an incidental product of this creativity. Things do go horribly wrong in his stories, but the horror is always balanced by comedy. It is as if the balancing of a sense of horror by a sense of humor was required to maintain a sense of values in an environment that was full of annihilative energies.

The native absurdist knew that laughter could in itself appear grotesque when a situation seemed only serious. Hawthorne's "My Kinsman, Major Molineux"—a story well within the native genre—has grotesque laughter as its subject. To save himself, Robin joins with the crowd in laughing at his kinsman. Robin's laughter is in one way creative; it has the power to save him from the absurd situation and to help him overcome his own absurdity. But in another way his laughter is not possible unless he suppresses his own sense of the wrongness of his kinsman's treatment. Hawthorne was postulating a very bleak possibility: when laughter saves, it may be at the expense of moral feeling. George Washington Harris's Sut Lovingood stories are not exactly comic in any ordinary way; one must agree with Edmund Wilson that Sut is a sadist as well as a rogue hero.[5] Sut's view of the absurdity of everything lets him excuse himself from all responsibility. Sut's laughter at his own vicious antics is grotesque. We do not laugh at them at all, unless we laugh in derision of Sut himself. The humor of the native absurdist ventures into very dangerous paradoxes indeed.

A native absurdist who thrived upon the absurd ambivalence of the comic-horrible life was Henry Clay Lewis ("Madison Tensas, the Louisiana Swamp Doctor"). Lewis wrote a number of stories during his brief career as doctor and contributor to the *Spirit of the Times* that would delight any modern connoisseur of grim humor. His life itself was a harrowing yarn. On the day he died, at the age of twenty-five, he was in the midst of an exhausting effort to look after scores of patients stricken during an epidemic of cholera in northeast Louisiana. The bayous were swollen by water from the flooding Mississippi; every road was a rut in the mud. The doctor was nearly blind with fatigue, but he had continued personally to care for his patients, all of whom lived miles apart. Plunging into a dark, swirling stream, the doctor and his horse were toppled; Lewis drowned in the mire.[6]

In addition to the horrors of the geography which eventually led to his death, Lewis encountered all the jolly and gory facets of the education and practice enjoyed by most physicians of the early nineteenth century. His stories reflect those encounters directly; they are populated by needlessly suffering innocents, cadavers, and disease-stricken cripples. (Perhaps one should say Lewis's stories are not populated but depopulated.) These subjects are enhanced by storytelling techniques that Lewis learned in the Yazoo swamps listening to the yarns of hunters. (Thus, also, some of his stories are tall tales or comic sporting yarns.) All of Lewis's tales reflect a sharply-honed ability to recognize and re-create the absurd. Being a medical student and doctor reinforced his absurd view. All men are equally ludicrous when stripped of their clothes, and all are equally vulnerable to grotesque deformities and embarrassing diseases.

One of the most famous of the stories to come out of Lewis's experiences as a medical student tells how he and two roommates play a ghastly trick on their landlady with the intention of curing her of her incessant curiosity. Since her habit is to poke about in their room while they are gone, they decide to hide something special for her to find—something they are sure will scare her out of her wits. The students are at the time engaged in dissection, so they carefully remove from their specimen a face that is especially appropriate to their trick. This face is so horrific that "even after working a week upon him I never caught a glimpse of his countenance but what I had a nightmare in consequence." The face has a gaping harelip and two gruesome exposed tusks, and "Every feature was deformed and unnatural. . . ." This face greets the landlady the following night, when she carefully unwraps the multilayered package the students have left to tantalize her curiosity. The roomers watch through a crack at the outside door as she takes the bait. All of this would lead to a predictable conclusion in a lesser story—the landlady would faint, and the students would have their joke and win the field. Lewis's landlady turns out to be the sharpest character in the story, however, and it is she who wins the game and has the last laugh.

When she first looks at the face, the boys think she is stopped cold: "Ay, but she was a firm-nerved woman. If metempsychosis be a true doctrine, her spirit must have once animated in the chivalrous times a steel-clad knight of the doughtiest mold. She did not faint—did not vent a scream—but gazed upon its awfulness in silence as if her eyes were riveted to it forever." After a moment, she begins to laugh a laugh which is called "hysterical." But this is not, as it turns out, the laugh of hysteria. A crowd gathers, the students enter the room, she laughs louder and more wildly, and then suddenly she stops. She puts on "an expression of the most supreme contempt" and says coolly, " 'Excuse me, gentlemen . . . I was just *smiling aloud* to think what fools these students made of themselves when they tried to scare me with a dead nigger's face when I had slept with a drunken husband for twenty years!' " The crowd departs, "and we, too, I reckon, between that time and the next upheaving of the sun." (The word "upheaving" in the last sentence must have been chosen quite deliberately.)[7]

In this story, Lewis displayed a knowledge of how to reverse a situation for a double humorous effect. The reader predicts a stock response from the landlady but is surprised by a new revelation underneath the package of appearances. Her response is not reasonable from the students' point of view, and it is not so from the reader's point of view until the very last. By first calling her laughter "hysterical," the teller reinforces our predictions. The reader enjoys his epiphany when he learns that what he had reason to expect is reversed. His revelation is a revelation of the absurd, because he sees suddenly that the unreasonable can occur even in a situation which has been carefully planned (by the students) and anticipated in confidence (by the reader). Moreover, some of this knowledge of the absurd is shared by the landlady, the real heroine of the piece. She has been living with the grotesque and horrible all her life. What she laughs at is the ludicrous naïveté of the students, who until now thought that they were masterful manipulators of rare absurdities. It did not occur to them that she would see a grim joke in the face of the cadaver; they thought the joke would be theirs alone. She knows the joke firsthand, however; they are the ones who have not understood the ambivalence of the face of death.

At times, Lewis's persona seems harsh and unfeeling as well as innocent, as in "Cupping on the Sternum," wherein the medical student acts upon his belief that his order to cup an old Negro servant woman on the sternum means that he should relieve the blood pressure on her stern.[8] Her agony is supposed to be the rest of the joke. But Lewis could in turn have the joke fall totally on the persona and thus indicate that the persona's view was ludicrous. In a perfectly emblematic story called "Stealing a Baby," the medical student's capacity for seeing everything as absurd becomes the focus of the story's satire. In this case, of course, the student is not being satirized as an unfeeling sadist but is being depicted as a victim of his own obsessions. He is at this time deeply involved in his studies of human anatomy, and it is his exaggerated "scientific" view which distorts his vision (or perhaps it clarifies his vision to the point of excluding all sentiment). Anatomy, the narrator reports, "was a passion with me. Whenever I met with persons extremely emaciated or finely developed, my anatomical eye would scan their proportions, and instead of paying them the usual courtesies of life, I would be thinking what glorious subjects they would be for museum preparations or dissection." He cannot separate anatomy from romance: "Even when my audacious lips were stealing a kiss from the pulpy mouth of my ladylove, instead of floating into ecstasies of delight, my anatomical mind would wonder whether, even in death, electricity by some peculiar adaptation might not be able to continue their bewitching suction. When holding her soft hand in mine and gazing into the star-lit ocean of her soul, I would wonder if there was not some peculiarity in the formation of her optic nerve which gave her eye such brilliancy."[9] Here the absurd view is itself humorous because it provides the light which throws the clash of science and myth into hilarious relief.

Later, in further pursuit of his studies in dissection, the student steals a dead black baby. Unfortunately, he shortly meets his beloved and is required to walk along with her, struggling to keep the infant corpse hidden under his coat. He is confronted by her angry father (who hates southerners and has brought the constable to force our hero to stop seeing his daughter) and is attacked by a huge bulldog (which may have gotten a whiff of the corpse)—all at the same moment. He is knocked over, his feet fly up, and "out in all its hideous realities rolled the infernal imp of darkness upon the gaze of the laughing but now horrified spectators."[10] No one else in the story appreciates this delicate balance of comedy and horror, this hilarious revelation of "hideous realities." The constable nearly arrests him, his girl rejects him, and he has to return the baby to the deadroom.

The humor of the absurd permeates all of Lewis's stories, obliterating sentimentality. They are splendid examples of how early rough humor in America rejected the romantic view in favor of the hard reality. The country doctor, Lewis once wrote, is a man who is always deeply moved by a patient's departure from the vale of tears, a noble healer who feels knit like a brother to all to whom he ministers—manly fathers, weeping women, sobbing children, and grieving Negroes. When the doctor dies, a sunbeam strikes his brow, "a sweet smile pervades his countenance," and he sinks to rest "amidst all that is beauteous in nature or commendable in man." After saying all this, Lewis added: "True to the instincts of his profession, he, no doubt, in the battling troop

of the angels above, if feasible, will still continue to *charge*."[11]
The story of the doctor's death was a matter for travesty, the bad
pun its proper end. It is probable that for Lewis humor was an
answer to horror. In the face of disease and death, he constructed
ways to laugh while feeling pain. It would be only appropriate
to note that he once predicted with characteristic irony that he
would die in the swamp.[12] Lewis had a morbid view, but his absurd
sense did at least have its curative powers.

Not all of the best yarns from the frontier were told as Lewis
told his, the persona himself being the teller and the manipulator (as well as the victim) of the absurdities. Some are narratives about characters who exercise the possibilities of absurd
manipulation by playing practical jokes on gullible victims.
John S. Robb's "Swallowing an Oyster Alive" is a definitive example of this kind of story, a "saw" in which an innocent is made
to look silly because he takes the world seriously and believes
in appearances. The victim in this story, a country lad from the
Sucker state, enters a tavern in St. Louis and orders oysters for
the first time in his life. He has heard of their reputation as a
delicacy. He is not aware that one of the regular patrons of the
tavern is about to spring a joke on him. As the Sucker downs the
first oyster, the wag drops his knife, looks up in horror, and exclaims, " 'Swallowed alive, as I'm a Christian!' " This is a perfect
ploy; the Sucker's mouth falls open in fear, and he asks, " 'What
on earth's the row?' " The reply is " 'the creature is alive, and
will eat right through you. . . .' " In his confusion, the Sucker
swallows a bottle of pepper sauce which the wag has said will
"kill" the animal. He thinks it does, since the sauce makes him
feel like the oyster is squirming violently as it "dies." The yarn
ends with the whole tavern company in a fit of laughter as the
Sucker darts out the door.[13] The victim's lot is the lot of the
stranger—he must take the word of the citizens of the place or
else forge ahead on his own. He will probably suffer from his
ignorance in either case. The relationship between himself and
his new world will remain ambiguous, and his dilemma will
remain absurd. The laughter of the crew in the tavern is the
laughter of those who for the moment have created the Sucker's
fate instead of falling victim to like circumstances themselves.

One of the most famous gory stories of the Old South is "The

Fight," by Augustus Baldwin Longstreet. The contestants in this battle, Durham and Stallings, literally tear each other to pieces. Here are the archetypal eye-gouging, ear-biting, bone-breaking details of the frontier fight story. The grotesqueness of the battle is heightened by the fact that Ransy Sniffle, a cowardly bystander who loves to watch fights, has deliberately manipulated Durham and Stallings into fighting.[14] In this story and in others, Longstreet displayed a full awareness of the meaninglessness of the common events of his time and place; his subjects include, besides the fight, the tricky horse swap and the cruel game of gander pulling.[15] His stories are written from the point of view of a civilized, literate observer who seems to believe that the world is disorderly when it should not be. He was not, as he has been called, a sadist and a nihilist.[16] He was simply perceptive and thoughtful enough to be simultaneously amused and appalled by the ill effects of the manipulation of appearances by the Ransy Sniffles of the world combined with the raw power of men like Durham and Stallings. His stories always imply that something is wrong and correction is possible. At the end of "The Fight," he stated that Christian religion and institutions had displaced the barbarity of such customs as these men exercised, and he called their behavior "a disgrace to that community."[17] It is quite possible, of course, that Longstreet was being sarcastic; surely he knew that such violence was scarcely abated anywhere and that the fight was indicative of all the tragic and absurd encounters between men. But whether or not he was being sarcastic, his final remarks would still imply that the dangerous absurdity of the relationships between men is unacceptable and correctable.

The native humorist also enjoyed sketching predicaments symbolic of the potential absurdity of all situations. William Tappan Thompson's very short yarn, "A Coon-Hunt; or, A Fency Country," is a fine example; it neatly recapitulates in microcosm the senseless aspect of man's wanderings. In this story, Bill Sweeney and Tom Culpepper go on a raccoon hunt at night, with their torch "a blazin" and their dogs far out ahead of them "yelpin like forty thousand." They have to stop often to pinpoint the dogs' location, and each time they do, they drink one another's health. "Bimeby they cum to a fence. Well, over they got, 'thout much difficulty." But this fence turns out to be just one of many in a very "fency" country. Moreover, in between each fence is "a terrible muddy branch." Each fence is higher and each creek muddier and wider than the one before. The joke hinges on the fact that the creeks and fences are only apparently multiple; the hunters are traveling in a circle. The apparently increasing obstacles of height and width and muddiness are so only because the two men keep getting drunker. Eventually they discover what they have actually been doing all night, and Bill says later that if the liquor hadn't run out "they'd been climbin the same fence, and wadin that same branch till yet."[18]

Not to be forgotten in the broad genre of fictional humor before Twain are the milder and quieter absurd characters such as B. P. Shillaber's Mrs. Partington (whose picture was used both for her own book, 1854, and as a representation of Tom Sawyer's Aunt Polly in 1876).[19] She is the one who told Ike to " 'drownd them kittens,' " but then in a gesture of mercy added, " 'Stop . . . and I'll take the chill off the water; it would be cruel to put 'em into it stone-cold.' " She did feel guilty afterwards, the author wrote, and the cat who had mothered the excess kittens received many a dainty bit ever after. She had done the awful deed, but who could criticize? "Perfection belongeth not to man or woman," and none could pretend "that Mrs. Partington was an exception to this universal rule."[20] There was Seba Smith's Jack Downing, recorder of and participator in the absurdities of political and military life in Downingville, Maine. A sharp observer of absurd character was Frances M. Whitcher, whose Widow Bedott sets out to tell about a declaration her late husband had made one night while sitting before the fire. She interrupts her own story constantly with irrelevant gossip, never getting beyond quoting her husband's nominal of address until the climax of the joke (her nickname was, appropriately, "Silly"): "He says to me, says he, 'Silly,' I says, says I, 'What?' If I dident say 'what' when he said 'Silly,' he'd a kept on saying 'Silly,' from time to eternity. He always did, because, you know, he wanted me to pay pertikkeler attention, and I ginerally did; no woman was ever more attentive to her husband than what I was. Well, he says to me, says he, 'Silly.' Says I, 'What?' though I'd no idee what he was gwine to say. . . ."

All of this humorous byplay leads up to an important statement: what husband Hezekiah had been trying to say all along was, simply, *"We're all poor critters!"* [21] The yarn ends there, the Widow Beddot having proved that she, at least, is comfortable in her absurdity. She missed the point, but we don't. When the native absurdist made his reader laugh, he did so in the full awareness that he and his reader were choosing to see the humor as well as the pathos of the recognition that *"We're all poor critters!"*

2 · THE TELLER IN THE TALL TALE

In a fully developed written tall tale, the writer describes a framing scene in which he is himself present and then introduces a character who tells the fabulous yarn. The writer thus pretends to be part of the audience, claiming that his only role has been to record the teller's story in the teller's own words. The writer of the story and his literary audience may appear to be detached from the teller in several ways: they may think they are of a higher social class than his, they may feel they are more literate than he, they may believe their own speech is more correct than his dialect. The reader's initial interest in the story will be in the teller's humorous language and his fabulous lie. But if the reader examines the story more closely, he invariably finds that the real focus of the writer's attention is the psychology of the teller himself, which proves to be far more complex than was first evident. The tall yarn in the story may or may not have been about the teller, but he is nonetheless always the main character of the story as a whole. A tall tale is a search for the wonderful, and the searcher, the man who is testing the limits of the possible, is the teller. The teller of the tale seeks to prove to strangers that this event, this animal, this hero, this locality, exceeds all their expectations. The reader is finally compelled to examine the teller's character because it is he who has embellished the fantasy with realistic detail and the real events with fantasy. It is the teller who is the manipulator of appearances and the creator of myth. He tries to take advantage of his listener's suspicion that the possible and the probable are not separable. He shows his listener that meaning is a matter of invention, not observation. He always starts his story in a completely plausible way so that the crossing into the fantastic will occur unperceived.

The teller's deliberate blurring of the real and the fantastic is an experiment in an activity which is potentially both dangerous and delightful. He may be so experimenting because he is fascinated by his discovery that the real and the fantastic are already blurred in the world, or he may be doing so unconsciously in an effort to order his inexplicable experiences in a mysterious wilderness. Two very simply structured tall tales which have analogues familiar in many countries illustrate this blurring process in a concrete way. (These stories sometimes are and sometimes are not told in a frame; they are used here as simplified examples of how any teller can combine fact and fantasy.) One of the stories concerns a piece of fabulous hunting luck. The hunter fires a shot (shoots an arrow or throws a spear) which not only hits the target—a deer for example—but passes through or bounces off the target, striking a number of other desirable targets—a leaping fish, a hidden rabbit, a tree full of honey. The hunter collects all of his catch and happily returns home. The other story occurs either in a sandy country (the dune hills of western Michigan) or in a snowy country (Prussia, New England). A hunter who makes it a habit to spend the night in a tree whenever he is caught away from home at nightfall finds himself far out in the wilderness on a particularly windy evening. He relaxes comfortably in the branches of a small tree and goes to sleep. When he wakes the next day, he finds himself high above the ground, the wind having blown the snow or sand away, revealing that his small tree is actually the top of a very tall one. This story usually ends with the hunter's relation of what he did to get down: "I just waited for the wind to blow the snow back under me again." Stories like these are fantastic but are not totally the wild invention of their tellers. Wind does blow masses of snow and sand around in peculiar ways, and it is quite possible for an errant missile to hit more than one target.

Aside from the style of the presentation, the pleasure of these stories arises from our awareness that the event could be possible in a universe where anything not only can happen but does happen. It is the teller who recognizes this. Consider again what the reader of the *Spirit of the Times* faced when he found all those wonderful animals; which were real and which were not? The observer of any situation is faced with the same dilemma; if a hoax is being perpetrated, he has no real defense against it. If the hoaxer is as careful as the good tall tale teller, his details will all be plausible and his own psychology ambiguous. The result will be a mock event which cannot be tested for factuality. If the hoax has a benevolent motive, or if it is perpetrated in pure fun, nobody cares except those few who might have been embarrassed. Americans love this kind of hoaxing. If the hoax is a Big Lie, its consequences are disastrous. But the teller in a tall tale is not a Big Liar; he is a creative storyteller. The literary man who recapitulates the teller's story and psychology in written form works only in the spirit of fun. The teller of tall tales always keeps his lies moderate. What he loves to do is re-create and celebrate the way the human mind receives and combines the real and the fantastic. Why should he not be believed, in the deep sense? Who can with more certainty believe that men fly to the moon, even when they have seen the shadows of reality on the face of the television tube? It is no more difficult to believe that giants lived in the woods.

At the heart of the American tall tradition in the pre-Twain era was a phenomenon known as "tall talk," which was characterized most succinctly by Nimrod Wildfire's sterling speech in James Kirke Paulding's *The Lion of the West*. Wildfire recalls a time when he was challenged by a riverboatman who had declared, " 'Mister . . . I'm the best man—if I ain't, I wish I may be tetotaciously exflunctified! I can whip my weight in wild cats and ride strait through a crab apple orchard on a flash of lightning—clear meat axe disposition!' " Wildfire rose to the challenge of language with "Poh . . . what do I keer for that? I can tote a steam boat up the Mississippi and over the Alleghany mountains. My father can whip the best man in old Kaintuck, and I can whip my father. When I'm good natured I weigh about a hundred and seventy, but when I'm mad, I weigh a *ton*." This speech is a perfect example of comic self-creation. Nimrod is tough, but he is also not sure that his toughness will always suffice. What happens when the half horse, half alligator meets up with the half elephant, half tiger? Wildfire says that once he hit a man so hard "He disappeared altogether; all they could ever find of him was a little grease spot in one corner."[22] Does he not fear that some superior energy will thus annihilate him? Nimrod is not on his own ground in this scene; he is in the big city and his audience is genteel. He has reasons for insecurity. Like Franklin in Paris, he is being what he is expected to be and making it fit what he knows he can be. Coincidentally, assuming a mask which suits him also enlarges him. A fairly ordinary backwoodsman imitates Nimrod Wildfire and is Nimrod Wildfire. If there is a "real" Wildfire, he is not distinguishable. To maintain the mask is to maintain courage in the face of doubt.

Another well-known mythical character whose psychology is directly analogous to Wildfire's is "The Wild Boar of Tehama." This original, a ferocious-looking tough, wins several hundred dollars from a quiet little man at poker, and seems "to have won a little ambiguously." The loser leaves the game, looking plenty hateful, and bystanders warn the tough that it would be prudent for him to leave by the back door. " 'Why, gentlemen, you don't know me. You don't know who I am. I'm the Wild Boar of Tehama! The click of a six-shooter is music to my ear, and a bowie knife is my looking glass—.' " At this point, the little man re-enters wielding a fowling piece. " 'But a shotgun lets me out,' " yelps the Wild Boar, and he dives out a window.[23] The Wild Boar creates his image and wins with it when he can. But he never lets his fantasy keep him from seeing real dangers; a shotgun is just a wee bit more powerful a reality than he cares to meddle with. It can all too abruptly kill even his mythical self.

Tall language in America does reflect tall experience, but, just as importantly, it indicates a creative impulse in the psychology of a character (or of a real man who tells tall tales in the traditional spirit). The teller of a tall yarn in a framework story shares with Nimrod and the Wild Boar the linguistic ability to create new realities.

Mark Twain's Jim Baker, the creative teller of one of the most perfectly constructed written tall tales, the "Blue-Jay Yarn," is a deliberate builder of mood, point of view, and story. He is a satirist and a master of the comic twist. In the end of his yarn, jays come from all over the world to see the hole that absorbed all those acorns, and an owl from Nova Scotia can't see the point of the joke about the hole being in a cabin roof. The owl, Jim says, didn't care for the "Yo Semite" country, either. Every reader has met that owl. Ironically, Jim's creative psychology is not fully open to the reader. Can the reader know whether or not Jim really thinks he talks to jays? He says he does, and he expects us to go along with him for the purposes of the story. Twain as outside narrator says simply that Jim "believed he could accurately translate any remark [birds] made." Jim's story begins with a pat assumption: " 'When I first begun to under-stand jay language correctly. . . .' "[24] Twain is "putting us on," of course, but there is no way to be sure to what extent Jim is deliberately putting us on.

The success of such a story depends on the author's ability to keep his teller ambiguous. This is a difference between a written framework tall tale and an oral tale heard directly from a yarn-spinner. The listener probably knows when the yarnspinner is deliberately lying. But Jim's story, as are many in the American horde, was carefully written down and elaborated upon by a man who had a real sense of the artistry of written storytelling. The psychology of the teller in a frame story is ambiguous for the same reason that James's governess in *The Turn of the Screw* or Poe's "I" in "Lygeia" is ambiguous. In Poe's or James's yarn, the reader innocently takes the story on the character's own terms until he begins to discover evidence that the character might be crazy. Then the reader is still stuck because all of his evidence is presented in the point of view of the ambiguous char-acter himself.

The framework tall tale often does give us a clue about the teller because the writer can assess his teller for us. However, the skillful writer will let his teller remain ambiguous or even con-tribute to that ambiguity, as Twain does by pretending to believe that Jim Baker talks to animals and birds. He introduces Jim's yarn by referring to some widely accepted beliefs: animals probably do have languages of their own; close study reveals many secrets about nature (Twain's was the new age of science —anything could be discovered); Jim is one of those noble and simple men who live close to nature and thus "know" nature deeply and directly. Our assessment of Jim is complicated be-cause this pretended acceptance of three common beliefs is satirical; Twain was poking fun at the beliefs themselves. If we miss the satire, we are tricked into believing that Twain himself may have been fooled by Jim's story, at least at first. If we do get the satire, we are nonetheless at a loss to know whether Jim thought of himself as a natural man or whether he was trying to satirize his listeners' beliefs by assuming a pose they expected and in which they had confidence.

An even more complex example of ambiguous teller psychology is that of Jim Doggett, the hero of Thomas Bangs Thorpe's classic, "The Big Bear of Arkansas."[25] The setting in which Jim tells his story is the tavern of a steamboat named the *Invincible* upon whose decks is gathered a heterogeneous crowd: a planter, a jockey, a bishop, a gambler, "professional men of all creeds and characters," and "Wolvereens, Suckers, Hoosiers, Buckeyes, and Corn-crackers, beside a 'plentiful sprinkling' of the half-horse and half-alligator species of men. . . ." The recorder of the tale, Thorpe in the role of himself as observer and writer, is one of this crowd, which is to be taken as symbolic of American society. Jim Doggett startles the crowd by entering the tavern and whooping, " 'Hurra for the Big Bar of Arkansaw!' " Jim immediately reveals that he feels out of place here or anywhere except his home state. New Orleans, where he has just been, can't compare to Arkansas; he declares that he was " 'thrown away in that ar place. . . .' " He is a hunter, he says, and hunting is so good in Arkansas that he never bothers to kill birds—except forty-pound turkeys. He specializes in big bears. Arkansas is, he continues in a loud voice, the " 'creation state, the finishing-up country—a state where the *sile* runs down to the centre of the 'arth. . . .' " Mosquitoes are also large, he admits, but that's actually a natural advantage: " 'If they ar large, Arkansaw is large, her varmints ar large, her trees ar large, her rivers ar large, and a small mosquito would be of no more use in Arkansaw than preaching in a cane-brake.' "

Jim's homestead is at a place called Shirt-tail Bend, on the forks of the Cypress. This locale is the tallest place in tall Arkansas. Jim tried farming, he says, but it was dangerous; turnips grew as big as cedar stumps, and potatoes as big as Indian mounds—both crops were useless. A pig once lay down on top of two or three kernels of corn and was killed when the stalk exploded out of the ground. When Jim begins to talk about Shirt-tail Bend and Arkansas, his manipulation of reality begins to dominate the story. By describing progressively taller and taller details, he nudges his listeners imperceptibly from reality into fantasy.

When Jim first roared into the saloon, everyone immediately recognized him as an orginal: "Some of the company at this familiarity looked a little angry, and some astonished; but in a moment every face was wreathed in a smile. There was something about the intruder that won the heart on sight. He appeared to be a man enjoying perfect health and contentment: his eyes were as sparkling as diamonds, and good-natured to simplicity. Then his perfect confidence in himself was irresistibly droll."[26] Jim exudes this confidence as he tells his story; the world he is drawing his listeners into is a world apparently under his full control. It does not awe him, so it appears; he seems the master of its truths, unharmed by its appearances. He knows that world, and he is ready to define and re-create it for his audience.

To convince listeners who doubt his tall generalizations, Jim agrees to tell a story of some particular bear hunt. After some hesitation about just which hunt to describe, he decides to tell about " 'the greatest bar . . . that ever lived, *none excepted. . . .* ' " His hesitation suggests that he may be making the whole thing up from the very beginning (though it does not prove that he is doing so): " 'Yes, I have it! I will give you an idea of a hunt. . . .' " He first knew of the great bear's existence by its claw and tooth marks high on a tree. (Bears proclaim their size and strength to other bears by stretching up and clawing stumps much in the same way cats do.) These marks were different from any Jim had ever seen before: " 'Says I, "them marks is a hoax, or it indicates the d------t bar that was ever grown." In fact, stranger I couldn't believe it was real, and I went on. Again I saw the same marks, at the same height, and *I knew the thing lived.* That conviction came home to my soul like an earthquake.' " The emphasis is Jim's; he knew. The "facts" before him imprinted themselves upon his soul. Thereafter, the pursuit of the Big Bear became his one obsession. But at every turn he was met with frustration, and each time the bear eluded him, it took on for him more aspects of the supernatural. The bear seemed to know that Jim was after it and made a regular business of selecting his hogs to steal while ignoring the neighbors'. Jim began to see the bear as a constant and evil presence, and finally he says, " '*he hunted me,* and that, too, like a devil, which I began to think he was.' " His involvement with the bear became complete, and its evilness turned to mystical ambivalence: " 'But wasn't he a beauty, though? I loved him like a brother.' "[27] Once Jim was sure he had caught the bear when his dog, Bowie-knife, drowned one in a lake. But this was just a big old she-bear, and the incident convinced Jim that he was hunting a supernatural bear for certain.

Finally, Jim's obsession became a comic monomania. He packed up all his ammunition, cleaned and "iled" his rifle, and informed his neighbors that " 'on Monday morning . . . I would start THAT BAR, and bring him home with me, or they might divide my settlement among them, the owner having disappeared.' " But Jim did not have to set out on his quest; the bear came to him. On Sunday, he strolled out into the woods to answer a call of nature, " 'taking my gun and Bowie-knife along, just *from habit. . . .*' " While " 'sitting down also from habit,' " Jim looked up to see the bear less than a hundred yards away; it loomed up " 'like a *black mist*' " and walked right towards him. Jim fired; the bear wheeled, gave a yell, and " '*walked through the fence* like a falling tree would through a cobweb.' " Before it walked very far, however, it dropped dead in a thicket. Jim can now say truthfully that the bear, dead and measurable, really is the biggest bear he has ever seen or heard of. But after his long experience with the mysteries of this particular hunt, and especially after his careful telling of the story, he is ready to declare without qualification that the bear " 'was in fact a creation bar. . . .' " The creation bear of his mind and experience has become a creation bear in reality.

Next Jim delivers the tallest twist of all: " 'But, strangers, I never like the way I hunted him, and *missed him*. There is something curious about it, I could never understand,—and I never was satisfied at his giving in so *easy at last*. Prehaps he had heard of my preparations to hunt him the next day, so he jist come in, like Captain Scott's coon, to save his wind to grunt with in dying; but that ain't likely. My private opinion is, that that bar was an

unhuntable bar, and died when his time come.' " At this point,
Thorpe as the recorder steps in to make Jim's character totally
and finally ambiguous: "When the story was ended, our hero
sat some minutes with his auditors in a grave silence; I saw
there was a mystery to him connected with the bear whose death
he had just related, that had evidently made a strong impression
on his mind. It was also evident that there was some superstitious
awe connected with the affair,—a feeling common with all
'children of the wood,' when they meet with any thing out of
their everyday experience."[28]

The writer's observation that Jim is a child of nature, that the
affair has "made a strong impression on his mind," and that
clearly "there was some superstitious awe connected with the
affair," suggests that it is only in Jim's view that the big bear
was really fantastic or supernatural. Two phrases quoted earlier
show how Jim's view of the bear's mysterious actions shifted
from a level in which he used a simile to compare the bear to
the devil to a level of equation using a metaphor: " *'he hunted
me* . . . like a devil, which I began to think he was.' " Finally
Jim's belief in the supernaturalness of the bear shifts from a
matter of metaphor to a matter of fact: " 'It was in fact a
creation bar.' " We cannot really know whether or not Jim has
convinced himself through a beautiful lie. The bear is real;
Jim has the bedspread, an actual piece of evidence (but we're not
with him at home to see it). We can be sure that it is Jim who
is responsible for the supernatural elements of the story, but we
do not know whether Jim thinks that he observed them or created
them. We do not know whether to take the big bear as the supernatural bear of a lie or a real bear exaggerated by Jim's imagination. Moreover, there is always the third possibility: it might all
be just exactly as he has seen it. But we are practical, so we
reject that possibility. Knowingly or unknowingly—and that we
cannot tell is what makes the story attractive in its ambiguity—
Jim has created his own hunting grounds, his own hunt, his
own identity as super hunter, and his own bear—the only
quarry to match his identity as hunter—a creation bear.

Thorpe's closing description suggests that Jim himself is
vaguely aware of, and a bit surprised at, his own creative abilities.
He has been, he knows, deceived by the appearances of things

in the woods. He has created, out of fact and fantasy, a reality which may or may not be the reality of big-bear hunting in Shirt-tail Bend. He has implicitly admitted this all along, expecting his audience to know what he is doing and expecting them to accept the story along with the man. For just a moment, in the silence following his story, we feel his confidence slip. But then he sees that the audience has responded rightly, and his confidence is instantly restored: "He was the first one . . . to break the silence, and jumping up, he asked all present to 'liquor' before going to bed,—a thing which he did, with a number of companions, evidently to his heart's content."[29] Jim is content indeed; a "number of companions"—and the author who created or re-created him—have accepted his story as a reflection of the reality of his consciousness.

A really fine writer of tall fiction during the late 1830s and early 1840s, a man whose work has gone almost unnoticed, was William P. Hawes, a northeastern contributor to the *Spirit of the Times*.[30] His stories are worth mentioning because Hawes was a keen observer of absurd situations and a writer who knew how precarious was the difference between a man's escaping a dangerous dilemma to live with laughter and falling prey to the dilemma's terror. He was also exceptionally skillful at inventing different ways to present an ambiguous inside narrator.

One of his yarns is not told in the conventional framework but in the first person by a character-narrator to an implied audience, in the manner of a dramatic monologue. The teller is in this case even more emphatically the focus of attention. The story begins with the all-important declaration of the reliability of the facts: "'Well, gentlemen, I'll go ahead, if you say so. Here's the story. It is true, upon my honor, from beginning to end— every word of it.'" The teller then spins a yarn about a fishing trip on Long Island Sound which he took with Tim Titus, a heavy-drinking friend. Tim and he fished from a boat for a while, catching several good tautaugs, but their whiskey quit before the fish did. Tim left the hero on a rock surrounded by good fishing water while he returned to the dock to pick up another jug. The narrator enjoyed the fun alone for some time, basking in the sun and catching fish. Tim failed to return, however, having apparently gotten sidetracked by the jug. The tide began to come in, and the little rock island grew smaller and smaller. The hero began to grow uncomfortable. His ludicrous situation became horrifying when, retrieving his fishing line, he noted a heavy pull on the other end. Whatever it was came up all too willingly. He soon discovered it to be a large shark, which ominously followed the pull gently and without resistance. The shark " 'came up to the rock, laid his nose upon its side, and looked up into my face, not as if utterly unconcerned, but with a sort of quizzical impudence, as though he perfectly understood the precarious nature of my situation.' " Fortunately, the shark decided not to make a pass at the fisherman and glided back into deep water, breaking loose from the line.

The tide continued to rise, however, and darkness began to fall. The hero then saw a sight which chilled his blood: " 'Something glided by me in the water, and then made a sudden halt. I looked upon the black mass, and, as my eye ran along its dark outline, I saw, with horror, that it was a shark; the identical monster out of whose mouth I had just broken my hook. He was fishing, now, for me, and was evidently only waiting for the tide to rise high enough above the rock, to glut at once his hunger and revenge.' " The fisherman beat the shark's first harassing attacks off with his rod, but it soon became evident that the tide and the shark's patience would win out. The shark sliced off his jacket on the next attack, and then, much to his dismay, more sharks joined in the fun.

Things looked very grim indeed until the fisherman noticed that the sharks always attacked singly, never together (a convenient twisting of natural history on the storyteller's part). In desperation, the fisherman stabbed at one with his knife and happened to cut out an eye: " 'In an instant, hope and reason came to my relief; and it occurred to me, that if I could only blind the other, I might yet escape.' " On the next pass, the shark lost the other eye and was forced to sink back into the depths. The narrator concludes: " 'Well, gentlemen, I suppose you'll think it a hard story, it is none the less a fact, that I served every remaining one of those nineteen sharks in the same fashion.' " Old Tim, by the way, did come by at last to save our hero from drowning.[31]

What Hawes did in this story shows how the conventions of

the tall tale can produce mythical overtones of some significance. The shark is the perfectly appropriate (even archetypal) symbol of the evil that can be masked by the surface of things (the sea). In telling the story, whether he has actually performed such a deed or not, the yarnspinner enacts an ancient human ritual: he raises the evil and conquers it. In its way, the story is designed to have the kind of tension, suspense, and climax that characterizes nonliterary rituals of the same order—the bullfiight, for example.

In another yarn, Hawes used a double framework device, starting with a conversation among a group of tavern sportsmen sitting around swapping lies. The inside narrator, Venus Raynor, proposes to tell a tale told to him by another teller—a story about " 'what I've heard tell on Ebenezer Smith, at the time he went down to the north pole on a walen' voyage.' " (In spite of the phrase " 'what I've heard tell on,' " the original storyteller was Ebenezer himself, as it turns out.) The others consent to listen to the story if it's true; they have their doubts.

While whaling in Baffin's Bay, Ebenezer left ship to stalk a huge polar bear. He loaded his gun with two bullets. He got a shot from a kneeling position just as the bear charged down upon him. The double load broke both the bear's front legs, and it sank to its knees just in front of Eb. Eb tried to get up and found that *his* knees were frozen to the ice. Pretty soon the bear was frozen to the ice, too, and the hunter and hunted squatted facing each other, just out of each other's reach. This is a perfect image of man's absurd dilemma; there Eb knelt, face to face with a hard fact of nature, having touched it at a distance, yet unable to master it or even be subjected by it. The ice which Eb and the bear were on broke loose from the floe and floated off to sea, with bear and man staring each other down.

At this point, the listeners express doubt about the facts of the story and ask Venus how Eb kept warm. " 'Them polar bears is wonderful hardy animals,' " he replies, " 'and has a monstrous deal o' heat into 'em.' " So whenever he was cold, Eb would just beat on the bear with his ramrod and make him roar and squeal, " 'and then the hot breath would come pouren out all over the captin, and made the air quite moderate and pleasant.' " Starvation? A seal stranded itself on the ice and Eb was fast enough with his knife to grab his half before the bear got it all. Finally they drifted into warm seas, the ice cake broke in two, and the bear floated off in the distance. Eb was later rescued. The listeners want to know what happened to the bear, but Venus says Eb had no way of knowing. Venus adds that he would like to know himself, since the bear had been real polite, letting Eb have the big half of the seal and keeping him warm and all. Venus maintains his mask throughout, preserving the story as a twice-created absurdity. He concludes, " 'That's all, boys. How many's asleep?' "[32]

The characters of Hawes's stories are realistic, the situations artfully contrived and emblematic, and the tone humorous. His heroes are ludicrous men who look a dilemma in the form of shark or bear in the face and live to tell their stories only because a combination of luck and invention saves them. Their dilemmas are absurd, their rescues are absurd, and their stories (and since they are all liars, one must concede that it may be only their stories) are absurd.

This discussion of the teller in the tall tale can best be concluded by referring again to Benjamin Franklin, who was not only a good teller but knew the social value of the teller's absurd creation. Franklin parodied American tall tales and at the same time created them himself. Let ignorant people know, he said, that "Whales, when they have a mind to eat cod, pursue them wherever they fly; and that the grand Leap of the Whale in the Chase up the Fall of Niagara is esteemed, by all who have seen it, as one of the finest Spectacles in Nature." It is lack of confidence, Franklin said, that hurts us all: "Really, Sir, the World is grown too incredulous."[33] In a way, Franklin meant this seriously as well as satirically. All his life, he found that tall tales, disguises, and hoaxes were excellent methods for conveying benevolent political and religious notions.

One of Franklin's hoaxes provides an insight into the moral value of the twin processes of telling and accepting tall stories. In 1768 he published in the *London Chronicle*, in two parts, a parody of adventure yarns called "Extract from an Account of the Captivity of William Henry in 1755, and of his Residence among the Senneka Indians six Years and seven Months till he made his Escape from them." The purpose of this "Account" seems to be the presentation of a mock cosmogony. The Indians, in response to Henry's unqualified praise of European institutions, discourse upon their view of creation. Canassatego tells a "true" story about how the gods shaped the destiny of man and concludes, " 'Every country has its great god Manitta, who first peopled that country.' " Canassatego's account of creation is comic in itself, but the target of the mock cosmogony's satire is made to look even more ludicrous. Franklin was attacking directly the common belief of Christians that the dogmas of Judeo-Christian theology were exclusive and correct. His hoax tries to demonstrate that the major tenets of Judeo-Christian theology are analogous to those of so-called pagan cultures.

The main point here is, however, that all the lie-swapping between Henry and the Indians yields a creative moral, a statement about how men ought to behave. Henry doubts a point in old Canassatego's account of creation, arguing that it is a story handed down through many generations and thus subject to much distortion, whereas the Christian account was written down hot from the pens of men inspired directly by the Great Spirit. Old Canassatego scolds Henry for impoliteness, regretting that his stay among the Indians has not taught him basic civilized manners. He asks Henry a question, and through the question Franklin delivered another of his creative rules by which men can live and build together: " 'You see,' " says Canassatego, " 'I always believed your stories, why do you not believe mine?' "[34] The role of the teller is to tell stories which require that men believe in one another—on the basis of appearances and in confidence.

3 · BITERS AND BITERS BIT

As a confidence man, Benjamin Franklin knew that the game of manipulating appearances has its limitations. He used the simple tests of pleasure-pain to measure what was good. If the streets are dark, light them; if there are fires, organize a fire department. He knew people sometimes want or need to be conned into overcoming their immobility or skepticism. Franklin was a creator of values as well as appearances; he could con the troops into attending prayer meetings, or he could con the separated colonies into rebellion, independence, and nationhood. He knew how dangerous a power his was, and he tempered his deceptions with benevolence.

The confidence man as a character in native American humor before Twain is seldom so benevolent. He has a Satanic streak. (This statement does not apply to Melville's Confidence-Man in the same way as it applies to his lesser analogues in native humor. Melville's Confidence-Man is a mythic figure with a creative purpose.) In his Satanic role, he is the antagonist of the American innocent—the emblem of the serpent in the Garden. He neither sees nor establishes any moral limitations to his manipulation of appearances, and he always plays the confidence game to see how far he can go with it. The game gives him a feeling of mastery over appearances, but his implementation of the game may have nihilistic motives and disastrous results. He is not a pleasant character, but he is educative: he teaches his victims the dangers of innocence. He may or may not be aware of the absurdity of his own actions, though he is probably well aware of the world's absurdity. Sut Lovingood knows himself very well. Billy Fishback, on the other hand, never seems to know that he is not only conning others but himself.

The long line of confidence men in American literature includes a vast variety of characters, some real, some fictional. The real ones are, since we know them by their autobiographies or by the descriptions of men who tend to exaggerate, fictional in the way that is appropriate to stories by or about con men. (Of the world's confidence-man fiction, Thomas Mann's *Felix Krull* best defines the jokes that develop when the con man tells his own story.) The American confidence man is Captain John Smith, rewriting his first account of the history of Virginia to enhance his own role and adding the story of noble Pocahontas. John Smith rewrote history to improve his image and to improve on history. (How can Pocahontas become myth if she is drawn only true-to-life?[35]) The American confidence man is the Yankee—peddler, practical farmer, mechanic, businessman—that lean sharper who, as Constance Rourke said, would spring up anywhere you might scratch the soil and come up carved complete, without discernible birth or breeding, and begin to exercise his wits.[36]

He is Haliburton's Sam Slick, who is certain that he will sell his wares at exorbitant prices to each new prospect because he has a sure knowledge of *soft sawder* (flattery) and *human natur*. The confidence man is Dreiser's Cowperwood, overcoming all reverses by his confidence in his knowledge of confidence, or Lewis's Elmer Gantry, creating ludicrous appearances of spirituality but managing to convince and convert thousands, including himself. Dickens recorded the American confidence man in *Martin Chuzzlewit;* there the character was a representative of the Eden Land Corporation. His type was real enough; the actual confidence man of the early and middle 1800s did very well selling shares in communities that were going to be nothing less than new Paradises.[37] The confidence man was a stock character in countless yarns and tales in nineteenth-century journals and newspapers. He was not always victorious, and his story has two forms. Both forms could occur in one book. The first is the story of the biter: con man wins. The second is that of the biter bit: con man wins, then is caught by his own game or by a new game invented by his victim, who becomes the biter of the biter.

These confidence men have the educative function: from two of their kind Huckleberry Finn learns how manipulation of appearances can on the one hand implement survival and on the other oppress and injure. Huck is himself a confidence man, assuming disguises or faking the smallpox, but all of his deceptions are necessary for survival. Readers are always on Huck's side, watching him try to make moral sense out of chaos. His confidence games are comic because they affirm life, and we are pleased by his success. The King and the Duke are at first comic because their deceptions are creative, too; their activities reveal to Huck and to the reader the ludicrous traits of human nature in the people they bilk. They are also comic when their deceptions are turned against them. But the King and the Duke stop being comic when their games go beyond survival or satire. When they try to cheat the Wilks girls out of their inheritance or sell Jim down the river, then they have crossed the line between games of life and games of death.

Billy Fishback, illiterate poor white and Confederate Army straggler, is one of the cruelest of such confidence men. Billy has no redeeming virtues and very little rascally charm. He is the creation of Kittrell J. Warren of Georgia; his book, which bears the ironic title *Life and Public Services of An Army Straggler,* is one of the few contemporary realistic and comic treatments of the Confederate soldier and is even rarer in that it describes a definitely antiromantic nonhero.[38] Billy is occasionally joined in his trickery by one Captain Slaughter, a bogus officer whose real rank is private and who eventually double-crosses Billy. Slaughter speaks a high-flown, Latinate language which Billy says smacks too much of the dictionary to suit his tastes. When the two of them work together (or against each other), they seem to anticipate the pair who spoil Huck's quiet existence on the raft. Warren had one of the sharpest eyes for the absurd of all the southern humorists. His book is a brilliant exploration of the way in which confidence games work and how they can suddenly turn against their manipulator. In it, funny scenes turn horrible, and creative invention all too easily and unexpectedly becomes destructive reality.

Billy is amoral and sinister. Warren refused to acknowledge him as his creation: he is "not my hero" he said in introducing Billy; "He's his own and his country's hero."[39] That statement tells us that Billy is a real and common type and that he is the ironic product of a nation which had been designed for better things. The setting of the story—its geography and the time in which it takes place—is drawn sharply and economically; at first, it scarcely seems there. But its weight is enormous. Here is the ravaged Virginia countryside; across it moves the remnant of Johnston's army, retreating towards Orange in March, 1862. All is chaos and the army itself is disintegrating. Billy is, as Floyd Watkins pointed out, but one of a hundred thousand stragglers and deserters preying off the countryside.[40] The scene is hellish—a nightmare world infested with vultures, winged and human.

Fishback's deceptions are intentionally vicious and deadly. At one point, he steals a horse from a poverty-stricken widow who believes she has lost her husband in the war. The horse is practically her last asset. In another horse theft, he double-crosses his "friend" and accomplice, Dick Ellis, sending a pursuer on Dick's trail who will kill him on the spot when he catches him. His worst deception is posing as a rich Georgia plantation owner in order to get a promise of marriage from young Caroline Graves. He persuades her father to sell his lands at half their value, which, as it turns out, impoverishes the old man. Fishback promises that when they all get to Georgia, Graves will be able to buy twice as much and twice as rich land as he had before for the same money. Billy says that he will take Caroline, the cash, and some slaves and start ahead to Georgia to get things ready; secretly he plans to sell the slaves, keep the cash, abandon Caroline and disappear.

The book would hardly classify as comedy of even the grim variety were it not that all of Billy's vicious tricks turn back on him. He is always first the biter, then the biter bit. Dick Ellis turns up alive and makes it impossible for Billy to get back in his commanding officer's good graces. When Billy returns to the widow's house to rob her a second time, he catches a glimpse of a man he believes must be the woman's new husband, and he springs out the door and runs. The man Billy sees is actually Caroline's brother, and later, when Billy is about to take Caroline as his wife and make off with the fortune, the brother comes up the walk. Billy, thinking that it is the widow's husband coming to get him, aborts his mission again, this time going out through a pane of glass. Warren made all of this doubly ironic: the woman's husband has returned (a sentimental miracle injected into the midst of the comic realism), but Billy never sees him. The brother, whose simple presence ruins both of Billy's schemes, has no knowledge of Billy whatsoever. The manipulator of appearances is the one most vulnerable to appearances.

Warren satirized Billy as a born fool, a man for whom any concept of higher laws was nothing but a joke. Billy perverts and exploits all the cardinal virtues of southern morality: duty, honor, honesty, pride, and respect for women. These are nothing more than tools in his trade. His parents were "married" as the result of "a great many trifling accidents," and Warren elaborated upon this in a comic discussion of the determining influence of blind natural chance.[41] Warren's point is that abstract moral concepts belong to a world entirely different from Fishback's world.

It follows that Warren would emphasize the ironies of Billy's uninformed confidence in his own ability to know the truth beneath the appearances he so blithely manipulates. In the following piece of mock dialectic, Slaughter speaks to someone else and is

overheard by Billy, who makes the counterpoint remarks to himself:

"Inferences are excluded from the analytical dissection of
metaphysical topics. Madam Necker truly observes, 'les limites
des sciences sont comme l'horizon, plus en approche, plus elles
reculent.' They are boundless as space, fathomless as infinity,
and limitless as the range of conception."

Fishback paused, "them words is Slaughter's," thought he,
"nobody never said no sich, but him."

"The clime of Utopia is alone congenial to the growth, expansion and development of doubts, speculations, and uncertainties. They yield to the power of dialects, like a gossamer to the
sturdy stroke of a giant—"

"Sich a dod-dratted fool. Wonder what creek he catcht them
big words outen?"

"There is no such reality as an occult science. Because a
man loses his eye-sight, is no reason why he should proclaim
that the luminous world is an occult and benighted globe. The
fault exists in the vision, not in the great, eternal and immutable
principle."

"Whar on yeath is the fool-killer? he ought to be cash-sheared
for bein outen place. Oh yes, hits Slaughter. Allers talkin gram-
mar, and I can cheat him outen his eye-teeth. Sich talk as that
don't do no good."[42]

Thus Slaughter seems to believe optimistically in a reality that
can be readily perceived, while Billy knows that reality is usually
obscure except to the juggler of appearances (namely himself).
Ironically, however, Slaughter is only pretending to subscribe
to the theory; Billy takes him seriously because he thinks that
what he overhears comes from the Slaughter behind the mask
usually presented to Billy. Later, Billy is duped by Slaughter because he relies on his overheard impression of the "real" Slaughter. Slaughter proves to be the superior confidence man whose
masks are multiple and always in place.

Billy is an absurd man whose character has no positive facets.
He is caught forever in absurd circles, many of his own making.
To Warren, Billy and his prototypes were absurd because they
could not see clearly, were not morally straight, and were totally
detached from the moral abstractions which could guide them.
Billy was born absurd and thus his world would always be absurd.

But Warren did not stay completely aloof from his character. The chaos of the background indicates that Billy's machinations are part of a disintegrating world—a South losing a war and a people losing integrity and human kinship. What finally happens to Billy seems to indicate that Warren knew that the barrier between what was and what was not could evaporate at any moment in any situation. Billy's last big trick occurs on a train crowded with women, children, and wounded soldiers. He wants a seat— he doesn't like to be uncomfortable. He looks around until he finds a young man who is obviously ill, his head down in a manner of indisposition. " 'You're sick,' " says the hero, and when the man admits he is, Billy goes into a pose as physician. He shouts, " 'Got the small-pox—got it bad—they put you in here to kill rebs. Yankee bullets can't kill em fast enough.' " This alarm, of course, causes a general panic, and the whole crowd retreats to the platforms and tops of the other cars. Billy declares that he personally needn't worry: he says he's been inoculated, so he will stay and nurse the sick man. This he does by relieving the poor fellow of all his traveling rations. Billy is satisfied. But then Warren closes the circle. When the train pulls into its next station, a real doctor discovers that the young man does have smallpox. Billy later discovers he has caught it. It kills him.[43] The laugh is on Billy— but what kind of joke is that? Billy's dilemma has suddenly become universal.

Johnson Jones Hooper's Simon Suggs (another confidence man Twain probably knew) is less hateful than Billy Fishback because his methods and attitudes seem more purely creative and less motivated by sheer cruelty. No reader loves Suggs or even sympathizes with him, but he does not inspire the same fear and disgust that Fishback or Sut Lovingood does. Simon is not a great misanthrope; in fact, his attitude towards people seems neutral. His motives for bilking others are not particularly complex: he loves to exploit people for fun and profit. Like Huck, he uses the disguise for survival. "His whole ethical system," wrote the author of his hero, "lies snugly in his favourite aphorism—'IT IS GOOD TO BE SHIFTY IN A NEW COUNTRY'— which means that it is right and proper that one should live as merrily and as comfortably as possible at the expense of others. . . ."[44] And, as Simon constantly finds, the country is always "new"—not only in the sense that it is frontier, but in the sense that every situation is a new opportunity for exploitation. He knows in turn that one's ability to exploit a situation is mathematically dependent upon the number of particular facts he commands about that situation.

The first confidence game Simon plays indicates that, even as a boy, he possesses all the abilities and motivations required of a good player. The game begins when he is caught gambling by his daddy, "an old 'hard shell' Baptist preacher; who, though very pious and remarkably austere, was very avaricious." When Simon sees his father coming, he immediately contrives with Bill, a younger and innocent Negro boy, to pretend that they have been playing mumble-peg. But first, Simon picks up all the money down on the last bet, folding up the cards and stating that his hand had been good enough to win anyway. Bill says, " 'Well, but mass Simon, we nebber finish de game, and de rule—.' " Simon's answer displays the budding confidence man already capably distorting abstract morality to fit the contingencies of the immediate situation: " 'Go to an orful h--l with your rule,' said the impatient Simon—'don't you see daddy's right down upon us, with an armful of hickories?' " Simon then tricks Bill into taking the first licking and subsequently prevents the second licking, scheduled for himself, entirely. He entices his father into a little game. He appeals first to his father's incredulity and pride by saying that he can cut cards better than any sharper in Augusta. His daddy has visited that thriving place and is convinced this makes him a traveler and a sophisticated man. Then Simon penetrates to the heart of his father's greed and vanity by wagering to draw a jack on a cut, just like the local rascal, Bob Smith. (The stakes are Simon's ten dollars and seventy-five cents against his daddy's best horse.) Daddy takes the bait because he feels a keen rivalry with Smith: " 'if it's book knowledge or plain sense, and Bob kin do it, it's reasonable to s'pose that old Jed'diah Suggs won't be bothered *bad.*' "[45] But what Simon knows is not a matter of book knowledge or plain sense; it's a twist of the wrist, and daddy loses.

The chapter in which Simon cheats his daddy contains some illuminating machinations on Simon's part involving his daddy's belief in predestination. Simon wonders if he really has to remain "predestinated" to take the same licking that Bill takes. He counters this apparent inevitability by calling on the paradox of inevitability itself—a masterful ploy, since it involves turning his own absurd predicament inside out and directing his father's most precious philosophical tenet back upon him. " 'It ain't no use, daddy,' " says Simon, as his father approaches menacingly; " 'I'm gwine to play cards as long as I live. . . . So what's the use of beatin' me about it.' " This argument leads his daddy into partial acquiescence, softening him up for further arguments bearing on predestination. Simon next cons his father into believing that the loss of his horse is God's providence. He is delighted that what daddy thinks is God's will is actually his own simple trickery. Simon nearly collapses laughing, repeating over and over his father's own line: " 'Oh, it's so funny that it could all a' been *fixed aforehand!* ' "[46] The next day Simon leaves home on his new horse to make his fortune in a world he will "fix aforehand," stacking the deck and "predestinating" the outcome, whenever and wherever he can.

Simon's success is contingent upon a sharp sense of how appearances rule lives and how human nature actually prefers to rely upon appearances. He knows exactly what his victim takes on faith, exactly how far his victim's logic goes, exactly how this man or that will respond to certain selected stimuli. He is, the author said, a "miracle of shrewdness. He possesses in an eminent degree, that tact which enables man to detect the *soft spots* in his fellow, and to assimilate himself to whatever company he may fall in with." The flexibility Simon needs, he has; it derives from "a quick, ready wit." Nature gave him exactly what he needed to be what he was: "if she made him, in respect to his moral conformation, a beast of prey, she did not refine the cruelty by denying him the fangs and the claws."[47] Hooper saw his character as morally repulsive but showed how Suggs is morally neutral from Suggs's own point of view. To Simon's eyes, the world is either a dangerous trap or a waiting prize. The way he escapes the dangerous trap and wins the prize is to become himself first the perceiver of traps and then their maker. Simon becomes captain of the Tallapoosa Volunteers during the Creek War of 1836, and he does it by exploiting fear and knowing the facts. The " 'badly-scared' mortality"—the frightened population—gathers in the center of town. Suggs, delighted in the confusion, declares himself to be well informed as to the Indians' attitudes and whereabouts. He knows that there are no Indians within ten miles but does not disclose this fact to the terrified people in front of the store: "Suggs was never the man to destroy his own importance in that sort of way." He magnifies the danger, in fact, and impresses upon the crowd "that he, Simon Suggs, was the only man at whose hands they could expect a deliverance from the imminent peril which impended." He is quickly elected leader.

Rascally as he is, Simon is drawn as actually being an appropriate captain for the Tallapoosa folk. " 'Suggs is the man,' " they shout in accord when in his oration he declares that they need a leader who is, " 'more'n all, a man that's acquainted with the country and the ways of the Injuns!' "[48] In short, they are unacquainted, and he is acquainted—with the country and with the facts. He is the man the unacquainted ones need, or, at least, the one they will inevitably get. Hooper implied that they deserve him.

Hooper apparently intended his portrait of Suggs to be a very general satire. The book's structure is itself a lampoon of campaign biographies, two specific objects of satire being Andrew Jackson and biographies of Jackson.[49] The satire is broadened by Hooper's discussion of biography writing and image-making. First he pointed out that a totally "true" biography of any man could be no better than an embarrassment: the Grocer Tibbetts, for instance, would blush mightily with "pangs of wounded modesty" if a biographer should "present him to the world in all the resplendent glory of his public and private virtues!" It would be kindest to wait at least until the subject was dead. Nothing could be more revolting than "that everybody should know all about us in our life-times, notwithstanding our characters may present something better even than a fair average of virtue and talent." Hooper is, of course, satirically pointing out that a biography always revises something, tailoring the man to fit the writer's idea of the man or, more commonly, the writer's idea of the way his audience wants its man to be. In his satirical persona, Hooper says that since Suggs may soon run for office, it is desirable to present to the public his image. The word *image* is Hooper's, and he added that the object of a campaign biography is to "create an idea of [the candidate's] *physique*." The biography of Suggs, the author continued, will do no more nor less than furnish his supporters "with such information respecting himself, as will enable them to vindicate his character whenever and wherever it may be attacked by the ruthless and polluted tongues of [his] enemies."[50]

Hooper's characterization of Suggs is a study in a universal comic phenomenon. His hero is ancient and ubiquitous. Suggs is the type of the perceiver and manipulator of absurdity; he manufactures his world as he goes along, tailoring it for his own well-being. His flexibility is enhanced by the fact that the world of his victims is a moral vacuum. That vacuum allows him room to operate. He is never encumbered by the feeling that he needs to create a morality to fill that vacuum; he scarcely sees his opportunities in the light of morality in the first place. He simply knows that there is a vacuum, and it is all new country waiting to be exploited by his shiftiness. He is the perfect amoral pragmatist.

George Washington Harris's Sut Lovingood is not unconsciously and blissfully amoral. He is consciously certain that there is no definitive abstract morality in the universe. He is convinced that he is predetermined by neutral forces to be what he is—Sut and nobody else. He naturally believes that he is absurd, too, and that any morality he might create would be absurd in turn. Therefore he spends his life exercising his absurdity to the fullest. " 'Men,' " says Sut, " 'wer made a-purpus jis' tu eat, drink, an' fur stayin awake in the yearly part ove the nites; an' wimen wer made tu cook the vittils, mix the sperits, an' help the men du the stayin awake. That's all, an' nuthin more, onless hits fur the wimen tu raise the devil atwix meals, an' knit socks atwix drams, an' the men tu play short kerds, swap hosses wif fools, an' fite fur exersise at odd spells. ' "[51]

Sut says that he is going to be "king fool" one day—unless his daddy never dies. As long as his father is alive, Sut has to take second place. In a story about how his daddy once acted like a horse, Sut, ever aware of the importance of the face of things, says his dad did better in the role of horse than in the role of husband and father. Sut's vision includes the awareness that a man's evaluation of a situation depends on where he stands in respect to it. When his daddy goes over the river bank with hornets on his tail, Sut points out, " 'Dad cudent see the funny part frum whar he wer, but hit seem'd tu be inturestin tu him frum the 'tenshun he wer payin tu the bisness ove divin an' cussin.' "[52]

Sut has been called an existential hero because he admits that he has no soul (he has instead a " 'whisky proof gizzard' "), that he is a fool, that he is funny-looking, and that the things he can do best are hold liquor and get in trouble.[53] Sut becomes, of course, a sadistic monster when his awareness of his own depravity pushes him to the extremes of the actions made possible by that awareness. For him to watch his daddy floundering in the creek without trying to help him is funny, all right, and innocent enough from his point of view and the reader's (perhaps). But then Sut casually remarks that he hasn't seen his daddy since. Did he drown? That doesn't seem problematical to Sut. Sut's vicious joke on Mrs. Yardley—he frightens a horse which runs through her yard and drags away a clothesline holding all her prize quilts—leads to her death by heart failure. But Sut sees it all as Mrs. Yardley's own fault, because she insisted on getting worked up over such trivial things.[54]

Harris used Sut as a vehicle for a variety of satirical and philosophical statements. On the one hand, he was able to reveal the destructive possibilities of the casually nihilistic activities growing out of Sut's backwoods brand of absurd creation. On the other hand, the fact that Sut is a sharp iconoclast served Harris well for the purposes of satire. Sut is responsible for a number of attacks on hellfire preachers, and he relishes nothing more than routing all the excitable worshipers at a camp meeting. Sometimes, when his viciousness is not dominant, Sut gains the reader's admiration by asserting his own total independence of the institutions and customs designed to impose order on human eccentricities.[55] Thus Harris satirized beliefs commonly accepted as immutable truths. The implication of many stories is that Sut's victims (like Suggs's) deserve what they get, and it requires the sharp eye and unique talents of the creative Sut to bring their ludicrous faults out into the open.

Ultimately, however, the reader tends to hate Sut, and it is difficult to accept the idea that Harris tried to make his character perceptive. It is easy to see that Harris was being perceptive about human nature and the problem of the absurd view. He was, however, being extremely critical of Sut as well. He gave Sut the absurd view but made him an absurd and dangerous man. Sut's absurd perception limits his vision instead of expanding it. Harris's satire focuses on the conflict between the deliberately nihilistic Sut and the blindness of archaic institutions and customs. The satire falls on both. Sut's world is a world in which all is not well, and only the comic response to his absurdity and that world's absurdity—a response shared by Harris and his reader —contains any shred of saving grace.

Billy Fishback, Simon Suggs, and Sut Lovingood are, at last, implicitly and explicitly condemned by their creators. These characters have enough sense to manipulate their worlds and to create a structure that suffices to maintain the sensual life for a time. But Billy, Simon, and Sut are ludicrous because they find no way to create meaning in their worlds. Most of the figures of the genre—Sut excepted—are not even aware of their own absurdity. Sut is the conscious absurd man, but he, too, has no desire to try to invent meaning. That is why he is appealing for his honesty and repulsive for his nihilism. By assuming a detached and superior point of view from which author and reader can watch absurd manipulators in an absurd world, these authors created an alternative to that kind of nihilism. Simon's amorality or Sut's absurd view does not have to be accepted by the reader; these authors have provided the reader the option of laughing the Satanic confidence man out of existence.

IV

The Descent to Faith: Herman Melville

Since this *world, then, can baffle so—*
Our natural harbour—it were strange
If that *alleged, which is afar,*
Should not confound us when we range
In revery where its problems are.—
Such thoughts!

CLAREL

I · CAPTAIN COOK'S TOE AND OTHER JOLLY PUZZLES

HERMAN MELVILLE had double vision. He habitually used sentence structures which are inherently ambiguous. He could deliberately generate numerous ambivalent statements while letting his style itself precipitate automatically other unanticipated ambiguities. He favored phrases such as "not unlike" and "to all appearances." He was master of the simile, which always leaves a comparison hanging as comparison, inviting the reader to make the connective leap if he wishes while the author need not admit any intention on his part. When White-Jacket says that in a storm "You become identified with the tempest; your insignificance is lost in the riot of the stormy universe around" does he mean that we have then found our significance or that we are an insignificance lost in the gale?[1] What could be more ambiguous than "Call me Ishmael"? That is what we are willing to call you, the reader must respond, but who, indeed, are you? The crucial opening sentence of *The Confidence-Man,* besides fixing the whole story as an April Fools' Day event, compares the man in cream-colors to Manco Capac, the first Inca, the sun's incarnation. The reader is led immediately to identify this first avatar of the Confidence-Man with the sun god, Christ, Prometheus—light-bringers of history and myth. But this comparison reads "there appeared, suddenly as Manco Capac at the lake Titicaca, a man in cream-colors. . . ."[2] The use of "suddenly as" is the author's own April Fools' joke, the first of many: he leaves the reader no way to know whether he intends the comparison to be simply a comparison or the Confidence-Man and the light-bringer to be metaphorical equivalents. Melville was also master of the ambiguities fostered by the variance in characters' points of view within a story. Ishmael tells what the white whale was to him, Starbuck has a different—and practical— view, and Ahab expands the whale's meaning constantly. Ahab says, " 'To me, the white whale is that wall. . . .' "[3] The character alone makes that judgment, and the author behind the book remains inscrutable.

The ambiguities of Melville's techniques reflect directly the theme in all his books that the meaning of the universe is not available to men because all evidence contradicts itself. This theme is the source of the tragedy of *Moby-Dick, Billy Budd,* and the last half of *Pierre.* It is also the source of the absurd humor in all of his books. This means that Melville's comedy always yields that laughter in the face of ambivalence which must be strictly arbitrary. Camus was probably not thinking of Melville's humor when he called *Moby-Dick* a truly absurd work.[4] In context, Camus was apparently referring to *Moby-Dick* as one example of a book whose central point was the impossibility of discovering abstract meaning. In this view, Ahab is the imaginative man, striking through the mask in the traditionally heroic attempt to discover essential truth. Ahab appears at first to be the absurd creator because he assigns meaning to the whale and shapes the quest for himself and the crew. On the other hand, Ahab does not re-create reality, solving the problem of how to live in the world. In Camus's view, Ahab is the suicide. The creators in the book who "live doubly"—Camus's phrase—are Ishmael and Queequeg, and these two are comic characters. And they have an affirmative sense of humor.

Melville displayed his sense of the absurd best in *The Confidence-Man* and there showed most clearly how the comic response to the absurd is a matter of purely arbitrary confidence. But the comedy which arises from the absurd view appears everywhere in Melville's fiction, and it developed as his own ironic sense developed. It is well, then, to begin with his travel narratives. These are the books in which he consciously imitated the satiric forms used by Swift, Fielding, and Smollett, and it is in these books that he explored the fascinating results of the abrupt combination of the practical, humorous, native American character and a primitive, mysterious environment.

Melville's first book is a comedy of terrors. In *Typee,* potentially dangerous and horrifying encounters are infused with light irony, and rescues are effected by unlikely coincidences. Melville based *Typee* on his experience and was following the tradition that demanded of story-telling travelers plenty of harrowing adventures and hairbreadth escapes. He drew upon the already popular themes of frontier humor, which always combined the terrible and the funny.[5] Furthermore, the setting of *Typee* is exactly right for ambivalent comedy: a sailor on a whaling ship knew various basic hardships by direct and unequivocal experience, and a prolonged visit among South Sea natives was a life of ambiguity among a people whose intentions and attitudes towards their visitors were always obscure. By putting the story into the words of a narrator susceptible to confusion who elaborates generously upon the facts, Melville enhanced all the implications of his comedy.

The ambivalence of the world as metaphorized by the ambiguity faced by a white man among the islanders is precisely expressed by the apocryphal story Tommo tells about Captain Cook, the famed circumnavigator. The Sandwich Islanders, he noticed, were always unwilling to allude to the fate of Cook, because rumor had established the belief among both islanders and whites that cannibals had devoured him. Whether or not this is true could never be known because "The Polynesians are aware of the detestation in which Europeans hold this custom, and therefore invariably deny its existence, and, with the craft peculiar to savages, endeavor to conceal every trace of it." At Karakikova, the scene of Cook's demise, a post marks the place where the explorer was supposedly buried, but the narrator does not believe that Cook was given a Christian burial, as the natives claimed. That claim "was a piece of imposture which was sought to be palmed off upon the credulous Englishman." There was, Tommo recalls, an old chief on the island of Mowee, who "gave himself out among the foreign residents of the place as the living tomb of Captain Cook's big toe!—affirming, that at the cannibal enter-tainment which ensued after the lamented Briton's death, that particular portion of his body had fallen to his share." This chief was prosecuted in the courts by his countrymen—not for can-nibalism, but for lying. This amounted only to defamation of his character, for none could prove whether or not the chief told the truth. The only evidence was the story under question. The result was the making of the chief's fortune; from the trial he received tremendous advertising, and ever afterward he exhibited himself to all who came as the man who had indeed eaten "the great navigator's great toe."[6]

This blackly funny story is no joke to Tommo because it is one of a series of dark imaginings which contribute to his dilemma in Paradise. All of his thoughts become colored by suspicion as time wears on in Typee. He discovers in the midst of bliss that he can no longer trust the natives who care so well for him. Do those packages hanging in one hut represent some concrete evidence that the Typee are indeed cannibals? His suspicious and confused vision sees them as nuggets of veiled truth, and an instant's glimpse convinces him that they do contain shrunken heads. Another bundle appears to hold a fresh skeleton, and the natives' assurance that the bones are those of a pig does nothing to allay his fears. He knows that he might be jumping to conclusions, but this possibility only complicates matters: "My imagination ran riot in these horrid speculations, and I felt certain that the worst possible evils would befal me." In scene after scene, he glimpses something which he first believes is conclusive evidence that the Typee are or are not cannibals only to have his evidence dissolve into ambiguity even as he reflects upon its concreteness. Further observation results only in renewed confusion.

It is important to note that his apprehensions occur just when Tommo is beginning to feel the constraints, the boredom, and the little annoyances of confinement to one way of life, no matter how ideal it seems in terms of creature comforts. "I had," he says, "grown familiar with the narrow limits to which my wanderings had been confined; and I began bitterly to feel the state of captivity in which I was held." Kory-Kory, his friend and transportation, is still devoted to him, the beautiful Fayaway is still enchanting, and the king Mehevi is just as gracious as before. But now Karky the artist and some of the other natives harrass Tommo daily by demanding that he submit to tattooing. The disappearance of his shipmate Toby weighs more heavily than ever upon him. His injured leg flairs into infection again. He is, as he admits, in an "unhappy frame of mind," a state in which "every circumstance which evinced the savage nature of the beings at whose mercy I was, augmented the fearful apprehensions that consumed me." So it is that Tommo decides to escape from the ambiguous island as soon as he can.[7]

Melville was not trying to show that Tommo simply imagined all the dangers on an actually harmless island. He was instead showing how the reliability of apparently factual data disappears when the mind cannot manufacture confidence in the data's factuality. For Tommo, data and perception work together in such a way that he not only thinks his situation is ambiguous, he knows that he cannot be sure whether that ambiguity is real or in his mind. Only a fool would remain in this ambiguous Paradise. The natives' attempts to recapture him when he tries to escape do give him a moment of assurance. Under the stress of pursuit, the ambiguities disappear—for the moment. He is finally rescued but, ironically, not as a result of his own efforts, except for his having forced his way to the sea's edge. An Australian ship has come to get him, sent by a native who chanced to inform the captain that he could find a much-needed sailor at the bay of Typee. This time, the capricious unknown yields safety instead of danger. Tommo's numerous alarms, escapes, and ambiguous experiences do not cause him any lasting misery, and he now has a remarkable horde of comic stories with which to amuse his fellows on board the *Julia*. Furthermore, it is in his character to proclaim a love for ambivalence once the danger is removed. He sees the ambiguity of Typee as perilous but responds continually, without hesitation, to the urgent appeal of new mysteries: "however ignorant man may be, he still feels within him his immortal spirit yearning after the unknown future."[8]

Melville implied in *Typee* that creatures in Paradise can be only creatures of Paradise. They are indistinguishable from their environment; having never made a choice, they have no viable identity. If Tommo were to remain on the island, he would have to become Typee. He would get tattooed, succumb to Fayaway's charms, and adopt all the customs of the place. By escaping, he can continue to become himself. This dilemma is a joke because Melville has refined it by a fitting gastronomic pun. If Tommo were to stay, he would run the risk of being absorbed into the Typee literally—by being devoured and digested.

To understand fully the intention of Melville's humor in *Typee*, the comedy about the ambiguity of Paradise should be seen in conjunction with Melville's diatribes (delivered directly through the persona) against Christian missions. His view was that Christian "civilization" had brought nothing more than disease and moral confusion to the islands. Melville was attacking both a Christian idealism that had degenerated and the romantic belief that primitive life is untainted and "true." He was not idealizing the primitive mode of existence, as a casual reader of the book might be led to believe. It is true that he made life in Typee—before Tommo falls prey to ambiguity—appear to be more sane, more common-sensical, more orderly than what American and European Christians thought to be the civilized way of life. But Tommo does not escape paradox in that haven of bliss, and the comedy of his dilemma is the product of an authorial rejection of any idea that life could be made easy by a "perfect" environment. It is also important to remember that Tommo is not capable of solving mysteries or determining his own fate. *Typee* is a book that does not offer any solution—either in the form of a system or in a character—to the universe's ambivalence.[9]

The Descent to Faith: Herman Melville

In *Omoo,* Melville shifted focus from the world's general ambivalence to its specific comic absurdities. Whereas Tommo in
Typee seems, in his quest to find and solve mysteries, forever to
discover and flee ambiguity, the narrator of *Omoo* (who is the
same man as the Tommo of the first book), in his quest for a
stable and productive situation, finds and again repeatedly flees
continuous sequences of grotesque events and scenes. The whole
book is designed to present men, systems, and situations as the
grim and funny realities of an absurd world. Doctor Long Ghost
plays pranks on the black cook and perpetrates variations on the
ship's favorite practical joke of hoisting sleeping sailors into the
rigging. Cockroaches and rats occupy the sailors' dishes and food
tins in the forecastle and are so numerous no one bothers to kill
them. The ship, a rotten hulk, is named the *Julia* and ironically
nicknamed the *Little Jule.* Graveyard humor based on the grim
realities of life at sea is plentiful: the hero wakes several times
to find a sick man's hand resting on his chest and, not wishing to
disturb the fellow, removes it carefully. The fourth time this
happens, the arm falls stark and stiff; the man is dead. This
sailor is buried without compunction, and his belongings distributed among the crew. At the time, in spite of the fact that a number
of sailors are ill, a state of mirthfulness pervades the ship, in
"shocking contrast," states the narrator, "with the situation of
some of the invalids." This hilarity on the part of the sailors seems
an alternative to grief and immobility—they are all grinning
fatalists. "Behold here the fate of a sailor! They give him the last
toss, and no one asks whose child he was."[10]

The most important elements of this picture of the absurd world
are the settings of the book itself. Melville developed in *Omoo* the
technique of making the ship a microcosm of the world, a metaphor he was to explore seriously in *White-Jacket* and *Moby-Dick.*
The ship in *Omoo* is a setting created strictly for dark comedy. Sailors stick their knives into the hull, and great chunks of wood fall
away. In this ship, being afloat means being about to sink. The
ship's edibles are inedible: everything was bought at an auction of
condemned navy stores at Sydney. The pork is rusty and spoiled,
the beef like mahogany-colored rope, and the biscuits honey-
combed with worm tunnels. An apocryphal story runs about the
ship that the cook found a horseshoe in the bottom of a beef

cask. As the narrator eats the last of a precious can of molasses, he finds the body of some unmentionable creature at its bottom. The *Julia* is a comic Inferno. Everything is so grotesque that the sailors cannot avoid laughter, but their hilarity is defensive: underneath this grim joking lies the constant awareness that only rotten timbers form the barricade against the sea and death.

The setting shifts that occur in *Omoo* do not take the reader out of the absurd when they take him away from the ship. Part of the crew, including the doctor and the narrator, refuse to remain on the *Julia* and are arrested for desertion and confined in the *Calabooza* on Tahiti. This is an outdoor "jail," an open place, a "beautiful spot," through which flows a mountain stream descending from a green hill. A beach sparkles nearby. This beauty is deceptive; close inspection reveals the place to be "extremely romantic in appearance" but "ill adapted to domestic comfort." At first, it seems that the sailors' discomfort has nothing to do with this setting. The prisoners are locked in manacles, a punishment which turns out to be a form of medieval torture: "there was no way of lying but straight on your back; unless, to be sure, one's limb went round and round in the ankle, like a swivel."[11] This posture precipitates nightmares. The manacles are eventually removed, and for a while the "prisoners" enjoy an idyllic life on the island, but, like the paradise of Typee, the island itself soon proves to be an intolerable prison. Long Ghost, ever the shrewd and careful man of the world, recognizes the uncertainty of their situation by saying, " 'In my poor opinion . . . it behooves a stranger, in Tahiti, to have his knife in readiness, and his caster slung.' "[12] Like Simon Suggs, he knows one has to be shifty in a new country, even lovely Tahiti.

Two other important settings also prove absurd. One, the immaculate, brand-new, ornate French man-of-war, the *Reine Blanch,* is actually a bedlam of pointless activity: the sailors spend their hours in repeated and unnecessary maneuvers, sail changes, and combat practice. They are, the hero says, "forever at quarters; running in and out the enormous guns, as if their arms were made for nothing else."[13] This kind of explicit attack on military discipline and practice is, of course, the kind of satire that characterizes *White-Jacket*. The world of the tight ship ought to be the very essence of orderliness; instead it is the very epitome of ludicrousness. The other setting is part of another satire on the primitive and rural life so readily romanticized by Melville's enchanted contemporaries. The narrator and Long Ghost hire themselves out to two men who own a plantation on the island of Imeeo. Here is their emblematic chance to start anew, seek fresh prospects, make a better living, and above all to work harmoniously in God's nature, with the sun above, the earth firm under their feet, and green life all about them. All of this turns out to be a matter of pulling stumps and laboriously hunting wild cattle. Everything they do is ludicrous and futile, profitless and without pleasure. It is little wonder that the hero is last seen heading out again, the islands sinking under the horizon behind him, the wide Pacific stretching before him.

Of Melville's later two travel books, *White-Jacket* is the more deliberate comedy of absurdities, and *Redburn* the more serious satire, containing definite implications about the kind of reform that is always needed in the world. *White-Jacket*, of course, did have as a rhetorical objective the informing of the American public about the criminal utilization of flogging as punishment, but this institution is attacked simply and directly instead of being satirized artistically. The narrator voices the attack by addressing the reader; his opinions are Melville's. In *Redburn*, Melville's opinion is not stated so directly; it is woven into character psychology and plot. It is revealed by Redburn's experiences, his contact with the horrors of Liverpool, and his reactions to the world's grotesqueness. There are few laughs in *Redburn*; its comedy lies in the exposure of the hero's innocence and in the rare moments when he is able to transcend his isolation. *White-Jacket's* comedy is simpler, though it is also the comedy of the absurd. The difference is that White-Jacket himself has a point of view that allows him to maintain a sense of humor, and it is he who tells the tale.

The narrator's white jacket itself begins its life as a joke, reflecting the awkward vulnerability of its impoverished and footloose owner. It is a patchwork affair, an old shirt quilted together and lined with ersatz rags. It is not waterproof. In a rain it is a burden, and its brightness makes White-Jacket stand out in a crowd, an easy mark for an officer seeking a hand for extra duty. The jacket is a perfect comic ambiguity. It covers the hero but keeps him wet and cold at the same time. It more than once nearly causes his death, but it is also the catalyst for his education. When he sheds it for the last time, its removal symbolizes departing innocence but also a new acquisition of the strength that allows him to save himself. It is the object of a metaphysical cosmic joke that begins with a pun: "Jacket," says the narrator, "I cannot consent to die for *you*, but be dyed you must for me. You can dye many times without injury; but I cannot die without irreparable loss, and running the eternal risk." The pun is extended by the fact that White-Jacket never does find a way to color or waterproof his jacket—the paint is locked up. This in turn precipitates a very funny identity crisis. White-Jacket pleads for paint because his whiteness makes him look like a spook aloft, an illusion which almost gets him killed when the frightened sailors lower him in the halyards. He pleads for paint because he thinks that it requires only a little visible marking to make a man a man. But paint is in short supply, and he is appalled at being refused: "What! when but one dab of paint would make a man of a ghost . . . to refuse it!"[14]

The setting of the book is an even more extensive comic paradox. This is a man-of-war world, programed to be orderly and perfectly disciplined. Everything is preset, predetermined, and accounted for ahead of time by strict regulation. This system's hierarchy is complete, and the rule of obedience to higher command covers all contingencies. It is totally appropriate to the absurd view, then, that this highly structured world be morally chaotic. The duties of all the various ranks are endless and "would require a German commentator to chronicle."[15] In war or peace, maneuvers are ludicrous: if there is no battle, then sailors man their stations for the purpose of pretending to fire at an absent enemy and tack endlessly for the purpose of eluding nothing. If there is a battle, then blood and brains are splattered about in a contest without winners. The ceremonials of a man-of-war are just as irrational, particularly those designed to flatter dignitaries ashore: "while shore pomp in high places has come to be regarded by the more intelligent masses of men as belonging to the absurd, ridiculous, and mock-heroic . . . there still lingers in American men-of-war all the stilted etiquette and childish parade of the old-fashioned Spanish Court of Madrid."[16] The very symbol and epitome of naval order, honor, and majesty, observes White-Jacket, is the commodore. What are those messages he passes to his secretary, so carefully and secretively handled, so obviously full of destiny for nations? White-Jacket finds one in the scupperhole: " 'Sir,' " it reads, " 'you will give the people pickles to-day with their fresh meat.' "[17] This world's absurdity is compounded by the fact that certain non-actions which would appear to be meaningless are actually not absurd in comparison to actions commonly accepted as meaningful. Sailors may say they believe men are immortal, but they put their faith elsewhere: "let us candidly confess it, shipmates, that, upon the whole, our dinners are the most momentous affairs of these lives we lead beneath the moon. What were a day without a dinner? a dinnerless day! such a day had better be a night."[18] This remark is being satirized and is to be taken as an innocent absurdity. But, in another sense, it is a seriously presented moral alternative. Those in the man-of-war world who attend to their dinners do nothing more than create themselves, directing cannon at no one. In this world, inaction yields some small meaning; action yields annihilation.

Against the background of this ordered chaos with its absurd formal structures, the novel's darkest comic observations are made. Commodores are gentlemen, says White-Jacket, and would never fire a dirty shot into a foe; thus the men are made to clean all rusty cannon balls until they shine. How are officers promoted? Over the buried heads of dead messmates.[19] The officers' continual invention of work usually has no more purpose than glorification of the command, as in the furling and unfurling of sails done in port to impress other ships, and is not only meaningless but dangerous. In one such maneuver, poor Baldy falls out of the rigging, crushing all his bones. The deaths of uncounted sailors, says White-Jacket, are to be attributed to nothing less than "the souls of those officers, who, while safely standing on deck themselves, scruple not to sacrifice an immortal man or two, in order to show off the excelling discipline of the ship."[20]

Some of the best grim jokes in the book center on the actions of the ultrascientific and objective Doctor Cuticle. It is he who performs the famous grotesque amputation, voicing in his running commentary his indifference to the value of life. When his patient dies, he bats not an eye, and invites his onlookers to a second showing: " 'The body, also, gentlemen, at ten precisely. . . .' "[21] Cuticle is absurdly creative in a terrifying way—in the face of death, he coolly proclaims a postmortem. The details of the operation—the cutting, the sawing, the bleeding—are not presented as Gothic nightmare; they are to be taken as realities. A moment's reflection finds them all too real. When Cuticle commences to cut, the other doctors take out their watches to see if he can live up to his reputation of being able to "drop a leg in one minute and ten seconds from the moment the knife touches it. . . ."[22] Cuticle himself has been bested only once in a lifetime of playing the game of scientific objectivity. This occurred when a lieutenant presented him with a sago pudding, claiming it to be a specimen of cancer. The good doctor believed him and was surprised and angry when the lieutenant proceeded to taste it. His anger only increased when he discovered he had been duped.[23]

Melville knew that the comedy in the presentation of the world of *White-Jacket* as absurd was contingent upon the ability of an observer to shift his viewpoint. Such a shift produces new insights into the ludicrousness of accepted patterns of behavior. This also means that two divergent opinions can coexist. Melville has White-Jacket perceive and express these observations as truths. A savage wandering the gundeck in his barbaric robe, White-Jacket remarks, seems to be "a being from some other sphere," and though his tastes may be "our abominations," our tastes will be his as well. "We thought him a loon: he fancied us fools. Had the case been reversed; had we been Polynesians and he an American, our mutual opinion of each other would still have remained the same. A fact proving that neither was wrong, but both right."[24] This kind of relativistic reasoning lies behind the long diatribes against the arbitrariness of naval law. White-Jacket attacks especially the ludicrousness of a legal system that allows instantaneous punishment for anything some capricious officer believes to be an infraction of a rule. The rule in turn may have nothing to do with the demands of the situation and may not even be obeyed by the officer himself. When White-Jacket uses the word "absurd" in this connection, it is a pejorative term and implies nothing creative. Corporal punishment was justified in the navy Melville knew because it could be inflicted quickly and effectively, without losing time or allowing the victim and his mates a chance to mull it over. This and other arguments are coldly logical, White-Jacket says, but are also "Absurd, or worse than absurd, as it may appear . . . and if you start from the same premises with these officers, you must admit that they advance an irresistible argument."[25] This absurd reasoning, which is a blind logic proceeding from ludicrous assumptions, led to obvious abuses, not the least of which is that thirteen of some twenty penal offenses a seaman might commit were punishable by death.[26]

White-Jacket occasionally reflects upon the comedy of the ironies of moral relativism, and it is this sense of humor that saves him. "We perceived," he reports, that sin was really warped understanding and "evil was but good disguised, and a knave a saint in his way; how that in other planets, perhaps, what we deem wrong may there be deemed right. . . ." The sailors on the warship were aware, he remembers, that it often seemed that the millennium had arrived, all distinctions had been wiped out, and their apparently miserable condition had become that state in which a man could be happy even in a pit of death, with cold clods being thrown on his face. He tells us that although he accepted this stoicism, it was a joke, for his philosophy was often "taken aback" by events on board. After all, "philosophy—that is, the best wisdom that has ever in any way been revealed to our man-of-war world—is but a slough and a mire, with a few tufts of good footing here and there." How can he joke?—"we never forgot that our frigate, bad as it was, was homeward bound."[27] What does a sailor do when he finds himself regretting his chosen profession? There is no substitute in this condition for "a shelf of merrily bound books, containing comedies, farces, songs, and humorous novels." *Gil Blas* and *Peregrine Pickle* would do for a start.[28] White-Jacket is able to take the irony of his own condition as comic, but his is, after all, a relatively safe laughter, since his ship is homeward bound.

Finally, White-Jacket realizes that not only is the man-of-war a comic world, but the world is like the comic man-of-war. The world, too, is made up of opposites, peopled by men with "counterlikes and dislikes" which dovetail into one another, the whole cleverly united "like the parts of a Chinese puzzle." Furthermore, he notes, "as, in a Chinese puzzle, many pieces are hard to place, so there are some unfortunate fellows who can never slip into their proper angles, and thus the whole puzzle becomes a puzzle indeed, which is the precise condition of the greatest puzzle in the world—this man-of-war world itself."[29] Would White-Jacket change it? He would have his story end in the middle of everything, with the *Neversink* still at sea: "I love an indefinite, infinite background—a vast, heaving, rolling, mysterious rear!" This mystery is reality; the earth sails securely through space as the man-of-war *Neversink* sails through the sea. White-Jacket thinks of the planet as "one craft in a Milky-Way fleet, of which God is the Lord High Admiral." We sail, he says, under sealed orders, ourselves "the repositories of the secret packet, whose mysterious contents we long to learn." But this voyage will be more than an endless circumnavigation of space, he believes, because the evidence of this life shows that a port awaits us. White-Jacket draws a moral from his optimistic and sentimental cosmology by saying that men must save themselves: "the worst of our evils we blindly inflict upon ourselves; our officers cannot remove them, even if they would." He then ends with a statement to the effect that ultimately our Lord High Admiral will interpose, and all will be well, just as the *Neversink* will eventually reach port. His reasoning, of course, is entirely circular. He says in one breath that God will intercede, and in another he demonstrates that He cannot or will not intercede.[30] This reasoning is a function of White-Jacket's sense of humor. Melville is satirizing it as circular and weakly pantheistic, but at the same time he shows its power to enable White-Jacket to live with ambivalence.

Redburn is a dark book in which occasional bits of unmistakable rough humor and satire do not outweigh unambiguously serious mysteries. Redburn continually encounters dire events which have no apparent rationale; the world he sees is absurd but usually without comedy. Situations are never clear to him, and all that he sees is threatening, fearful, and tragic. He cannot understand (and since he is the narrator we never learn) what is wrong with Harry Bolton. Harry generously offers to show

Redburn England, but wherever they go Redburn is puzzled because Harry doesn't tell him where they are. Redburn sees Harry's England in a vacuum; it is a set of visible places without names or identities. His tours of Liverpool are descents into hell. He sees a woman clutching a dead baby, another two children clinging to her rags, starving to death in the bottom of a black hole. He has no way to help them, cannot find anyone in authority willing to send aid, and finally, returning to the place, discovers only a pile of quicklime. Emigrants, he learns, are often crammed into the holds of unsafe ships without the owners having provided food or sanitary facilities; this means nothing less than that men have killed others for the price of passage.

All of these things and more are the observations that change Redburn from the comical and bumbling novice sailor of the first chapters to the enlightened and worldly moralist of the last. Redburn is the object of ridicule at first, but, as he is exposed to the absurdities of the real world, he learns how to perceive these absurdities and thus become the observer of the ludicrous himself. It is the Redburn of the last chapters that can say, "We talk of the Turks, and abhor the cannibals; but may not some of *them* go to heaven before some of *us*? We may have civilised bodies and yet barbarous souls. We are blind to the real sights of this world; deaf to its voice; and dead to its death. And not till we know that one grief outweighs ten thousand joys will we become what Christianity is striving to make us."[31]

Redburn carries a quite clear moral. In the face of mysteries, ridicule, misanthropy, injustice, pain, disease, and death, Redburn creates an idealized alternative. He sees that people are senselessly indifferent to anything outside themselves, that the apparently generous rich have nothing but cold and meaningless charitable intentions, and that institutions formulated to relieve miseries actually compound them. His alternative is primitive, unassuming human love which rejects the misanthropy of "the diabolical Tiberius at Capreae; who even in his self-exile, embittered by bodily pangs, and unspeakable mental terrors . . . yet did not give over his blasphemies. . . ."[32] Men must become, if they are to save themselves, deeply civilized, not "blind to the real sights of this world; deaf to its voice; and dead to its death." To eradicate grief must be all mankind's effort. That he is unable to eradicate Harry Bolton's grief makes Redburn's idealism ironic in the reader's view, and this irony contributes to the book's darkness. Redburn is capable, however, of achieving at least an ideal moment. When Carlo, the Italian boy, plays the organ, all the sailors and emigrants gather on the deck to listen. The rich cabin passengers sit aloof, unmoved by the music. Redburn responds fully to a fusion of his own perception and imagination with the creation of another's: "Play on, play on, Italian boy! what though the notes be broken, here's that within that mends them . . . while I list to the organ's twain— one yours, one mine—let me gaze fathoms down into thy fathomless eye;—'tis good as gazing down into the great South Sea, and seeing the dazzling rays of the dolphins there."[33] Redburn's vision here is like Ishmael's privileged glance revealing whale amours in the deep. Of course, Melville could be satirizing Redburn as a sentimentalist. But he isn't.

In *White-Jacket* and *Redburn* Melville did tend to be corrective; he was less so in *Typee* and *Omoo*. In all four books he had his central characters perceive and report on absurdities. His heroes occasionally achieve a partial or temporary solution which generally amounts to the brief and limited establishment of a primitive human relation based on the most elemental precepts of love. This solution is a state of open and unequivocal forgiveness, affection, and spontaneous charity; it transcends relative differences and accepts organic and spiritual sameness. It requires the utmost effort of the will and imagination, which in turn must reduce the individual's dependence upon will and imagination. Redburn hears the music of another's soul when he is in a state of calm, without conscious intentions. None of the three narrators is capable of sustaining this solution, and the moments in which they do achieve it are rare. They do learn that there are a few worldly traits which provide some help in surviving dilemmas. These are honesty, common sense, and a desire to act nobly. But the most important thing the heroes of these books learn has little to do with spiritual concerns or worldly virtues. They learn that what is most required in the absurd world is sharp eyes and quick feet.

2 · QUEEQUEG'S COFFIN

The narrator of Mardi believes that the best thing he can do about an intolerable situation is to step out of it. Where that step will lead, he can only surmise; he knows that every exit from an old situation is an entrance into a new one. He jumps ship in the middle of nowhere and, with fear balanced by eager anticipation, sets sail westward with his companion, away from the ill-fated *Arcturion* towards islands he hopes will lie in his path. The sea is awesome in its beauty and terror, and to go upon the sea in a small boat is to know that that beauty and terror are the same thing. One moment, all the horizon is visible; the next, the mariners are buried in watery hollows. But the voyager at the beginning of his quest does not despair; indeed, his optimism is an inevitable part of being at the beginning. " 'But drown or swim, here's overboard with care! Cheer up, Jarl! Ha! ha! how merrily, yet terribly, we sail!' "[34] All of Melville's novels set author, characters, and reader to sailing merrily and terribly. But this is most intensely so in *Mardi, Moby-Dick,* and *Pierre.* There is in these three an unremitting reminder that the world is always double, that it is made of beautiful and dangerous, serious and comic mysteries, and that to shift points of view is continually to find new ambiguities rather than solutions to the old ones. The quest for the center of things does become in these books that circumnavigation which White-jacket feared was the totality of man's experience.

All three of these books start in comedy; all three are deliberately humorous and satirical in the early chapters. They all end with the death or, in the case of Taji, the symbolic death of the questing central character, whose search thus ends without an answer. Surprisingly, the most coherently structured book of the three in terms of its developing comic-tragic pattern is *Mardi,* the one that might seem most chaotic. *Mardi* progresses from genial, rough humor and adventure—the kind of appealing narrative that had already made Melville popular—through satire of the Swiftian kind to the intensely symbolic and quasi-mystical events of the last chapters. The darkness of the late chapters is forecast in the early chapters, and the comedy of the early chapters permeates the seriousness of the closing ones. The satire overlaps nicely into Babbalanja's final stages of intellectual achievement and Taji's final despairing commitment to the shade. It is as if we ascend through increasingly complex layers of humor and seriousness until the two are at last indistinguishable.[35]

This blending technique is so successful that it is impossible to define one exclusive tone in *Mardi,* be it tragic or satirical, seriously corrective or nihilistically sarcastic. Often this fusion is accomplished by a skillful and abrupt pairing of some affirmation of life's comedy with a startling reminder that death can terminate the comedy at any moment. The inscrutable and funny Annatoo is killed just as her characterization begins to fulfill its comic potential. Her husband, Samoa, declares her the most virtuous of women, and the narrator is making fun of this innocent pronouncement when the joke is suddenly displaced by catastrophe. A killer squall capsizes the boat. Jarl saves the ship by cutting the mast, but a block at the end of a shroud strikes Annatoo as the mast falls away. The same action that saves the ship spells the end of Annatoo, who, without a word (for once), slides down the slanting deck into the sea.[36] In a later scene, as Taji, Media, Babbalanja, and Mohi listen to Yoomy sing " 'Ho! merrily ho! we paddlers sail!' " there is a sudden splash, and a man in the bow disappears into the lagoon without so much as a bubble. This event is a metaphor for Melville's recognition that while men must be merry if they are not to be sad, they nonetheless will one day drop just as they lean gleefully forward. The incident is followed by Babbalanja's heavily ironic discourse on predestination. He says first, " 'Oh, Oro! this death thou ordainest unmans the manliest.' " But then he modifies his despair by a statement of faith and resignation: " 'Yet what seems evil to us may be good to [Oro].' "[37]

Taji's quest is in its first stages motivated by his growing egoism. Melville's characterization of this egoism accomplishes several things. He first satirizes Taji's narrow view of the world and then shows Taji's view expanding to allow him to see the absurdities of almost all situations. He can then show that Taji's egoism can be of the heroic sort; Taji will see but refuse to accept the absurdity of his own final position. Taji jumps ship largely because he is bored and because, although the captain is a "trump" and the sailors all good fellows, "There was no soul a magnet to mine; none with whom to mingle sympathies. . . ."[38] He assumes control over the pliable Jarl, talking him into going along with his desertion, and later he simply usurps command of the *Parki* from Samoa. In rescuing Yillah, he thrusts himself into a situation about which he knows very little. He takes advantage of Yillah's concept of herself and dupes her into believing that he is a god from the same mystical realm as the one from which she thinks she came. When the islanders of Mardi treat him as a divinity, he plays the part to the hilt: "erecting my crest, I strove to look every inch the character I had determined to assume."[39] Taji is a bit let down when he discovers that he is but one of an indefinite number of demigods. This toying with appearances— or should it be called lying—reflects the narrator's awareness of how "truth" is really a matter of what is believed. In all his deceptions, he is clumsily creative, maintaining a position as top man, but to our eyes he is hypocritical and ludicrous. His egoism is comic through most of the voyage but develops gradually into a more heroic awareness of the world's absurdity. This leads at last to an awareness of his own absurd condition. This development is largely due to his exposure to Babbalanja and his discourses; his refusal to accept his absurdity and resign himself to it is a function of his rejection of Babbalanja's final synthesis.

In spite of his early egoism, Taji does display a readiness to be educated about the absurd even before he meets Babbalanja. He has a sense of meaninglessness and often describes the state of being possessed by that feeling. He also knows what kind of experiences overcome this sense. These experiences cannot occur without the belief that although reality itself is the source of mysteries, the way to understand the mysteries is to observe real things closely. He recommends to whoever would make direct contact with the world a journey in an open boat. Look into the sea, he says, "wherever saw you a phantom like that? An enormous crescent with antlers like a reindeer, and a delta of mouths." The manta is a phantom, but its phantomness is a matter of fact. "Doctor Faust saw the devil; but you have seen the 'Devil Fish.'" The sea is an arena, full of "God's creatures fighting, fin for fin," just as is the land world, but the attuned observer sees even such battles as part of God's harmonious universe.[40] All men are seen as they really are when they are at sea, he says. When all is well we see the organic unity of all, and at such a time "no creed is absurd."[41] But these experiences and affirmations depend on the inner serenity of the observer and upon his world's placidity. Everything must be going smoothly without a threat to contemplation and forward motion. When this ideal state of things is changed in the slightest—as when the ship finds itself becalmed—then the sailor's mind becomes unsettled, he is tempted "to recant his belief in the eternal fitness of things," and he is surprised to find himself in "a state of existence where existence itself seems suspended." He then closes his eyes "to test the reality of the glassy expanse." If he is a reader, "Priestley on Necessity occurs to him," and "he grows madly sceptical." Suddenly, "To his alarmed fancy, parallels and meridians become emphatically what they are merely designated as being: imaginary lines drawn round the earth's surface." The log is a liar, the captain an incompetent ignoramus who has lost his way, and "Thoughts of eternity thicken." Then "He begins to feel anxious concerning his soul." The becalmed sailor is nowhere.[42] This is the condition of the absurd.

Babbalanja's philosophical quest parallels Taji's search for Yillah. Curiously, both journeys turn out to have no real-world goal. Yillah grows more and more mysterious, more and more remote, until Taji at last disappears into the world of unknowns to continue his search for what has become an unknown. This brave act adds to the stature he has acquired; he has become a perceiver of absurdities and commits himself finally to what may be an eternal absurd quest. In doing so, he pursues meaning where none is visible. Babbalanja's quest has as its object not a symbol of deep mysteries but Oro Himself, the source of everything. His quest must necessarily end in his learning that a leap of faith is always required when a man comes to the

edge of the center of things. In his famous vision, Babbalanja ascends through layers of heavenly knowledge with the
bright angel, only to ask the last question, "'why create the
germs that sin and suffer, but to perish?'"[43] This question
of "why?" could not be more basic. It cannot be answered—only
Oro knows. Thus the prime motivation behind all events in the
universe must appear to man's intellect to be unintelligible, and
all worldly endeavor must prove circular. Babbalanja's intellectual quest can carry him to the mystery but not into it.

It is Babbalanja who tells stories which define the absurd
condition precisely. (His stories are never digressions.) One is
about King Normo's fool, Willi, who, although he had to obey
his king's every word, fancied himself free. One day Normo
commanded Willi to go to a tree and wait there. Willi, bowing
beneath his bells, asked permission to walk there on his hands.
It was granted, but the effort proved uncomfortable indeed, so
Willi turned a somersault and leaped to his feet. Said he,
"'Though I am free to do it, it's not so easy turning digits
into toes; I'll walk, by gad! which is my other option.'"[44] Thus
did Willi manufacture a choice out of nothing. Babbalanja is
full of such tales. Once nine blind men, he tells his listeners,
set out to find the original trunk of a huge banyan tree whose
secondary trunks were so old and so numerous that no one
could tell where the center of the tree was. Each blind man,
upon blundering into a secondary trunk, was certain that he
had the primary one. The moral is, in the words of the local
king, "'Will ye without eyes presume to see more sharply than
those who have them? The tree is too much for us all.'"
Mohi claims he can make no sense of Babbalanja's story,
"'obverse or reverse.'" "'It is a polysensuum,'" claims Babbalanja. He means that all men are blind men, taking data in
their own way and mistaking the multiple and contradictory
evidence of the immediate world to be the central truth of
the universe. "'A pollywog!'" exclaims Mohi.[45] Melville's implication is that the universe is a polysensuum and a pollywog
—a cosmic joke on man.

Mardi continually raises the question of what responses to
this joke—besides Babbalanja's act of faith—are tenable. The
satires in the book directly reject several kinds of behavior which

are commonly accepted as solutions: hermits claiming to have the answer but talking in circles, ludicrous communal attempts at living together, deadly war games, the invention of endless numbers of strolling gods. Sensuality is rejected when Taji rejects Hautia. Melville shows that one can justifiably compromise: Media recommends expediency, acceptance, good-humored contentment, and philosophical generalization: "'Meditate as much as you will, Babbalanja, but say little aloud, unless in a merry and mythical way. Lay down the great maxims of things, but let inferences take care of themselves.'"[46] Mortals live in Mardi and do not need to know any more than Mardi requires for life. Media's attitude is appropriate to the man of state, the man who must deal with worldly structures. When he returns to a nation torn with dissension, collapsing in his absence, he does not despair but sets out to rebuild. In committing himself to the state, he identifies his fortunes with it and as a result identifies himself.

Taji's other companions, too, realizing that their world must always appear absurd to the finite mind, create solutions that allow them to live in the world. Yoomy is a poet, albeit a bad one. But at least he creates structures of meaning. And, since he can manipulate symbols, Yoomy can read the figures of the universe; only he can interpret for Taji the mysterious flowers of Hautia. Mohi sees structures in history. Babbalanja accepts the paradoxical message of the angel in the vision: to know all would be to be all; to have great mystical love is to be sad. He knows that his Mardian happiness is no more than freedom from great woes, that ultimate tranquillity will be sadness, and that "'tranquillity [is] the uttermost that souls may hope for.'"[47]

Taji accepts no solution and instead plunges into endless pursuit in the circles of the absurd. The vision of Yillah has been lost, but he nonetheless chooses to pursue her shade forever. This means also that he chooses to be chased forever by his avengers in turn. Were it not for the serious tone of the last lines he speaks and Melville's comparative success at capturing the high style of tragedy ("Now, I am my own soul's emperor; and my first act is abdication!"), Taji's commitment would be ludicrous.[48] We would come away laughing at the picture of a comic egoist searching madly for nothing, three angry natives in hot pursuit, showers of arrows streaking the intervening space to thud against his boat's hull for all eternity.

A simplistic love is once recommended by the narrator before he begins his quest, and the reader feels that this is to be taken seriously, just as was Redburn's occasional unassuming acceptance of the self of others. Taji says, "to hate, a man must work hard. Love is a delight. . . ."[49] Babbalanja himself seems at times resolved when he is able to fall back into a quiet belief in a transcendental essence: " 'All are parts of One. In me, in *me*, flit thoughts participated in by the beings peopling all the stars.' "[50] This offsets his earlier despair at having perceived a total relativism: " 'Who in Arcturus hath heard of us? They know us not in the Milky Way. . . . We point at random. Peradventure at this instant, there are beings gazing up to this very world as their future heaven. But the universe is all over a heaven: nothing but stars on stars, throughout infinities of expansion. All we see are but a cluster. . . . With marvels we are glutted, till we hold them no marvels at all.' "[51] Finally, what is taken to be the wisest and most ancient solution in Mardi is in itself enigmatic and absurd but also, in terms of man's knowledge and perception, sensible and logical. It comes from the last testament of the ancient prophet Bardianna; his dying advice to the people of Mardi is " 'live as long as you can; close your own eyes when you die.' "[52]

But it is Babbalanja's solution which is to be recognized as the central paradox of the book. In a soliloquy, Babbalanja paraphrases Ecclesiastes I. 4-9, reversing some of the text's essential ideas.[53] His paraphrase begins nihilistically: " 'Nothing abideth,' " he says in contrast to the Bible's "the earth abideth forever." Ecclesiastes says that the rivers of the earth run forever into the sea without filling it, but Babbalanja says, " 'the river of yesterday floweth not to-day; the sun's rising is a setting; living is dying; the very mountains melt; and all revolve:—systems and asteroids; the sun wheels through the zodiac, and the zodiac is a revolution. Ah gods! in all this universal stir, am *I* to prove one stable thing?' " His answer to himself ought to be no. He knows that he is dust, that he carries his own skeleton, and that eventually he will lie down to be walked upon by his children's children.[54] In another meditation, he quakes to discover that " 'We die, because we live.' "[55] But ultimately his answer to "am *I* to prove one stable thing?" is yes, with an affirmative emphasis. In the end, he settles for his own search for wisdom in lieu of final wisdom. He says that his voyage has both ended and just begun. He stays behind in the land of Serenia " 'to grow wiser still. . . . Within our hearts is all that we seek: though in that search many need a prompter.' "[56] That prompter is Alma, Melville's metaphor for the true Christ, who can be sought only in Serenia, the land where decayed "Christianity" has never obstructed the clear and simple light. Those in Serenia have left institutions, priests, and Scripture behind. Babbalanja commits himself to a lifetime of exploring the means by which men can live together in love and serenely investigate the workings of their own finite minds in relation to the infinite mind of Oro. Babbalanja cannot at last be nihilistic; he accepts a solution while realizing its absurdity.[57]

Ahab will not so yield, even though he knows just as Babbalanja does that he is in the absurd condition and can never see finally. He must strike through the mask. Babbalanja accepts the final "No"; Ahab does not—and that is the difference between the high comedy of Babbalanja's story and the majestic tragedy of Ahab's. Since Ahab's tragedy necessarily involves the death of all the mariners but Ishmael, one must go on to say that the condition of all the crew, who are to be taken as all the world, is the same as his, whether they know it or not. They are jolly, they laugh and joke, they hunt the whale and re-create his fat into light. But the blunt forehead of Moby-Dick gets them all in the end.

Ahab's story is not the only definitive tale of the absurd in *Moby-Dick*. Starbuck's story, for example, summarizes in a stroke the absurd dilemma. Starbuck is a tragic hero of another sort than Ahab. His dilemma resembles that of Oedipus, Hamlet, Lear, or Milton's Adam. Starbuck stands before Ahab's door, the captain asleep just behind the thin boards. The musket is leveled; his hands tremble. " 'Great God, where art thou? Shall I? shall I?' "[58] But law and conscience contradict each other, and he cannot decide to shoot. The captain at sea is God's representative—that is one law, and it is supported by another—no man shall kill. His conscience tells him that if Ahab lives, the ship and the crew will go to destruction. Starbuck knows true indecision. He does not fire, but not because he decides between law and conscience. He cannot fire because he cannot decide. Starbuck's dilemma is permeated by the essence of the cosmic joke, but no one is laughing.

The outright laughter in *Moby-Dick* arises from light treatments of good-humored solutions to man's dilemmas. Here we have the comedy of love, Queequeg and Ishmael learning to accept one another in bed. The two swap religions, Queequeg's proving more sensible, even in its apparent grotesqueness, than Christianity. Later, at sea, Queequeg and Ishmael are tied together in a truly dangerous mutual venture, one descending into the whale, the other holding tight on board. This is a ludicrous picture, too, as the pair teeter on the brink of nothingness. This hilarity will not end in the squashing of the mariners if both hold tight and keep confidence in one another. Finally, the comedy of love reaches its peak in the raw humor of the chapter called "A Squeeze of the Hand" as Ishmael and his shipmates blend together their hands and their souls in the pot of sperm: "Come; let us squeeze hands all round; nay; let us all squeeze ourselves into each other; let us squeeze ourselves universally into the very milk and sperm of kindness."[59] Even as the end descends, there is still one comic solution remaining. Stubb creates a laughing confidence out of doom: " 'I grin at thee, thou grinning whale! Who ever helped Stubb, or kept Stubb awake, but Stubb's own unwinking eye? . . . I grin at thee, thou grinning whale! . . . Oh, oh! oh, oh! thou grinning whale, but there'll be plenty of gulping soon!' "[60] One can always go out laughing.

That *Moby-Dick* is full of such humor was recognized even by its first reviewers, many of whom commented extensively upon its comic scenes. J. Watson Webb, of the *Courier and New York Enquirer*, thought it "enlivened with the raciness of [Melville's] humor" as well as "the redolence of his imagination." A famous British reviewer was insulted by the mixture and called it a "tragic-comic bubble." The British edition, *The Whale*, did not, of course, contain the epilogue in which Ishmael was saved (a crucial difference for the reader who loves the absurd), and it was practically ruined by the deletion of some of the best bits of racy and rough humor.[61] Interestingly enough, the American journal that most appreciated the book's humor was William T. Porter's New York *Spirit of the Times*. The anonymous *Spirit* reviewer lauded the comedy of the work to the exclusion of almost everything else and added a few jokey things himself: "Moby Dick . . . is all whale. Leviathan is here in full amplitude. Not one of your museum affairs, but the real, living whale, a bona-fide, warm-blooded creature. . . ." The *Spirit* loved confidence games, and the reviewer's comments were followed by a reprinting of Chapter XCI, in which Stubb cons the captain of the French whaler, *Rose-bud,* out of a valuable ambergris whale.[62]

Not only the readily observable humor but the whole of *Moby-Dick* is permeated by Melville's sense of the absurd. Ishmael's commentaries on man's attempts to structure meaning reflect the author's absurd sense directly and comically. Probably the best known is his comment on the sight of the *Pequod* with a whale's head hoisted up on each side of the ship. Whereas when just one head is hoisted, the ship leans over sharply, with two, she regains her even keel. "So," says the narrator, "When on one side you hoist in Locke's head, you go over that way; but now, on the other side, hoist in Kant's and you come back again; but in very poor plight. Thus, some minds for ever keep trimming boat. Oh, ye foolish! throw all these thunder-heads overboard, and then you will float light and right."[63] Melville is again being ambiguously comic and serious here. On the one hand, he does mean that to find a balance between differing systems of thought (he did not necessarily see Locke's and Kant's systems as contradictory) is extremely difficult and, when achieved, only leaves the man who does the balancing in an overweighted condition. Drop one, capsize; drop both simultaneously, and be free to start anew. On the other hand, Melville did occasionally present such a balance as a plausible solution. Ishmael says quite seriously, in describing how whales are often obscured in their own spout's vapor, that his perception is often similarly fogged but occasionally struck through by "divine intuition . . . enkindling my fog with a heavenly ray." For this he thanks God, "for all have doubts; many deny; but doubts or denials, few along with them, have intuitions. Doubts of all things earthly, and intuitions of some things heavenly; this combination makes neither believer nor infidel, but makes a man who regards them both with equal eye."[64]

Just as Ishmael recognizes that philosophy is a game, so does he recognize that law, which should help men stabilize things, can be manipulated endlessly. What is a fast-fish and what is a loose-fish? The law on who owns a whale or does not own it seems quite clear:

I. A Fast-Fish belongs to the party fast to it.
II. A Loose-Fish is fair game for anybody who can soonest catch it.

A brife law, and to the point. But this is trouble in itself; volumes are required to explain it. Ishmael cites as just one example of possible confusions arising out of this law a case wherein a crew was forced to abandon both whale and whaleboat, which were connected by the line. Another ship killed the whale and recovered the boat and line of the first ship as well. Whose property was whose? The owners of the first ship considered themselves damaged and brought the matter to court. The way out of this bind for the judge of the case was to award the boat to the plaintiffs, for they had abandoned it to save their lives, and the whale to the defendants, who killed it. But the judge also awarded the harpoons and line to the defendants because this gear had become the whale's property. This judgment is a masterstroke of absurd manipulation. Melville extends the implications of the story in a comic comment on the impossibility of finding abstract constants upon which to found clear judgments, be they civil, political, or moral: "What are the Rights of Man and the Liberties of the World but Loose-Fish? What all men's minds and opinions but Loose-Fish? What is the principle of religious belief in them but a Loose-Fish? What to the ostentatious smuggling verbalists are the thoughts of thinkers but Loose-Fish? What is the great globe itself but a Loose-Fish? And what are you, reader, but a Loose-Fish and a Fast-Fish, too?"[65] Attach a fish firmly to a boat, and its place is known; its status is relative to the boat and fixed as long as it is fast. A Fast-Fish is a Fish made Fast. Any condition outside of this definition, which in itself is circular and absurd, is Loose-Fish.

Ahab himself is not without humor. To the carpenter making him a new leg, he says, "'Well, manmaker!'" and from this remark launches into a series of heavily facetious metaphors. He likes the vise—which is strong enough to break bones—because it gives a good grip: "'I like to feel something in this slippery world that can hold, man.'" The blacksmith is Prometheus, forging for Ahab's leg a buckle screw, as the god forged men. As long as he's about it, says Ahab, "'I'll order a complete man after a desirable pattern. Imprimis, fifty feet high in his socks; then, chest modelled after the Thames Tunnel; then, legs with roots to 'em, to stay in one place; then, arms three feet through at the wrist; no heart at all, brass forehead, and about a quarter of an acre of fine brains; and let me see—shall I order eyes to see outwards? No, but put a sky-light on top of his head to illuminate inwards.'"[66]

Ahab's nihilistic joking reaches a peak in a later confrontation with the carpenter. The subject is Queequeg's coffin, which the carpenter is now converting into a life buoy, Queequeg having outlived its usefulness as coffin. "'Then tell me; art thou not an arrant, all-grasping, intermeddling, monopolizing, heathenish old scamp, to be one day making legs, and the next day coffins to clap them in, and yet again life-buoys out of those same coffins? Thou art as unprincipled as the gods. . . .'"[67] Not so unprincipled, the carpenter. His principles are practical ones. He does not have Ahab's complexity of vision, but he has tools to patch legs, boards in which to bury people, and caulk to make life buoys that won't sink. But Ahab is Ahab, and Ahab sees this practicality as equivocation. His jokes produce but bitter inverted laughter in his own throat.

Ahab is absurdly creative; he makes the whale what it is to Ahab. To Starbuck, the whale is a whale; to Stubb, to Flask, to the harpooners, the whale is a whale. Even to the captain of the *Samuel Enderby*, also the loser of a limb to Moby-Dick, the whale is a whale. To Ahab, who perceives his own absurd condition in precisely the way Camus described the process of perception, the whale is a force against which he strives to create his own meaning. But unlike Sisyphus, Ahab will not accept what is out of his power to will and control; were Sisyphus an Ahab, he would have shattered his frame against the rock.

The absurd creators in *Moby-Dick* are Ishmael and Queequeg. They create a friendship out of hostilities. They bind themselves one to another with the ridiculous rope. Ishmael is an absurd creator because he knows that to stare so long and so deeply from the mainmast that one falls into the sea, or to dive into the sea—to take the plunge as, in his way, Ahab violently does—is to be drowned. He is content to ride the sea's surface and chooses to be glad for those moments when the sea opens to reveal schools of whales. In the calm at the center of the Grand Armada, Ishmael looks down; "Some of the subtlest secrets of the seas seemed divulged to us in this enchanted pond. We saw young Leviathan amours in the deep." His response to the encounter is this: "And thus, though surrounded by circle upon circle of consternations and affrights, did these inscrutable creatures at the centre freely and fearlessly indulge in all peaceful concernments; yea, serenely revelled in dalliance and delight. But even so, amid the tornadoed Atlantic of my being, do I myself still for ever centrally disport in mute calm; and while ponderous planets of unwaning woe revolve round me, deep down and deep inland there I still bathe me in eternal mildness of joy."[68] Ishmael rests in himself, whether that self is known or not. He is content to be.

Queequeg's creativity is of the straightforward, practical kind. When he thinks he is dying, he calls the carpenter and orders a coffin. He lies in it to get a good fit. He assumes that his death is a beginning. He gathers about him the essentials needed for a journey—sea biscuits, a flask of water, a bit of cloth for a pillow, and an icon. For Queequeg, death is not absurd because he has his own perfect response to it. His response may seem absurd to Ishmael and the other mariners. When he fails to die—and he does not die because he remembers an undone duty and wills his own survival—all is not wasted. The coffin becomes a sea chest. That is prudence. Next, he carves upon it the tattooed hieroglyphics of his body, a theory of the heavens and earth, "a mystical treatise on the art of attaining truth." Queequeg and his coffin become in this way corporeal embodiments of The Riddle, which must remain "unsolved to the last."[69] Queequeg's coffin is the emblem of the absurd creator's answer to the unanswerable question posed by the gods.

It is irony of the darkest kind that the coffin will not save Queequeg himself; if the creator's creation cannot save him, what will? But at least the book does close upon the rescue of Ishmael, held up at sea by the product of Queequeg's practicality, simple faith, and firm acceptance of fate. There would be no alternatives left to the reader had Ishmael gone down with the ship as he did in the first English edition.[70] But as the ending stands, an alternative is given; men can hope to achieve acceptance, practicality, faith, and an appreciation like Ishmael's of the glimpses into the sea that are given. In the view of Ahab, such a hope is absurd, but, because of this hope, men who don't drown don't drown.

But drowning men do drown, and Pierre drowns. Pierre is "quite conscious of much that is so anomalously hard and bitter in his lot, of much that is so black and terrific in his soul. Yet that knowing his fatal condition does not one whit enable him to change or better his condition. Conclusive proof that he has no power over his condition. For in tremendous extremities human souls are like drowning men; well enough they know they are in peril; well enough they know the causes of that peril;—nevertheless, the sea is the sea, and these drowning men do drown."[71] The drowning of Pierre is not to be taken as a black joke, even though he is heavily satirized in the beginning of the book. Rather, the shift from the lavish and funny parodies of the first chapters to the heavy melodrama of the last chapters indicates that Melville intended to show that what is comic can, through nothing more than a single revelation of a dark truth beneath benign appearances, shift drastically and suddenly towards the deadly.

That *Pierre* has comedy at all may not be apparent to any reader inclined to believe that Melville expected him to take all the flowery rhetoric of the first chapters seriously. Actually, the book was probably begun as a parody of romantic literature. Pierre in his teens is prone to such statements as "It must be a glorious thing to engage in a moral quarrel on a sweet sister's behalf!"[72] He reads nature in terms of excessive metaphor and reacts accordingly: "She lifted her spangled crest of a thickly-starred night, and forth at that glimpse of their divine Captain and Lord, ten thousand mailed thoughts of heroicness started up in Pierre's soul, and glared round for some insulted good cause to defend."[73] This pure comedy turns dangerous when Pierre does elect to defend a cause—that is, the cause of Isabel; his discovery that she may be his half sister is the revelation that precipitates the book's gradual shift towards darkness. The relationship between Pierre and his mother is drawn in the broadest possible comic terms, its sexual overtones being not one whit suppressed, and the whole of it condensed in unsubtle nuggets such as Mother's " 'I thank heaven I sent him not to college. A noble boy, and docile. A fine, proud, loving, docile, vigorous boy.' "[74] His intended wife is docile, too, and that pleases her all the more. The comedy of *Pierre* does not entirely disappear after the book turns serious; burlesque permeates the scenes in the wild household of Pierre, Isabel, Lucy, and Delly, and parody is the only word that describes that enormity, Lucy's "I am coming!" letter.[75]

Edward Rosenberry's assessment of the book as a compendium of all the literary diseases of the previous sixty years of American popular fiction is informative and suggestive because it so accurately accounts for both the parodies and the faults of *Pierre*. First, Melville blithely ran roughshod over all the conventions of sentimental literature, drawing Pierre as a burlesque romantic hero spouting high-flown heroic drivel. Then, it seems, as the book turned darker, Melville could not resist the temptation to go ahead and dramatize Pierre's dilemma in the popularly approved mode, including all the requisite elements: sighs, tears, faints, hysteria, woe, and suicide.[76] This view could be extended even further than Rosenberry goes with it. Melville's fine sense of the absurd made it possible for him first to invert popular taste to produce a burlesque and then to invert the burlesque itself to reveal a dark reflected side of things that did not show before this double inversion took place. Inverting the burlesque does not necessarily mean (as Rosenberry suggests) that the author comes back to his starting point, the gross conventions themselves. It can mean that he intends with the first inversion to show how what we take seriously can be seen as funny and then with the second intends to show that what we've been laughing at can in turn become doubly serious in a new way. To illustrate: Pierre is funny to us at first because he is so completely unaware of the grossness of his language, the grotesqueness of his relationship with his mother, and the ludicrousness of the romance he is carrying on with Lucy. But when one more thing that he does not know—that Isabel is his sister, his father's illegitimate daughter—causes the second inversion by becoming known to him, then all of these laughable elements become starkly reflective of his awaiting doom. His language turns from sentimental to Shakespearian (albeit Melville did not always render its tragic rhythms convincingly), his mother disowns him and dies, and the broken Lucy devotes herself to her part in their common fate. That which changes his life, the author pointed out, is a shadow which comes "Out of the heart of mirthfulness. . . ." Later, we see that "a smile is the chosen vehicle of all ambiguities. . . ."[77]

This book helps us understand *The Confidence-Man* because the constant manipulation of appearances on the part of the author shows us how little is required to alter our view of any situation drastically. It is as if the author were toying with Pierre, and toying with us, drawing us off guard by the early burlesque, dropping an unexpected element into the scene, and leading us step by step into the endless confusions and fateful complications that ensue from that one revelation. In Book IX, appropriately entitled "More Light, and the Gloom of that Light, More Gloom, and the Light of that Gloom," Melville informs us that this novel is a picture of what happens to the overserious thinker who begins to peel back the layers of reality in search of some center:

> In those Hyperborean regions, to which enthusiastic Truth, and Earnestness, and Independence, will invariably lead a mind fitted by nature for profound and fearless thought, all objects are seen in a dubious, uncertain, and refracting light. Viewed through that rarefied atmosphere the most immemorially admitted maxims of men begin to slide and fluctuate, and

finally become wholly inverted; the very heavens themselves being not innocent of producing this confounding effect, since it is mostly in the heavens themselves that these wonderful mirages are exhibited.

But the example of many minds forever lost, like undiscoverable Arctic explorers, amid those treacherous regions, warns us entirely away from them; and we learn that it is not for man to follow the trail of truth too far, since by so doing he entirely loses the directing compass of his mind; for arrived at the Pole, to whose barrenness only it points, there, the needle indifferently respects all points of the horizon alike.[78]

This is Pierre's absurd condition; he penetrates to the center of himself only to find total contradiction.

In killing his cousin Glendinning (the last of the family), Pierre does at last assert a choice for one of the infinite directions pointed out by the spinning compass. The ending of this book is not effective as a tragedy, so it must be taken as melodrama or some kind of black comedy. The latter comes close to being correct; the ending is comic in the absurd sense, though it is without affirmation. We may even laugh at Pierre's grotesque behavior and language or his overdramatic suicide. Surely we have been grinning wryly all the while at his ludicrous household, and now we are all too disposed to snicker at the carnage in the jail cell, so obviously reminiscent of the end of *Hamlet*. (It is impossible to tell if Melville intended his ending to be an imitation or a parody.) But we do not have to condemn Melville for being unintentionally funny. Is it not possible that there is a saturation point for seriousness in any given pattern? Once the tragedy of the absurd has been epitomized in a character like Ahab, there may be nowhere for the same author to go but towards parody. Melville in *Pierre* parodies sentimental popular fiction, Shakespearian melodrama, and himself. It is also quite possible to come out of the book having made the point seriously. The compass spins.

Pierre's perception of absurdities is what ultimately drowns him. He reads *Hamlet* and Dante's *Inferno;* Dante makes him fierce, but *Hamlet* insinuates that there is no one to strike. Dante teaches him that he has cause to quarrel; *Hamlet* taunts him for faltering. He quizzes himself constantly: What, exactly, is his relationship to Isabel, and what is his real responsibility to her? Worse, does he really intend to become her hero? The most critical question at the point at which Pierre's career turns headlong towards his doom is, "Was the immense stuff to do it his, or was it not his?" He asks, "Who am I?" Finally, "Impossible would it be now to tell all the confusion and confoundings in the soul of Pierre, so soon as the above absurdities in his mind presented themselves first to his combining consciousness."[79] Pierre's perception is not satirized towards the end of the book. The persona's clear grasp of the universe's perfect duality is at last shared by Pierre: " 'Oh, seems to me, there should be two ceaseless steeds for a bold man to ride,— the Land and the Sea; and like circus-men we should never dismount, but only be steadied and rested by leaping from one to the other, while still, side by side, they both race round the sun. I have been on the Land steed so long, oh I am dizzy!' "[80] When Pierre understands his own absurd position, he is no longer the victim of the book's wit. But his recognition comes too late, as he well knows. Pierre drowns because he did not soon enough acquire "the immense stuff" to live with and re-create absurdity. His inability to write a coherent book symbolizes his failure as a failure of the imagination. Having failed to create, he chooses the other alternative, suicide.

No discussion of the absurd in *Pierre* could be complete without some comment on Plotinus Plinlimmon. The satire on Plinlimmon and his followers is generally accepted as a burlesque of the foggy aspects of Emersonian thought, in particular the cheerful and unqualified assumption that a pure and innocent exposure to nature's forms combined with a true inward opening of the soul produces a correct correspondence with absolute morality. The motivation for the satire on Plinlimmon was Melville's observation of what appeared to him to be a staggering innocence in conjunction with "a certain floating atmosphere" which seemed nothing less than "Inscrutableness."[81] But one thing ought to be added to the generally accepted interpretation of Plinlimmon. His famous pamphlet describes the absurd perfectly and then offers a ludicrous answer to it. The conceit comparing the soul to a chronometer is an exact comic metaphor of the absurd condition. In an artificial world, the soul of man is removed from God in the same way that a timepiece set at Greenwich time is removed from Greenwich time if it is carried to China without being reset. Its record of "correct time" will absolutely contradict local time. Thus our intuitions of abstract right and wrong will not match the apparent rights and wrongs of the artificial world in which we live. Some men have better-adjusted souls than others; Christ's was a perfectly set chronometer.

It is important to take this comic metaphor seriously. If a man has the sense of the absurd, then that sense is dependent on some source of what is not absurd, or normal. If the world appears constantly absurd, then it must appear so because the perceiver has a notion of something more "correct." Melville as persona apparently agrees with his character; up to this point, Plinlimmon's argument seems reasonable and is not satirized. But where Plinlimmon goes wrong in his view is in his assumption that men can be properly tuned to the correct time. Melville doubts that intuition will furnish the settings. When Plinlimmon says that the "earnest and righteous philosopher" (these are ironic words the author is putting into the voice of his target) cannot help but see the world in meridian correspondence to God, we know that Melville means that this solution is ludicrous. The cosmic joke delineated in all of Melville's fiction is that men are comic or tragic precisely because their chronometers—inner ones or outer ones—are always different one from another and from whatever Master Timepiece the believer might postulate. Plinlimmon is right when he says: "What man who carries a heavenly soul in him, has not groaned to perceive, that unless he committed a sort of suicide as to the practical things of this world, he never can hope to regulate his earthly conduct by that same heavenly soul?" But he is too optimistic when he follows that by: "And yet by an infallible instinct he knows, that that monitor can not be wrong in itself."[82] Melville's point is that although all men might have a sure feeling that the Big Clock in the Heavens does exist, none can ever read the dial from here.

3 · The Confidence of the Confidence-Man

Emerson precisely defined the perception of the absurd in his essay "The Comic" (1843). Humankind, he said, universally has a "taste for fun," but "The rocks, the plants, the beasts, the birds, neither do anything ridiculous, nor betray a perception of anything absurd done in their presence." As the lower nature does not create or perceive jokes, neither does the higher; "The Reason pronounces its omniscient yea or nay, but meddles never with degrees or fractions; and it is in comparing fractions with essential integers or wholes that laughter begins." Emerson did not agree with Aristotle that the ridiculous was merely the incongruous, that which was out of time or place. The essence of comedy to Emerson was "an honest or well-intended halfness; a non-performance of what is pretended to be performed, at the same time that one is giving loud pledges of performance." No other animal but man dons disguises; no other knows that there can be a difference between the appearance of the whole and the reality that is but a part of the whole. The heart of Emerson's argument is: "The presence of the ideal of right and of truth in all action makes the yawning delinquencies of practice remorseful to the conscience, tragic to the interest, but droll to the intellect." Men who have access to Reason by way of their intellect have access to a standard by which to test the events of this world. They test their deep consciousness of the organic perfectness of The Whole against those facts and events in the world which are out of kilter, which do not meet the standard of the sense of Wholeness.

Emerson put it another way:

There is no joke so true and deep in actual life as when some pure idealist goes up and down among the institutions of society, attended by a man who knows the world, and who, sympathizing with the philosopher's scrutiny, sympathizes also with the confusion and indignation of the detected, skulking institutions. His perception of disparity, his eye wandering perpetually from the rule to the crooked, lying, thieving fact, makes the eyes run over with laughter.

This "perception of disparity," Emerson said, constitutes the revelation of the "radical joke of life and then of literature." A joke exists because the perceiver and artist—the man in touch with his soul—sees man's fallen world in all its absurdity. Animals and things of wild nature do not attempt anything they cannot execute; even an "abortion," or apparent failure, in some species is a function of nature. Men, because their Reason supplies the knowledge of the parts as well as the whole, can perceive, create, or even fall prey to the differences between whole and part.

Emerson concluded this essay with a dark observation. Whenever we quit our soul, our "spontaneous sentiment," we do something laughable. "All our plans, managements, houses, poems, if compared with the wisdom and love which man represents, are equally imperfect and ridiculous." From this it is easy to see how laughter educates us, how farce and buffoonery rest and refresh us. But laughter has its limits, and mirth can quickly become "intemperate." It is possible to be tickled to death. "The same scourge whips the joker and the enjoyer of the joke. When Carlini was convulsing Naples with laughter, a patient waited on a physician in that city, to obtain some remedy for excessive melancholy, which was rapidly consuming his life. The physician endeavored to cheer his spirits, and advised him to go to the theatre and see Carlini. He replied, 'I am Carlini.'"[83]

It is not now known whether or not Melville ever read this essay.[84] The internal evidence of the piece, especially the equating of the elicitation of laughter and the manipulation of the confidence game, and the remark about the "joke so true and deep" generated by the pairing of the pure idealist and the man who knows the world, certainly do suggest that Melville had it in mind when creating the portraits of Mark Winsome and Egbert in *The Confidence-Man: His Masquerade*. But there is also the possibility that this is such an accurate presentation of the dark and light side of the ability to perceive the comic that had Melville read it, he would have drawn a more generous portrait. Whatever the case, something is missing from Emerson's essay—it is not a complete statement of the whole condition of the absurd, although it is a statement of how the absurd is perceived. What is missing from this essay is what Melville, in one of the major thematic phases of *The Confidence-Man*, tried to show was missing from the Emersonian mode of thought.

Melville called Emerson a humbug but said that at least he was an uncommon one. Melville respected Emerson as a man who dived, and "Any fish can swim near the surface. . . ." Emerson may sometimes have appeared to Melville to have been a fool, but Melville said that he would have preferred to be foolish in Emerson's way than to be what is commonly accepted as wise.[85] The characterization of Mark Winsome in the book does not seem to reflect the relatively temperate view expressed in the famous letter to Duyckinck; Winsome is attacked without compromise in the portrait. It must follow that what is being attacked in the character of Mark Winsome is some aspect of the Emersonian mode of thought that was not appropriate to the world Melville perceived. Melville had read Emerson at least as early as the late 1840s and had been developing his reactions to him during all of this time.[86] What *The Confidence-Man*, as well as those relevant passages in *Pierre*, shows is that Melville disagreed with Emerson on two basic points. As the satire on Plimlimmon indicates, Melville simply did not believe that men could deliberately attune themselves to some Omniscience and thereby perceive the organic unity and abstract value of the universe. Everything that has been said about Melville's recognition of man's helplessness in the face of appearances applies. It was more characteristic of him to see God as The Practical Joker rather than as the Supplier of Ideal Truth.[87] Secondly, as *The Confidence-Man* indicates, Melville knew that the very processes of knowledge-gaining, "Reason," "Intellect," "Experience," "Self-Reliance," "Idealism," and "Transcendentalism"—or any of the ways by which moral knowledge appears to be derived from experiential data—are in themselves absurd because the acceptance of any kind of data requires an act of pure confidence. Furthermore, this act of confidence has to be absurd in itself. The man who elects to have confidence does so arbitrarily, knowing that his act is ironic.

Melville's Confidence-Man is not the comic stereotype of tradition. He is not simply a crook or avaricious bird of prey making his living off the innocence of the American types encountered on board the *Fidèle*. His victims, as a matter of fact, are often shrewd and skeptical manipulators of appearances themselves. Furthermore, the Confidence-Man in Melville's book earns from his victims a very bare living indeed. He is instead a multiple mythical figure, appearing to be Christlike and Satanic at the same time. Since his figural nature is thus ambivalent, he is also an imitation of the traditional anti-Christ. In addition, it is apparent that Melville added to his character reflections of Prometheus, Vishnu, and Manco Capac. This combination of figures points to an interpretation of the Confidence-Man's character as that of the man or god of illumination, the light-bringer. The Confidence-Man's operations in the world of the *Fidèle* are not destructive but educative. He is a creator in that he recognizes that life is a masquerade, and, having perceived this, he re-creates that masquerade and becomes the master of it.[88] The Confidence-Man is ambiguous as a light-bringer in the way that the saviors of religious traditions are ambiguous. Whoever wishes to be saved must put his faith in the appearance of the savior. The convert has no empirical method for testing the genuineness of the savior. He must make an act of faith or confidence in the savior. But the Confidence-Man is even more ambivalent than this. Those who put their confidence in him are cheated out of money. They do not learn why confidence is necessary, in spite of his having told them why. And the Confidence-Man is the man who puts out the light at the end of the book.

Melville was not, however, saying that hope or confidence is futile. He was not repudiating Christlike love.[89] Instead, Melville's Confidence-Man teaches the reader, if not his audience, that, since there can be no perfection in an imperfect world, mere faith in some Perfection is the only possible source of hope. The book does see faith in itself as absurd, but that is not to say that the book sees faith as foolish. The Confidence-Man teaches that confidence is what holds the world together, that confidence in the "truth" of a proposition or set of data is the only thing that makes that proposition or data true. This rule applies not only in matters of religious faith but in all human endeavors. The Confidence-Man knows the irony of having to rely on confidence in the absence of any test for totally objective and provable truth. The subject of Melville's book is not the character of the Confidence-Man but the confidence of the Confidence-Man.

The name of the boat which represents the world in the book could have been, had Melville simply elected to use English, the *Faithful*. But instead he chose *Fidèle*, which shares a Latin root—*fides*—with the word *confidence*.⁹⁰ This equation of confidence and faith remains constant throughout the book. The captain, like God, is never seen—but we think he is there because the ship does go down the river. Similarly, men think there is a God because the universe "goes."

The Confidence-Man in his first avatar, that of the deaf-mute stranger, posts for the edification of a group of skeptical passengers several signs, including "Charity thinketh no evil," "Charity believeth all things," "Charity never faileth." The quotations are from I Corinthians 13. The stranger is looked upon as a lunatic by the observers. In the midst of this display, the ship's barber steps out of his shop and posts his sign: "No Trust." This is "An inscription which, though in a sense not less intrusive than the contrasted ones of the stranger, did not, as it seemed, provoke any corresponding derision or surprise, much less indignation; and still less, to all appearances, did it gain for the inscriber the repute of being a simpleton." Immediately after this, the "lamb-like" stranger is jostled rudely by two porters carrying a large trunk. He withdraws to a quiet spot near a ladder on the forecastle and drops down to sleep.⁹¹ The implication of this opening chapter is quite clear. People, as represented by the crowd, believe that the world is run without trust. If a gentle, simple soul were to admonish them to have faith and charity (and thus by implication hope), they would reject him as an idiot. The Confidence-Man in this avatar, significantly enough, withdraws. He has in this disguise no voice to admonish his listeners; he has no ears to discern their skepticism. The Confidence-Man in his first avatar wears no more disguise than Christ or Christlike men; his admonition is no more fake than is Biblical text itself. His message is simply "Have Charity." Obviously, the world rejects this. If the message is to be made clear, the world will have to be conned into accepting it. The Confidence-Man in this avatar knows this already and is preparing the audience for the game by the best double-con of all: he presents the simplest "truth" first. The audience is now ready to be conned because they think, as do all humans by implication, that truth can be—and must be—rationally demonstrated and is not so simply a matter of faith.

In his next appearance, as Black Guinea, the Confidence-Man proves that men are so skeptical that they do not believe their eyes. This in turn demonstrates that although the people in the audience have claimed to be rational, they are unwilling to put their confidence in what appears to be rational. Although he is twisted and deformed and gives a list of people who can vouch for him, few believe that Black Guinea is in legitimate need. Some doubt that he is a cripple at all. The passengers make a game of charity, throwing small coins at the beggar's open mouth. A country merchant does at last believe him and offers a half-dollar and a gesture of true sympathy and kindness. The point seems at first clear: all men are truly in need, and whether or not they appear "genuine" is something no one can really judge. True charity will believe because it cannot fail: whether the beggar is true or false, the beggar, like all men, needs charity, and the giver has been charitable. But after all, we the readers, even more than the passengers, are left in skeptical ignorance because we cannot really know who Black Guinea is and suspect that he is the Confidence-Man of the title.[92] We do not like to think that abstract charity has had no "true" visible object.

In the audience around Black Guinea, there are a Methodist minister and a man with a wooden leg. The combat between these two is definitive; it shows exactly what dilemma the book is going to explore. The minister, who is called the "church militant" and the "white cravat against the world," would shake into the skeptical wooden-legged man "charity on the spot." There can be no other kind of charity than charity accepted wholly and arbitrarily "on the spot." Love that has to be bolstered by reasons, causes, motives, and justifications is no love. But, of course, the minister is a confidence man, too. The wooden-legged man calls all the audience a " 'flock of fools, under this captain of fools, in this ship of fools!' " He sows the seeds of suspicion among his listeners:

" 'look you, I have been called a Canada thistle. Very good. And a seedy one: still better. And the seedy Canada thistle has been pretty well shaken among ye: best of all. Dare say some seed has been shaken out; and won't it spring though? And when it does spring, do you cut down the young thistles, and won't they spring the more? It's encouraging and coaxing 'em. Now, when with my thistles your farms shall be well stocked, why then—you may abandon 'em.' "[93] His message is the message of Genesis I and II. Once fraud has been perpetrated in the world—and it has to be so perpetrated but once—it is forever impossible to have trust. This planter of the thistle seed of skepticism is Satanic. He is also completely logical, for his awareness is exactly appropriate to the world. He is also comic, for he unintentionally helps spread the seeds of another kind of plant—the desire for trust that the Confidence-Man will harvest.

The collegian is one of the Confidence-Man's most comic victims. The Confidence-Man first preaches to him on the immorality of skepticism as manifested by Tacitus, the poisoner of confidence. He points out how little confidence there is between men. The sophomore, embarrassed, retires from the spot.[94] Later, the collegian is approached by the Confidence-Man again, in the person of the agent for the Black Rapids Coal Company. The collegian, having overheard a conversation about this agent between the man with the weed (also the Confidence-Man) and a Mr. Roberts, believes that he now has an inside tip on the market. He has heard that the stock of the Black Rapids Coal Company is about to increase greatly in value, an impression planted deliberately by the man with the weed. Certain he has the facts, the collegian proceeds to dupe the poor unsuspecting representative of the company into selling him some stock. "Sagely" turning over the agent's transfer book, the collegian puts on the air of a man who has investigated all the angles. " 'I hate a suspicious man,' " says the Confidence-Man, " 'but I must say I like to see a cautious one.' " " 'I can gratify you there,' " returns the collegian, " 'for, as I said before, I am naturally inquisitive; I am also circumspect. No appearances can deceive me.' "[95]

The joke is that appearances are at this very moment deceiving him and the Confidence-Man has used the collegian's immodest certainty in his own analytical abilities against him. Furthermore, in thinking that he is conning the agent, the collegian is putting his trust in his own ability to manipulate trust and mistrust on the basis of what he takes to be facts. After the Confidence-Man thus reverses the collegian's deadly combination of skepticism and reliance on an analytical method designed to beat the world's game, he launches into a diatribe against those who play for profit in a bear market by selling short. Such speculators drive the market down by their own suppression of confidence in themselves and those involved in the game with them. This sermonizing is in itself presented satirically. But the point to be made out of everything that happens between the agent and the collegian is that there is no way to beat a system built in the way the market's system is built. It is so structured that all profits and losses appear to be matters of cause-effect, the results of knowable factual events. But what happens in the market, or what happens between individual seller and buyer, is actually a matter of confidence and nothing else. The data can be manipulated. If one is sure that he has inside information, there is no way to be sure that the information has not been deliberately distorted and then supplied to him. If he thinks he has information behind that, he is still faced with the same perplexity. There is always between seller and buyer the effect of "I know that you know that I know that you know" ad infinitum. To complicate the matter, the market itself reacts to confidence; if holders lose confidence in a stock, they sell, and if this loss of confidence spreads, there is a bust. If everyone is confident, there is a boom.

The same applies to currency, about which much is made in the final chapter when the old man buys a counterfeit detector to test bills he has accepted. The old man does not know that the bills under question, which are on a Mississippi bank, are actually worthless because of a general failure of Mississippi banks.[96] The counterfeit detector he buys to test his bills proves even more of a joke since it points out such minute details to be checked that no one can really be sure if he has done the checking properly. On top of that, Melville has selected a beautifully ambiguous term in *counterfeit detector*. How can the old man know his detector is not itself counterfeit?[97] Is it a detector of counterfeits or a detector which is counterfeit? If he should lose confidence in his counterfeit detector, would he need a counterfeit counterfeit detector

detector? Finally, the concept of a detector for currency is doubly ludicrous because even "real" money is good only as long as those who use it have confidence in it. It doesn't matter what money looks like, or who prints it, if everyone in full confidence assigns to each denomination of currency the same value. Gold itself would not be immune to devaluation should the world suddenly decide that its intrinsic value was nil.

The Confidence-Man teaches the reader (if not the old man and the collegian) that everything people think about logical processes of acquiring and guarding wealth is a humbug. Logic does not apply, and researching the data involved in a transaction does not rid the participant of the need to proceed with confidence. Not to do such research, however, is shown in the cases of all the victims to be totally foolish; those victims who respond immediately to the Confidence-Man's pleas to their faith will never know whether or not their money goes to charity and stocks or into a swindler's pocket. But the simple irony is that those who go to great lengths to get all the facts are still in no better position. As the Confidence-Man's game with the dying miser shows, long experience in even a very specific, well-defined set of circumstances—the business of guarding money closely—does not help a man solve the problem of truth. The reader is left in no better position in respect to what is implied by these business transactions. He never knows what happens to the money, either. It is equally possible that the money solicited by the Confidence-Man in his roles as charity collector or stock peddler actually goes to charities and stocks or that it goes into his pocket.

That confidence is always required to establish the "reality" or "truth" of any situation—economic or otherwise—is both the great joke and the moral of the book. The satire is directed against those who believe confidence is not required. The rule of confidence applies in the game of fiction-making itself. In a mock defense of the inconsistency of fictional characters, one of several such comments on technique in the book, Melville indicated an awareness that the process of story is in itself a confidence game requiring acts of faith from both author and reader:

> If reason be judge, no writer has produced such inconsistent characters as nature herself has. It must call for no small sagacity in a reader unerringly to discriminate in a novel

between the inconsistencies of conception and those of life as elsewhere. Experience is the only guide here; but as no one man can be coextensive with *what is*, it may be unwise in every case to rest upon it. When the duck-billed beaver of Australia was first brought stuffed to England, the naturalists, appealing to their classifications, maintained that there was, in reality, no such creature; the bill in the specimen must needs be, in some way, artificially stuck on.[98]

Just as the reality of fictional characters must be taken on faith, so must the reality of whatever "truth" data dictate be taken on faith.

The end of the first phase of the game on the old miser epitomizes the confidence puzzle. The miser has rebuked the Confidence-Man at first, since he equates confidence with " 'bubble . . . fetch, gouge!' " The Confidence-Man does win his confidence, however, perhaps because the miser is physically and mentally weak from disease and senility. Having turned over a hundred dollars to the Confidence-Man, who disappears, the miser repents that he did not at least get something in writing: " 'Nay, back, back—receipt, my receipt! Ugh, ugh, ugh! Who are you? What have I done? Where go you? My gold, my gold! Ugh, ugh, ugh!' " This is followed by: "But, unluckily for this final flicker of reason, the stranger was now beyond ear-shot, nor was any one else within hearing of so feeble a call."[99] H. Bruce Franklin says in a note that "reason" here refers either to " 'My gold' " or " 'Ugh, ugh, ugh!' "[100] Actually, "reason" certainly refers to the miser's whole speech, and the implication is simply that confidence and reason do not coexist in a world where reason must, since it is a reason designed to deal with a world of deception, erode confidence.

In his disguise as the herb-doctor, the Confidence-Man performs an examination of the ironies of man's attempts to correct medicinally the body's chemistry. He tries to convince one victim that iron therapy is ludicrous because iron is a lifeless mineral and men are animals. The herb-doctor offers as a logical test for the effectiveness of remedies their naturalness. Whereas the well body is in a pure and natural state, it is proper to deduce that the best remedies are pure and natural. But the herb-doctor is the Confidence-Man, and he has assumed along with his disguise the highly debatable axiom: life is natural, herbs are natural, therefore herbs are naturally good for natural man. This is absurd reasoning; the Confidence-Man behind the mask of the herb-doctor knows that confidence in herbs is confidence pure and simple, without basis in "fact." The joke is compounded by the fact that the herb-doctor does have an occasionally valid prescription in " 'I am no materialist; but the mind so acts upon the body, that if the one have no confidence, neither has the other.' "[101] Probable connections between mental and physical health were generally accepted in Melville's time even as they are in our own. No one would argue against the statement: no man is well who thinks he is ill. The converse is not necessarily true, however, so the Confidence-Man does con his patient, to be sure. But the Confidence-Man's patient cannot be cured unless he is so conned!

The herb-doctor also prescribes that if a man is to be healthy, he will have to leave out of his serious considerations everything that tends to annihilate him. He quotes Shakespeare's Jessica in *The Merchant of Venice* to show that herbs are good things. He says:

> Is it not writ, that on a moonlight night,
> "Medea gathered the enchanted herbs
> That did renew old Æson?"

He stops his quotation at this point, leaving out Lorenzo's reply:

> In such a night
> Did Jessica steal from the wealthy Jew,
> And with an unthrift love did run from Venice. . . .[102]

In short, if the sick man is to be healthy, he will have to forget or ignore half of the possibilities in any situation—the dark half. A short time later, the herb-doctor paraphrases I Thessalonians 5: 21, which reads "Prove all things; hold fast that which is good." His rendition is " 'Prove all the vials; trust those which are true.' "[103] Whereas the Biblical text equates goodness and tested truth, the herb-doctor's version says ironically that truth is all that can be trusted but the only truth that is true is that which is already trusted. By an ingenious distortion of Biblical logic, the Confidence-Man has defined the absurd circle.

The Confidence-Man's greatest challenge before he meets Winsome and Egbert is the skeptical backwoodsman, Pitch. Approached by the herb-doctor, this worthy declares, " 'I have confidence in distrust. . . .' "[104] What the Confidence-Man will prove to him is exactly that—that even confidence in distrust is trust. But he will do more than this. The skeptic rejects all known tests for truth, including nature, which is thought to be gentle, but which breaks his windows with hailstones. In his role as the job-broker, the man who finds employers for boys, the Confidence-Man finally cracks Pitch's resistance. He does so by turning the backwoodsman's own skeptical logic back upon him. Experience has taught Pitch to mistrust boys; he has had five-and-thirty bad ones. The Confidence-Man pretends to presume that the process of reasoning by experience is the same as proceeding " 'by analogy from the physical to the moral.' "[105] This Pitch accepts. Pitch is, after all, the new man in the new age of science; he thinks that his method is empirical and inductive. The Confidence-Man argues that a boy is simply an unfinished man, and that, as empty gums in a baby are filled with unsound boy-teeth and these boy-teeth are replaced by sound man-teeth, so do boys become men, and their apparent badness is just an indication of a goodness that will come with maturity. The Confidence-Man can warp the analogizing process beautifully; he conveniently fails to point out that some bad first teeth are replaced by bad second teeth. After drawing a number of other such experiential analogies, the broker finally sells Pitch a boy. Concluding the sale, he adds, " 'Confidence is the indispensable basis of all sorts of business transactions. Without it, commerce between man and man, as between country and country, would, like a watch, run down and stop.' "[106] So, too, would mankind itself grind to a halt; for if we apply cold logic and explode the Confidence-Man's ludicrous analogies here (and, logically, they are fallacious and absurd), then boys will never get a chance to grow into men. But, as before, the reader is left holding the irony: we cannot know whether Pitch signed a good contract or a bad one. We are forced to believe the Confidence-Man's assertion that confidence is all we can be certain to get out of any transaction in which we put our confidence.

The Confidence-Man's parley with Charlie Noble, in which he assumes the name of Frank Goodman, is one of the outrightly funny passages of the book. Here are two con men, almost (but not quite!) matched, trying to get one another to drink just one more glass of wine, each himself refraining in order to keep his head clear, all the while claiming to have drunk his share and urging the other on. The Confidence-Man, now the Cosmopolitan, comments on the nature of humor, quoting Aristotle (a joke on the reader, since the passage apparently does not exist): " 'The popular notion of humor, considered as index to the heart, would seem curiously confirmed by Aristotle . . . who remarks that the least lovable men in history seem to have had for humor not only a disrelish, but a hatred. . . .' "[107] In short, confidence and humor go together; the pure rationalist cannot laugh.

Thus the Cosmopolitan exploits Charlie's good humor, flattering him and eventually playing the best joke of all on him, manipulating the manipulator of appearances by turning absurdities inside out. All the talk about confidence between the two confidence men demonstrates that the Cosmopolitan knows what man's condition is and Charlie does not. The Cosmopolitan knows all the dangers of confidence. He springs a trap on Charlie by abruptly asking for money and then, when Charlie, who has just declared himself without qualification a man of confidence, leaps up enraged, the Cosmopolitan circles him with gold pieces from his own pocket. Charlie recants by saying how well he played the part of misanthrope, knowing all the while what Frank was up to. The Cosmopolitan pretends to accept Charlie's explanation. Then he tells him the story of Charlemont, the St. Louis merchant who, after a youth spent in merry kindliness, suddenly became apparently embittered, went bankrupt, and disappeared. Years later he returned to his home and his friends again, once more a happy and prosperous man. One of these friends, after many years of frustrated speculation about the mystery, finally asked Charlemont what had happened. Charlemont would not tell him: " ' "No, no! when by art, and care, and time, flowers are made to bloom over a grave, who would seek to dig all up again only to know the mystery?—The wine.' "[108] If two men sit together drinking, the Cosmopolitan tells Charlie, they are able to do so because they are willing to take one another's story at its face value. When Charlie suspected Frank's motives, he was ready to depart in anger because he thought he had discovered the dark center of the Cosmopolitan's being. That impression proved to be just another appearance, and afterwards the two restored their pseudoconfidence. But the irony about pseudoconfidence is that the two are not drinking and they are not together. The dark joke is that those aware of the absurd game of deception all men are involved in know that the deception game is the only game that can be played. To believe in sincerity is foolhardy, but without sincerity, all relationships are lies. There is no way out of this bind; the Confidence-Man can do no more than play his game to the utmost of his abilities. He plays it better than Charlie does, and Charlie is a very good confidence man. Charlie asks if this story of Charlemont is true. The Cosmopolitan replies, " 'Of course not; it is a story which I told with the purpose of every story-teller—to amuse. Hence, if it seem strange to you, that strangeness is the romance; it is what contrasts it with real life; it is the invention, in brief, the fiction as opposed to the fact.' "[109] All of this circling in absurdity is too much for Charlie; he has been bested, and he slinks away.

The Confidence-Man next confronts Mark Winsome and Egbert, Melville's imitation of Emerson and Thoreau. Their place in the succession of opponents to the Confidence-Man is now quite clear. Neither of them is conned, and the reasons they are not conned make them look like icy philosophers indeed. They speak for an honest life, a life founded on the individual perception of moral truth. The Confidence-Man proves to us, if not to them, that men can have little more than an inkling that moral truth exists, let alone the wherewithal to tap such a source in their own souls. The satire begins with Winsome's equation of beauty, love, and truth. He says to the Confidence-Man with irony of which he is not aware, " 'yours, sir, if I mistake not, must be a beautiful soul— one full of all love and truth; for where beauty is, there must those be.' " The Cosmopolitan replies with a joke which we get but which Winsome cannot: " 'I am pleased to believe that beauty is at bottom incompatible with ill, and therefore am so eccentric as to have confidence in the latent benignity of that beautiful creature, the rattle-snake, whose lithe neck and burnished maze of tawny gold, as he sleekly curls aloft in the sun, who on the prairie can behold without wonder?' " As he says this, he assumes himself snakelike qualities; the Satanic side of the Confidence-Man is manifest, almost as a counterpoint to the developing joke. Winsome seems to agree that the beauty of the snake does indicate true benignity and indicates that he has felt, and suspects that the Cosmopolitan has felt, a true sympathy with that " 'irides-cent scabbard of death.' " Now the Cosmopolitan can push his joke to its limit because he has trapped Winsome by reducing the argument about beauty and truth to absurdity. The joke that the reader next gets is that Winsome does not know that his argument is so reduced, which means that what he takes to be rational analogizing is actually a colossal act of confidence.

When Winsome asks the Cosmopolitan if he would like to be a rattlesnake, the Cosmopolitan replies that he can't see that he would, especially since it would make him uncongenial, a " 'lone-some and miserable rattle-snake.' " This is mere prejudice, says Winsome, and adds, " 'And here we have another beautiful truth. When any creature is by its make inimical to other creatures, nature in effect labels that creature, much as an apothecary does a poison. So that whoever is destroyed by a rattle-snake, or other harmful agent, it is his own fault. He should have respected the label. Hence that significant passage in Scripture, "Who will pity the charmer that is bitten with a serpent?" ' " The joke is that, by Winsome's own argument, the beauty of the snake should tell the observer that the snake is safe, not poisonous. The label on the rattlesnake is just as reliable as the label on the counterfeit detector. Having caught Winsome in the contradiction, the Con-fidence-Man simply answers his last question, " 'I would pity him.' "[110]

The Confidence-Man himself is like a snake. He is also like a snake charmer. Whether he bites Winsome or Winsome bites him by winning the game, the Confidence-Man is going to feel pity for a victim. When the Confidence-Man succeeds in gaining his victim's confidence, he has saved him by getting him to perform an act of faith, but he has at the same time robbed him. The Confidence-Man in this case would feel pity if he should bite Winsome, who would be the charmer in the analogy because he is countermanipulating the Cosmopolitan's attempts to get him to act in conscious confidence. If the Confidence-Man loses the game, however, then he is like the snake charmer who got bitten, and he would have to pity himself. This makes the Confidence-Man both a creator of the absurd, a creator of acts of faith out of souls where no faith exists, and an absurd man, also vulnerable to the bite because he could be tripped up and exposed by the charmer, Winsome.

Towards the end of the rattlesnake discussion, Winsome implies that the rattlesnake is not accountable for its own deeds, phrasing his implication as a question. The Confidence-Man replies, " 'If I will not affirm that it is . . . neither will I deny it. But if we suppose it so, I need not say that such accountability is neither to you, nor me, nor the Court of Common Pleas, but to something superior.' " He adds,

> "You object to my supposition, for but such it is, that the rattle-snake's accountability is not by nature manifest; but might not much the same thing be urged against man's? A *reductio ad absurdum*, proving the objection vain. But if now . . . you consider what capacity for mischief there is in a rattle-snake (observe, I do not charge it with being mischievous, I but say it has the capacity), could you well avoid admitting that that would be no symmetrical view of the universe which should maintain that, while to man it is forbidden to kill, without judicial cause, his fellow, yet the rattle-snake has an implied permit of unaccountability to murder any creature it takes capricious umbrage at—man included?"

With this, the Confidence-Man pretends fatigue and breaks the argument off in spite of Winsome's renewed enthusiasm for it. The Confidence-Man has demolished Winsome's test of labels and his system of natural rightness, but Winsome does not know it. There is still a joke on the Confidence-Man, for his argument may suggest that men are no more nor less accountable than the rattler. If he is aware of that irony, and his total character shows that he is, then he is truly creating before our eyes the most ominous multilayered joke of the book.

Shortly after this episode, Winsome contradicts his philosophy of natural tests by saying, " 'The data which life furnishes, towards forming a true estimate of any being, are as insufficient to that end [of identifying the self] as in geometry one side given would be to determine the triangle.' " The Confidence-Man answers, " 'But is not this doctrine of triangles someway inconsistent with your doctrine of labels?' " Echoing "Self-Reliance," Winsome answers, " 'I seldom care to be consistent.' "[111] Emersonian reason as represented by Winsome (who is really only half an Emerson after all) is actually a mode of pure faith in the soul's ability to furnish the sense of rightness required to get by in the world. When neither Winsome nor Egbert acts in true charity and confidence, they are shown to be hypocritical, for their system should yield a trust that binds men together. Egbert's system of common sense, which, he claims, reveals high moral truth, tells him instead not to trust the Cosmopolitan when he asks for money. Moral philosophy succumbs when put to the test of cash values. Egbert's refusal comes in a hypothetical test case, in which the Cosmopolitan gets him to pretend to be Charlie (echoing the game with the second-best confidence man), and the Cosmopolitan again assumes his role of the needy Frank Goodman. "Frank" asks "Charlie" for a loan. Egbert, in response, tells his famous story of China Aster to prove how foolish confidence is when money is at stake. Reverting to his real character as the pose slips rapidly away, Egbert continues to demolish the Cosmopolitan's appeal for the moral rightness of confidence. Egbert is being satirized because his common sense does not yield moral truth. Confidence is the same as faith, and faith ought to be, in a Christian society, the highest moral good. But common sense demolishes faith.

Winsome and Egbert are safe from being afflicted by the awareness of the absurd condition that the Confidence-Man possesses. They stick to their system in the face of its loopholes. Their position is ironic, because as quasi-transcendentalists they ought to cleave to the view that an act of faith is literally a leap through and beyond the world and its evidences. This does not by contrast make the Confidence-Man an ultimate transcender, however, for the Confidence-Man knows, as we know, that his position is also absurd. China Aster's story would not have been tragic if everyone had confidence in others. This is the essential tragedy of the story of Adam and Eve's fall—confidence is the only thing that will yield love and a lovely world, yet confidence is stupid, even in a world in which it was not yet violated. In his discussion with the barber, whom he finally does con for a haircut, the Confidence-Man sums up the basic dilemma: " 'Don't you think consistency requires that you should either say "I have confidence in all men," and take down your notification; or else say, "I suspect all men," and keep it up.' "[112] The major theme of *The Confidence-Man* lies in the question the Confidence-Man poses to all his opponents (or are they partners?) and in the question Melville thus poses to us. We are all confidence men; we all put our trust somewhere. The center of the circle of truth is not ours to know. If we are to have any truth, we must create it. An act of faith is required, yet at the same time an act of faith is irrational and foolish. The question the book asks is why do men not accept the absurd act of confidence as the only creative act open to them. All the reasons that all of the potential victims give for not doing so are under satirical attack. Empiricism does not yield faith; it only proves that there is a Prime Cause that is unknowable.

The last chapter of the book puts even faith in faith into the realm of the irrational. It demonstrates that even the Confidence-Man's confidence in his ability to create confidence can be undermined. Even the logic against logic is shown to be illogical. The Confidence-Man expresses his fears about confidence, and then he finds support for his doubts in a Bible which he borrows from the old man, who is reading it in the dim light of the stateroom. He is relieved when the Christlike old man points out to him that he is reading from the Apocrypha, that part of the book which is not labeled approved, genuine, revelation. In short, the believer in warranted Biblical text, the complete Christian, can still have confidence based on Scriptural evidence and thus be saved. But the Confidence-Man knows that all things can be manipulated, and that includes Biblical text, the last thing he has turned to as a firm motivation for confidence.

The Cosmopolitan never uses a life preserver, though he recommends one to the old man. Why doesn't he? Is it that he doesn't need it or is it that he doesn't trust it? This recommendation is, moreover, complicated by the fact that it is a scatological joke. The life preserver referred to is designed to be a seat as well; the seat is designed in turn to serve as a chamberpot.[113] The Confidence-Man creates this joke for the reader's benefit, going through the motions of a lie that says he is supernatural—he doesn't even have to defecate. He is really doing so ironically, however, because he knows the old man will not get the joke and he knows that we will not believe it. The sad part of the irony is that the Confidence-Man cannot be supernatural and therefore complete and true; he does depend, if he is a man, upon the life-saver chamberpot.

(129

When the Confidence-Man puts out the light, he is emblematically suggesting that he has come to the end of this April Fools' Day absurd spiral. He has shown us, as he tried to show his victims, that confidence is the basis for all the truths we hold. But his own confidence in his confidence is also shown to be sheer arbitrary faith. There is no bottom to this spiral. The joke, finally, is on the reader. He must accept the Confidence-Man's message, yet he does not dare accept it. He now has no alternative in any sphere of action—religion, business, fellowship, or the act of reading *The Confidence-Man* included—but to create something out of nothing. This is the creative doom of Christ and all bringers of light and, as the reader has seen in reading the book, of the receivers of light, too. The Confidence-Man and *The Confidence-Man* admonish us to recognize that we, too, are men dependent on confidence in our confidence and thus must be Confidence-Men or nothing.

4 · THE JOKES IN *Billy Budd*

Whereas Moby-Dick, Pierre, and *The Confidence-Man* are Melville's fullest definitions of the absurd, his late short fiction is saturated by the absurd sense transformed into various concise and weighty jokes. There is grim humor based on the absurd sense in "Bartleby the Scrivener," "Cock-a-Doodle-Doo!" "Benito Cereno," "The Paradise of Bachelors and the Tartarus of Maids," and the sketches in "The Encantadas." But the best example among these pieces is *Billy Budd*, certainly a story not usually regarded as having a scrap of humor in it.[114] There are three jokes that occur in *Billy Budd* after Billy is hanged. The mere juxtaposition of these jokes to the hanging makes them grim, but more than that they throw into stark relief the theme of the book and display concisely Melville's complete sense of the absurd.

The first joke is the discussion between the ship's purser, a pseudophilosopher, and the "scientific" ship's surgeon. Billy's death has been described in beautiful and calm ascension imagery. He died without a twitch, passing from one life to another as though death were no event at all. The sailors have witnessed something comparable to the triumph of Christ. But these two wags—the purser and the doctor—proceed to have a debate over whether or not it is really possible to die by hanging without twitching. The purser begins to ask, " 'What testimony to the force lodged in will power . . . ?' " and the doctor interrupts by stating unequivocally that no will power could possibly be shown in " 'a hanging scientifically conducted. . . .' " Instead, he says, some absence of involuntary mechanical muscle spasm was manifested which cannot be said to be any the less involuntary for its being unusual. Baiting him, the purser asks him to account for this further, and the doctor replies that the event only appears phenomenal " 'in the sense that it was an appearance the cause of which is not immediately to be assigned.' "[115] The high rhetoric of this discussion of Billy's death is a device of comic reduction directed at the purser and doctor. Billy's "ascension" is seen by these two as nothing more than a curiosity.

The second joke is the account of Claggart's murder and Billy's execution given in the press. The newspaper report is a ludicrous distortion of the story as the reader has seen it: Billy has become the instigator of a mutiny plot, he has "vindictively stabbed" Claggart, and he was obviously no Englishman, but "one of those aliens . . . whom the present extraordinary necessities of the service have caused to be admitted into it in considerable numbers." His "crime" is described as a depraved enormity.[116]

These petty philosophical reactions and distortions prove that, ironically, men need arbitrary and unyielding institutions headed by captains like Vere. He is a man of expediency. He is identified with his military buttons; he has at his command the perfect solution for the absurd condition he finds himself in when he witnesses Claggart's murder, and his conscience tells him all of the ambivalent truths about the event: he follows the rule book. He executes Billy quickly. He is a man who can perceive the absurd but who has devices for overcoming it. Since Billy's execution and ascension do not elicit anything more from his fellow crew members than a comic argument and a ballad (albeit a good ballad), Captain Vere is just the man for them. He knows how to prevent mutiny. The implication is that the men who operate best in the world are the expedient and law-obeying Captain Veres.

They subscribe without deviation to arbitrary law in spite of their suspicion that law can destroy. Usually their consistency does yield order and not chaos. They are fit to lead.

The third and final joke centers on Vere. He is a man who has lived in imitation of the Old Testament God, the swift judge who divides good from evil with a stroke. He is killed by a shot from a French line-of-battle ship called the *Athée*—the *Atheist*. This is some kind of great joke, not all of whose ambiguities and incongruities are apparent.[117] But one thing is clear: that he should be cut down by symbolic disbelief shows that even the most efficient and systematic human being will eventually fail. Vere calls for Billy Budd as he dies. Has he saved himself by yielding at last to the mysteries? There is, by definition, no way to know. Even the Confidence-Man is forced to enter the darkness without knowing, conning himself into confidence to the very last.

V

The Prisoner at the Window: Mark Twain

"And yet when you come to think, there is
no real difference between a conscience
and an anvil—I mean for comfort."

HANK MORGAN

I · A HIGH AND DANGEROUS VIEW

A CONNECTICUT YANKEE IN KING ARTHUR'S COURT is Mark Twain's masterpiece of the absurd. Here, as in his other books, he exercised fully the traditional satirical technique of shifting points of view. But more importantly, it is in this book that he most clearly and effectively developed his darkest kind of satire—a satire directed at the very perception process which allows satire. This undercutting of the satirist's own moral vision is a powerful and serious experiment in the comedy of the absurd. The process is emblemized by Hank Morgan's analysis of his conscience. His remarks occur in the midst of his efforts to comprehend Morgan le Fay's mind and experience, which have tailored

(133

her judgment so that she automatically justifies extreme cruelty. He realizes that his conscience and hers are two different things; they have not been, as is commonly supposed, given by God to man as an instrument for dividing the "true" right from the "true" wrong. What he sees as wrong, Morgan le Fay takes to be natural, commonplace, and correct. If he were to be given a chance to re-make man, Hank remarks, he would not give him a conscience at all; "it would be much better to have less good and more comfort." "Good" is an illusion and is often "bad"; "comfort" is a reliable test of what is desirable. The joke about the conscience derives from the relativist's awareness that morality is nothing more than a function of a social frame which produces morals. Hank extends this view of the circularity of morality into a comment on the absurd: "I suppose that in the beginning I prized [my conscience], because we prize anything that is ours; and yet how foolish it was to think so. If we look at it in another way, we see how absurd it is: if I had an anvil in me would I prize it? Of course not. And yet when you come to think, there is no real difference between a conscience and an anvil—I mean for comfort."[1]

Hank's remark provides the key to Twain's double-faceted satire. The first facet of his satire is a combination of the viewpoint-shifting technique and the subject of relativism. Men suppose that the conscience shows a man the contrast between what is and what ought to be, but instead the conscience is simply at the mercy of what is. Nonetheless, some men have an intuition that there is a discrepancy between abstract rightness and what appears to be right in the world. This awareness of discrepancy is the first and most readily observable source of humor in Twain's works. Sometimes Twain as author displays this awareness, and sometimes his character does, too. It is an awareness analogous to that Emerson defined in "The Comic." The world men take to be normal and correct is seen as distorted from some vantage point that allows a more comprehensive view or a new angle of vision. Twain invented a number of very startling displacement devices, among them the familiar ones of letting Huck journey through a ludicrous world on a raft and taking Hank out of nineteenth-century New England into Arthur's world. Early in his career, Twain attempted to rewrite *Hamlet,* adding a new character, a commentator whose views were practical and iconoclastic. This character, who bears faint resemblance to Hank Morgan, was to make sarcastic asides to the audience about the characters and events of the play. Had Twain succeeded in developing this intention, the travesty might have been a splendid and grotesque inversion in which the absurd dilemmas of tragedy were abruptly transformed into the absurd trivialities of farce. The late fragmentary work, "Three Thousand Years Among the Microbes," features a character transformed from a human being into a cholera germ which takes up residence in the body of a juicy, disease-ridden bum. "Gulliver's Lilliput outdone," proclaimed Albert Bigelow Paine.[2] That praise may be excessive, but the device was perfect for examining the ludicrosities of man from the inside out.

The displacement process was, then, very serviceable to Twain; it is the basis of those revelations that delight and educate his audience. Twain extended and altered the technique in some of his books—*A Connecticut Yankee* especially—to produce the second and darker facet of his satire. When a new angle of vision is assumed, the formally normal-appearing world is not the only thing that can be shown to be laughable. The old point of view is often discovered to have been ludicrous, too. In turn, the second angle of vision can be scrutinized from a third point of view, and so on. By employing a series of such displacements and by reversing some positions (showing the *yeas* and *nays* to be perfectly balanced on any given question), the satirist can show that it is possible to shift from viewpoint to viewpoint forever. His satirical scrutiny then loses its moralizing function and becomes a quest among random points of view. It is crucial to note that what Hank is attacking is the source of moral knowledge itself, and he is surely not the only character through whom Twain made the point. Huck's conscience misleads him. Satan in *The Mysterious Stranger* argues convincingly that the "Moral Sense" is not moral but is actually a fabrication used to justify vicious aggression in behalf of arbitrary moral systems. The consciences of most men interfere with the forgiveness and understanding that the relativistic view would make possible. But, ironically, the satirist who condemns other consciences must have a conscience—one that dictates the "morality" of the relativistic view. In calling the conscience "absurd," Hank calls the inspiration of satire absurd.

It is this second aspect of his satire that makes Twain's humor serious.[3] In works like *Huckleberry Finn, A Connecticut Yankee, The Mysterious Stranger,* and "The Great Dark," Twain displayed, almost to the point of saturating the reader with arguments and examples, a sophisticated awareness of the comic ambivalence which characterizes the vision of the perceptive man. Often he saw the revelations of intuition—that source of moral knowledge so highly regarded by American thinkers—as absurd revelations. In Twain's books, the faculties of judgment are determined relativistically, exactly as are the qualities which judgment is testing. The nineteenth-century pragmatist Hank, the innocent Huck, or the sensitive and carefully intelligent Pudd'nhead are all absurd perceivers of an absurd world. It is when the view of a character who is obviously designed to draw our sympathies— a character created to be on the author's and reader's side in the war of values—fails that Twain most clearly reveals a dark sense of the absurdity of everything.

The difference between Twain's two kinds of satire is parallel to the difference between the humor emphasized in his early travel books and that emphasized in his late dark comedies. In the travel books, viewpoints are shifted to reveal sequences of new absurdities. The humor deriving from these shifts is designed to expose the ludicrous follies of the human race. The traveler generally perseveres; his viewpoint almost always proves superior. The travel books do contain occasional bits of grim humor, and Twain's deep concern with the ambiguity of vision displays itself from the very beginning. But it is the later books which have the ambiguity of vision as their main subject. Twain saw this dilemma of perception as tragic as well as comic, but when he put his sense of humor aside—as he did in "Which Was It," for example—the result is not tragedy but sadness, a tone of brooding melancholy. The reader is merely depressed by an endless spiraling through circles of ugly entanglements as the main character tries to create one solution after another only to have to undo one mistake after another. Twain simply was no tragedian in the technical sense. On the other hand, his genius was so perfectly balanced between the tragic and the comic view that the combination disallowed both tragedy and light comedy. Only serious comedy could result from his understanding of relativity.

The tragicomic limits of vision are sharply delineated by the story of the prisoner at the window in *A Connecticut Yankee*. Among those Hank frees from Morgan le Fay's dungeon is a man who was luckier than the others because he had a very small arrow slit from which he could peer out at the world. He could see his own home, and for twenty-two years he watched the lights shine there at night and people come and go. He could not make out who the people were. Five funerals had issued from the hut during those years, and, since he had left behind a wife and five children, he spent his time wondering which one was alive. Because he is so curious about the prisoner's question, Hank escorts him home personally. The homecoming turns out to be "an amazing kind of a surprise party . . . typhoons and cyclones of frantic joy, and whole Niagaras of happy tears; and by George . . . not a soul of the tribe was dead!" Hank is struck by Morgan le Fay's "ingenious devilishness": she had invented all the funerals merely to torment the prisoner's heart, and the finishing stroke of genius was to leave the family invoice one short.[4]

Here, as elsewhere, Twain depicted the vision of any man: tailored by experience, limited by the place in which he lives, constricted by the window from which he views the world rather than freed by it. Some windows are larger than others. Hank's window is very wide, but it has fatal blind spots; Huck's view changes constantly, but we agonize because it cannot expand very much. Some men's windows face the dark and do nothing but reflect. A few men (Twain included) have several windows. No one is outside the cell; all see only what their window allows. Every man is a prisoner at a window.

There is one more dark element in this emblematic scene. Not only is the prisoner's vision narrowly constricted, but what he sees has been distorted by a cruel manipulator of the view. That the viewer's vision should be limited is only part of his dilemma. The other part is that everything he sees is a practical joke. Often in Twain's book a joke-maker like Morgan le Fay is not present at all, or at least is not knowable. The joke then has a reality independent of causation. Existence is then a practical joke.

The re-creator of the joke, Samuel Clemens in the guise of Mark Twain, persona of the travel books and implied author of the novels, has the advantage in the joke world. He can use his imagination to see the view from different windows, creating laughter out of the absurdities that the shifts of sight reveal. He can do even more than that. Full sight—the comprehension of ultimate meaning—is of course impossible, but the highest artistry of comedy is to create meaning and laughter out of the perception of meaninglessness and tragedy. This is absurd creation which counters the absurd dilemma.

To Twain, creation of laughter once seemed a lowly mission: "I *have* had a 'call' to literature, of a low order—*i.e.* humorous. It is nothing to be proud of, but it is my strongest suit, & if I were to listen to that maxim of stern *duty* which says that to do right you *must* multiply the one or the two or the three talents which the Almighty entrusts to your keeping, I would long ago have ceased to meddle with things for which I was by nature unfitted & turned my attention to seriously scribbling to excite the *laughter* of God's creatures. Poor, pitiful business!"[5] It was far from a pitiful business; it was a high—and very dangerous—business. In his selection of a pseudonym, Clemens made a metaphor that conveys the precariousness of floating carefully between hilarity and nihilism. When the leadsman on a steamboat cried "Mark Twain," the pilot, the crew, and all experienced passengers knew immediately that the boat drifted at that thin edge of safety, the ambiguous water that is almost—but not quite—shoal. To one side (or perhaps even just behind!) lies enough water to float the ship; to the other, less water than she draws. James M. Cox recently wrote that the cry "Mark Twain" meant "*barely* safe water—a message which might bring either relief or fear to the pilot, depending on the circumstances."[6] Actually, the pilot could not know what the circumstances were. "Mark Twain" meant barely safe water under the boat, and what it indicated about the water ahead of the boat was anybody's guess. The condition of the pilot at Mark Twain is the condition of Mark Twain the humorist. His comedy is always just barely safe, and its direction is always ambiguous.

2 · THE INNOCENT ABSURDIST

Twain's primary subject in his first major works—the early travel books and the accounts of his experiences in the West and on the Mississippi—is the vision of one traveler. Traveling is the natural mode of life for the missionary who wishes to excite laughter by finding and revealing the world's absurdities. These books are thus something more than autobiography altered for the purposes of entertainment; they share with the novels that came later the basic device of motion, the continual displacement that allows intensive scanning of the varieties of absurd experience. In *The Innocents Abroad*, Twain and his companions are connoisseurs of the absurd on a voyage of discovery. In *Roughing It*, Twain portrays himself as the absurd man, the innocent victim of absurdities. In *Life on the Mississippi*, he investigates the comic and serious difficulties of learning where the snags are in the real world of a river whose realities are always hidden beneath a murky surface. The subject common to these books is the vision of the traveler. The effects of the limitations of the traveler's vision are told in retrospect by a storyteller, the older Mark Twain who wrote the books. The satire thus works in two directions: it falls upon the narrator as well as upon the eccentricities of other people and the discomforts of Europe, the West, and the river.

Twain prefaced his recollections in *The Innocents Abroad* with a note on vision, declaring that he would show the reader "how *he* would be likely to see Europe and the East if he looked at them with his own eyes. . . ."[7] The traveler is thus supposed to be the symbolic American who can look upon Europe and the East with the eyes of a rational man. His vision requires a firm American confidence in its own correctness. He sees the value systems of foreign countries as absurd when tested against his own. His values are simple: people should be honest and common-sensible, places should be clean, and institutions should be democratic. The satire that falls on old systems and cruelties is satire designed to evaluate and expose things that are wrong. But the big joke of *The Innocents Abroad* goes beyond the jokes the traveler discovers in Europe and the East. This joke starts in the narrator's discovery that he is prejudiced, that his all-essential confidence in the clarity of his vision can be undermined. The implications of his discovery are weighty: if the sharp American perceiver loses confidence in his vision, he loses confidence in his American values. The joke ends, however, with an affirmation of a new faith, a gradually developed confidence in a process which transcends the limits of vision: the creative art of telling and understanding stories. When reasoning and observation fail to discover some underlying truth, then the traveler accepts and enjoys an absurdly created truth or manufactures one of his own. Twain's kind of travel record produces not facts and figures but tall tales whose comic truth is superior to the sober pseudotruth of a selection of data.

Before this affirmation can occur the traveler must realize the circularity of reasoning and the comic inadequacy of vision. " 'Dan, just look at this girl, how beautiful she is!' " says Twain, thinking the girl speaks only French. She returns, in perfect English, a reminder that such an outburst is a serious breach of decorum. "We took a walk," the older Twain recalls; "Why *will* people be so stupid as to suppose themselves the only foreigners among a crowd of ten thousand persons?"[8] Such revelations of the ignorance of innocence repeat themselves throughout the journey, bringing the traveler through sad experience to a recognition of how easily his vision can be deluded in even the simplest circumstances. The problem of perception is complicated by the fact that even an orderly, beautiful reality can reasonably be judged absurd. Upon observing the landscaping of Versailles, the traveler seems to have discovered some consistent artistic principles. Precision and massiveness make the Versailles landscape seem beautiful and meaningful. By contrast, the puniness and distortion of the American gardens he is familiar with make a scene "look absurd enough." But the orderliness of Versailles is not necessarily reasonable; in fact, it is a mystery: he cannot fathom how trees can be made to grow to a uniform height, thickness, and, above all, shape. "I have tried," the retrospective narrator says, "to reason out the problem, and have failed."[9] All that orderliness imposed on nature is, from any rational viewpoint, absurd. It is not grotesque but is still an astonishing distortion. The older Twain realizes that to see an appearance of meaning is not to know how the appearance was wrought nor to understand the meaning itself.

Twain's responses to the comic scenes recorded in *The Innocents Abroad* have an even bolder implication about meaning: to see one of Europe's mysteries is often to see something that has no inner reality at all. The missing reality has been supplanted by a lie. The narrator and his companions love the lies that constitute antiquity. They are made ecstatic by being shown enough whole and fragmentary crowns of thorns to fill a bushel basket. The sad condition of *The Last Supper* makes bleakly ludicrous the raptures of those who see in it some greatness that is no longer there. The true original dust of Adam settles all questions about man's origin: no one, after all, can prove that the dust under that particular monument is not the dust from which Adam was made and to which he returned. Constantly, Twain's recollection of these artificial oddities and the record of his tongue-in-cheek response to them make it plain that he is embellishing the lies with creative expansions of his own. Instead of merely making all the superstitions and legends of the old countries look silly, he is displaying them proudly to us as the most entertaining facets of the trip.

The dirty city of Civita Vecchia, for instance, is disappointing but not because it is dirty. Its filth is, in fact, its one potential; Twain can make jokes about it. The real trouble with Civita Vecchia is that there is nothing to see: "They have not even a cathedral, with eleven tons of solid silver archbishops in the back room; and they do not show you any moldy buildings that are seven thousand years old; nor any smoke-dried old fire-screens which are *chef d'œuvres* of Reubens or Simpson, or Titian or Ferguson, or any of those parties; and they haven't any bottled fragments of saints, and not even a nail from the true cross. We are going to Rome. There is nothing to see here."[10] Of course, Twain the teller is being ironic about all the lies he is told by all the guides, saying that European civilization is a sham. On the other hand, "There is nothing to see here" is also literally true: where there are no lies, there is nothing. The travelers take great pleasure in watching the guides trying to fool them and watching themselves taking all stories with the necessary grain of salt. What they discover on their quest is more than the constant gap between illusion and reality—they discover that the reality is nonexistent. The lie that has filled the vacuum is perfectly satisfying to a traveler who knows exactly how the lie works. "Splendid lie—drive on" is their motto, complementing perfectly the subtitle, "The New Pilgrims' Progress." The New Pilgrims progress from one splendid lie to another.

Twain the retrospective humorist makes his book out of these splendid lies. How did the oyster shells get five hundred feet above sea level to form the veins unearthed by a cut made for the uphill road to the citadel at Smyrna?

> It is painful—it is even humiliating—but I am reduced at last to one slender theory: that the oysters climbed up there of their own accord. But what object could they have had in view? —what did they want up there? What could any oyster want to climb a hill for? To climb a hill must necessarily be fatiguing and annoying exercise for an oyster. The most natural conclusion would be that the oysters climbed up there to look at the scenery. Yet when one comes to reflect upon the nature of an oyster, it seems plain that he does not care for scenery. An oyster has no taste for such things; he cares nothing for the beautiful. An oyster is of a retiring disposition, and not lively —not even cheerful above the average, and never enterprising. But, above all, an oyster does not take any interest in scenery—he scorns it. What have I arrived at now? Simply at the point I started from, namely, *those oyster shells are there*, in regular layers, five hundred feet above the sea, and no man knows how they got there. I have hunted up the guide-books, and the gist of what they say is this: "They are there, but how they got there is a mystery."[11]

The scientific explanation of this phenomenon would only destroy the funny myth, breaking up the comic rhythm of the analysis of the oyster's artistic limitations. The satirist in this book cares less about the demand for truth than he does for well-told lies. What can be re-created out of error and mystery into a deep joke is what the traveler is looking for. Twain's primary accomplishment in *The Innocents Abroad* is not corrective satire, which in this case would be decidedly uninteresting. To eradicate follies and lies would be to spoil everything. The fiber of the book is the fun that traveling can be when it becomes a matter of discovering absurdities, magnifying them, and weaving them into a yarn. The book itself is the biggest fabrication of all, encompassing and exceeding all the original shams and fusing them into one large travel lie.

Roughing It is also a tall book as well as a funny one, and in many ways it represents the height of Twain's power as a creator of positive laughter. The book is full of graveyard jokes: fun is made of discomfort, injury, sorrow, and even death. But the humor is not sick; it is healthy. It overrides the potential darkness of the jokes. The older Twain writing this book distills out of his humiliating and painful experiences a comic essence that was less apparent to the young Twain in the middle of those experiences. Occasionally the retrospective teller speaks directly to the reader, suspending the device of depicting his earlier naïve self in order to make direct satirical comments. At these times, he is simply the man who witnessed the moral confusion wrought on the South Pacific Islanders by Christian missions or saw that real Indians were never noble savages. Sometimes this Twain tells on himself unintentionally: he talks of inferior and superior races, displaying, in spite of his intellectual recognition of the absurdity of racism, a feeling that equalization for some requires that they first be elevated.

But for the most part, the Mark Twain of the plot—and this book does have a plot—remains innocent and gullible throughout, in contrast to the experienced Mark Twain who, as the author, manipulates a humor dependent upon his recognition of himself as an absurd victim of appearances during the years of his quest for silver in Nevada. In writing the book Twain showed that he recognized the comedy of his own early innocence. On the other hand, he never did grow much less gullible than the Twain who is the hero of *Roughing It;* the man who would not give up hope of finding a silver mine was the same man who years later sank his fortune into the Paige typesetting machine. Nevertheless, there are two different kinds of confidence displayed by the two Twains in this book. The first is the naïve confidence of the absurd hero, and it is the fortunes of this confidence as it is tested against the disappointments of the quest for wealth that constitute the book's plot. This hero never learns about the nature of appearances, nor does he develop a consciousness of the dangers of his naïve confidence. In the opening chapter of the book, he believes that he will pick silver bars off the desert floor. As the book progresses, he is repeatedly duped either by others or by himself into high expectations only to have each end in disappointment. At the end of the book, he is left still searching, pocket-mining for gold in Calaveras County.

But the retrospective author's confidence has become sophisticated. (One should not forget that both Twains in the book are characters; for artistic contrast, the teller is made to seem almost as wise as the real Twain and the hero more ludicrous than Twain could ever have been.) The storyteller sees all the absurdities of his earlier confidence. His new confidence is in his ability to invent and control a comic myth of himself. The excellence of the humor of *Roughing It* shows that, at least at this time in his life, the confidence of the real Mark Twain was well-founded. Such confidence is precarious precisely because it is a function of mental attitude. But in *Roughing It* the humorous inclination perseveres and keeps the jokes from turning black.

Dark humor requires something that Twain deliberately left out of the travesty of *Roughing It*. A country woman in a stage-coach plays a crude and lovely game: "She would sit there in the gathering twilight and fasten her steadfast eyes on a mosquito rooting into her arm, and slowly she would raise her other hand till she had got his range, and then she would launch a slap at him that would have jolted a cow; and after that she would sit and contemplate the corpse with tranquil satisfaction—for she never missed her mosquito; she was a dead shot at short range. She never removed a carcase, but left them there for bait." The humor here depends upon a unique female behavior described in sporting terms. To be compared with this yarn is Jim Blaine's account of Mrs. Wagner's borrowed glass eye that fitted so loosely it constantly got twisted around, scaring all the children in the vicinity. She packed it in cotton but the cotton worked loose and stuck out around the edges, making it look worse than ever. She was always dropping it, and, after someone fetched it, all present would have to wait while she jammed it in again, usually backwards. This yarn worsens as we hear a catalog of items missing from the person of Mrs. Wagner, including hair and one leg.[12] (These ladies are of the same high class as Brown's girl friend in *Mark Twain's Travels with Mr. Brown*. She picked her nose with a fork. Brown could not live without her.) These travesties of femininity are not true grim jokes. There is no compulsion here to laugh in defense against terror. Grim humor draws on situations that leave no possible reaction but totally ironic laughter. Here the reader is delighted to see a skillfully handled transformation of romantic ideal into jolly grotesque, and there is no darkness in that.

There are in *Roughing It* a number of good stories about farcical trials, thefts, murders, massacres, and other happy incidents characteristic of western life. Even the water could be deadly, and, when talking about one alkali lake, the teller gives this picture of the predetermined circle all life moves in: "Providence leaves nothing to go by chance. All things have their uses and their part and proper place in Nature's economy: the ducks eat the flies— the flies eat the worms—the Indians eat all three—the wild cats eat the Indians—the white folks eat the wild cats—and thus all things are lovely."[13] And thus all is an absurd circle. The silver seeker's quest for nothing and the ludicrous events he encounters are part of the motion of a world busily going nowhere. But this does not mean that the jokes of the absurd in the book are grim; the author's sarcasm is, after all, cheerful. "All things are lovely" does mean that things are not lovely. But, at the same time, to the man willing to balance his tendency towards nihilism with a sense of humor, all things are lovely because, in the telling, they can appear to be so funny.

In *Life on the Mississippi* (and in its predecessor, "Old Times on the Mississippi") Twain began to develop his river metaphor, which was to prove a perfect symbol of ambivalence. He was to extend the metaphor even further in *Huckleberry Finn*. On the one hand the river represents escape, refuge, and a natural, happy state of primitive existence. On the other hand, the river hides snags from the pilot, produces a fog that keeps Huck and Jim from finding freedom, and carries Huck from one horror to the next. The river is as ambiguous as the stream of life it is intended to represent; like Ishmael's ocean, it can hide everything or, in moments when a man acquiesces, open to yield a moral revelation or a tangible danger.

It is the very real ambiguity of the river that causes the problems faced by the cub pilot in *Life on the Mississippi.* He is perplexed by the river's constant shiftings, by the way a snag can show clearly at the edge of a run one trip and be downriver submerged in the middle of the run the next. Bixby's skill, in contrast to the cub's perplexity, is nothing short of miraculous: "Fully to realize the marvelous precision required in laying the great steamer in her marks in that murky waste of water, one should know that not only must she pick her intricate way through snags and blind reefs, and then shave the head of the island so closely as to brush the overhanging foliage with her stern, but at one place she must pass almost within arm's reach of a sunken and invisible wreck that would snatch the hull timbers from under her. . . ."[14] Bixby's seemingly casual explanation shows that the river is even more hopelessly complicated. On a clear night the shadow of a shore hides snags and safe water alike. On a dark night, all shores seem to be straight, and a pilot must drive his boat directly into what appears to be a solid wall. He has to know where the real curves are. On a drizzly, gray night the shore has no shape at all. Moonlight changes the shore according to the kind of moonlight it is. The cub is naturally overwhelmed: " 'Have I got to learn the shape of the river according to all these five hundred thousand different ways?' " Bixby answers, " '*No!* you only learn *the* shape of the river; and you learn it with such absolute certainty that you can always steer by the shape that's *in your head,* and never mind the one that's before your eyes.' "[15]

The cub learns through bitter experience that his reliance upon his own confidence is essential. Bixby educates him by tricking him. He asks if the cub knows the next crossing, and the cub replies that he does. Bixby then leaves the pilot house with a curt " 'You think so, do you?' " This is enough to shake the cub's certainty. Slowly his confidence evaporates, and, as the leadsman begins to deliver false readings, he decides that he is in trouble. He ends by shouting an order to " 'back the immortal *soul* out of her!' " There is no danger, and Bixby's lesson is firm: " 'You shouldn't have allowed me or anybody else to shake your confidence in that knowledge. . . . And another thing: when you get into a dangerous place, don't turn coward. That isn't going to help matters any.' "[16]

These are brave words, and Bixby would have the cub believe that confidence can have a foundation in the knowledge carried in the mind. The pilot has his method: he memorizes a reality he sees by daylight and tests by experience. He uses his knowledge of this model to steer the boat at night and in fog. If he is truly confident in the model, he can ignore all deceptive appearances. But what Bixby either does not admit or refuses to recognize is that this confidence does not really have a foundation. The problem—and the ambiguity that underlies the pilot's absurd position—is that the shape providing the original for the mind's idea of the river is absolutely unreliable as model. It can and does change from day to day. The sandbar shifts, the snag floats into the run, a whole bank gives way; all of these possibilities and more are chronicled in the book. In the final analysis Bixby's reliance upon experience and visible facts is more pure confidence than absolute certainty. Whether or not the water is shoal or safe is something that no man can know for sure; a pilot steers by a confidence he has invented. Whether or not the experienced pilot is to have confidence is a matter of whether or not he's the confident type. Bixby's "lesson" is an outrageous joke: does he really want the cub to ignore the leadsman's cries? If the leadsman's readings cannot be relied upon, what can? Experience teaches the cub that he must invent confidence for himself.

3 · THE FAILURE OF ABSURD CREATION

The humorous action of both *The Adventures of Huckleberry Finn* and *A Connecticut Yankee in King Arthur's Court* grows out of the conflict between the absurd world and the heroes' vision. Both Huck and Hank are threatened by confidence men operating as extensions of corrupt institutions and societies; both win most of their battles because they are able to become wiser confidence men and better liars than their opponents. Their triumphs are comic because Twain has made it clear that he believes that Huck's and Hank's motives, while they could hardly be judged noble, are at least based on simple pleasure-pain principles and innocent democratic notions about justice. The humor of both books darkens and disappears because the heroes are finally defeated by the same flaw. For all their creativity, neither Huck nor Hank has a wide enough field of vision. The implication is that, given the endless contradictions of the absurd world, no man can have a wide enough view. Even imagination fails because the information it acts upon ultimately proves false. Absurd creation can temporarily modify Huck's existence or give Hank his moments of glory, but it cannot give either of them the final victory.

Huck's life under Miss Watson's tutelage is civilized, calm, secure, and, therefore, intolerable. What Huck, Tom, and the other boys are doing when they conjure up and enact horrendous crimes and thrilling escapades is creating alternatives to the dull meaninglessness of schoolboy life in a small town. When they "ambuscade the A-rabs," Huck cannot see that their victims are anything but children on a picnic: "So then I judged that all that stuff was only just one of Tom Sawyer's lies. I reckoned he believed in the A-rabs and the elephants, but as for me I think different. It had all the marks of a Sunday-school."[17] Huck sees here no motives for deception. Unfortunately, although Huck does have a feeling that Tom's inventions are ludicrous, he is never able to reduce his susceptibility to Tom's kind of insanity. He does not resist Tom's cruel game with Jim in the last chapters, and he plays at least two stupid and vicious tricks on Jim himself—once with the dead rattler whose mate bites Jim, and once by trying to convince Jim that their separation in the fog was a bad dream. Huck can see the idiocy of Tom's games, and he can play good games of survival, but he never develops a conscious knowledge of what lies are for.

Huck's manipulations are trivial until his life is threatened by Pap, and then his ability to lie becomes a tool for survival. Pap tries to kill him in the cabin, passing out before succeeding, and Huck spends the night holding a gun leveled at the unconscious man's head. When he falls asleep and Pap wakes up, Huck is forced for the first time to think up a good lie quick enough to save his skin. " 'Somebody tried to get in, so I was laying for him,' " he explains.[18] The trick works. Because of Pap's murderous intentions, Huck cannot stay in the cabin even though it is comfortably dirty there and he has liked living off the land. His carefully planned escape symbolically kills off the old Huck by making it appear that he has been murdered and sets a new Huck free to become what he will. His discovery of Jim on Jackson's Island marks Huck's entrance into a relationship of interdependence with one other person, and his success from this point onward depends upon his ability to hide Jim and to protect the small society on the raft by his machinations. The necessity of providing this safety is the justification behind his continuing to practice deception.

Huck's flight down the river is a journey among the grotesque commonplaces of civilization. He exercises his creativity in response to these absurdities, succeeding or failing at random. In the chaotic interior of the floating house, he and Jim observe all the grim effects of man's sad petty sinning: the whore's tattered clothes, the grimy bottle with which her bastard was fed, the greasy cards scattered over the floor, the whiskey bottles, the profanity on the walls, the bit of stolen money, and the corpse of a gambler murdered by an anonymous hand. (The corpse is Pap.) From his entrance into the house on, Huck's trip down the river is like a descent into hell—a series of encounters with increasingly horrible absurdities. These include the Grangerford feud in which strong and beautiful people kill one another without motive, the cruel murder of Boggs and the senseless rage of a cowardly crowd, and the dangerous games of confidence men.[19] The confidence games are at first innocently hilarious, exposing the comic gullibility of men, but they eventually become vicious as the King and Duke sell Jim and attempt to steal a family's sustenance. At the end of the journey, Huck finds himself still in the midst of hellish absurdities, acquiescing to Tom's stupid and dangerous plot to "free" Jim. As in the beginning of the book, he has the same scrap of common sense telling him that Tom's escapade is ridiculous, but he has not gained the clear-sightedness to judge it as crazy or the ingenuity to do anything about it.

Thus Huck's creativity grows no more sophisticated, no more predictably successful, and no more certainly moral as the book progresses. (His tricks do grow more complicated, however.) The terrible reversal of the rattlesnake trick ought to teach Huck something about the requirements of living with others, but his lesson does not prevent his tricking Jim about their separation in the fog. After that, Huck sometimes seems to sense that his relationship with Jim rests on mutual trust, but he is not consciously aware of this knowledge, nor does he draw any moral conclusions from his educative experiences. When Tom's Aunt Sally, mistaking Huck for Tom, asks him why he's late in coming to the Phelps plantation, Huck, running on *instinct* (his own word), invents a lie about a steamboat accident. " 'We blowed out a cylinder-head,' " he says. Aunt Sally Phelps exclaims, " 'Good gracious! anybody hurt?' " Huck replies, " 'No'm. Killed a nigger.' "[20] This often-quoted passage is the best revelation of Huck's failure to generalize from his experience with Jim any moral view to overcome his automatic judgment of a black man as nobody.

Another of Huck's tricks, although designed for his own survival, results in the death of the robbers aboard the wrecked steamer, the *Walter Scott*. Huck feels bad about this even though he has tried to fix it so the law can find them and hang them properly. Clearly, Huck has no control in this situation over either the outcome of the conflict between himself and the robbers or his own rationalizations about his part in it. His beautifully constructed defensive lies succeed in keeping Jim safe, but their success does not help expand Huck's vision. Everything he does to save Jim contradicts his conscience. He has been taught that slaveholding is morally right. Of his smallpox trick, a brilliant act of creative lying, he says, "I see it warn't no use for me to try to learn to do right; a body that don't get *started* right when he's little ain't got no show. . . ."[21] Many of the book's jokes arise out of our recognition that Huck keeps finding excellent alternatives to ludicrous situations without being aware of the morality of these alternatives. The irony of his "moral" training is that it has taught him to resist a truer morality.

The one situation in the book that does not seem ambiguous and threatening is the short period when only Huck and Jim are aboard the raft. Then life is easy and happy as they give themselves over to the drift of the current. They fish, lie around naked, swim, and smoke; they acquiesce to the river. They never feel "cramped up and smothery" but only "free and easy and comfortable on a raft."[22] They enjoy absurd reasoning and comic myth-making at their leisure: "It's lovely to live on a raft. We had the sky up there, all speckled with stars, and we used to lay on our backs and look up at them, and discuss about whether they was made or only just happened. Jim he allowed they was made, but I allowed they happened; I judged it would have took too long to *make* so many. Jim said the moon could a *laid* them; well, that looked kind of reasonable, so I didn't say nothing against it, because I've seen a frog lay most as many, so of course it could be done."[23] Twain had double fun in this paragraph: the religious view (stars were made) and the scientific view (they just happened) are as absurd as the frog-moon analogy Huck and Jim invent. On a raft you can't go wrong; any response to nature has its own comic correctness. The trouble is that the river's easy security is an appearance. The same river which helps Jim and Huck to survive so well carries them past the Ohio River (and freedom) in a fog.

Furthermore, trouble can come to the raft, and it does. It is shortly after Huck's and Jim's idyllic interlude that the King and the Duke appear. Huck defends Jim and himself against these two first by accepting their stories—that keeps peace—and eventually by employing increasingly more complicated maneuvers designed to counter their increasingly evil machinations. Huck's eventual triumph over the King and the Duke prove that he has learned quick responses to dangerous confidence games. But immediately after recognizing the con men for what they are and beating them at their own game, Huck fails to see Tom for the dangerous fake he is. Huck thinks Tom must have good reasons for doing what he does, even though they are not clear. Again, Huck has excellent motives for resisting Tom but is unable to recognize his own morality. He is, after all, still convinced that he cannot be a good boy. The sad joke of this book is that Huck's vision remains limited by his ingrained inability to evaluate his own motivations.

It could be argued that Twain intended Huck's inadequacies to be merely those of a boy incapable of corrective reasoning being initiated into the deceptions of the world. But Twain did draw a character who represents the ultimate in pragmatic and rational thinking whose success is no more final than Huck's. Hank Morgan is this complete Franklinian man, the absurd creator in a position of power recognizing that much of what he creates is a sham, that he has invented his own image, and that the worldly ends of social betterment justify deceiving an ignorant population. He is, by his own description at the beginning of his history, a Yankee of Yankees whose first characteristic is practicality. His father was a blacksmith, his uncle a horse doctor, and he learned his trade in an arms factory; he thus has inherited or acquired all known mechanical abilities. He is head superintendent and full of fight. Plainly, the Yankee's character combines all the elements necessary for leading humanity in an orderly fashion through the mechanistic age. One thing is missing, however; he admits that he is so practical that he is "nearly barren of sentiment . . . or poetry, in other words."[24] He is the man of the times, much like Henry Adams's dark vision of the American yet to come who would harness the energy of the dynamo without worrying about meaning, a man so scornful of the religious traditions of Europe that he would have relegated theological speculation to the realm of useless superstition. There is, therefore, one initial clue to the limits of Hank's vision: he sees a great deal more than any Arthurian can, but he has at least one great blind spot. As it later proves, his vision is seriously limited by even greater debilities.

When Hank first discovers that he has somehow been transferred out of the nineteenth century into the sixth, he is not flustered because he has perfect confidence in his training and methodology. Having been told that the date is June 19, 528, he resolves to test that information by waiting to see if an eclipse will occur two days later, as he remembers it must from his own knowledge of astronomical history. Until that event, however, he will bide his time. He has made up his mind to two things: "if it was still the nineteenth century and I was among lunatics and couldn't get away, I would presently boss that asylum or know the reason why; and if, on the other hand, it was really the sixth century, all right, I didn't want any softer thing: I would boss the whole country inside of three months; for I judged I would have the start of the best-educated man in the kingdom by a matter of thirteen hundred years and upward. I'm not a man to waste time after my mind's made up and there's work on hand. . . ."[25] Hank knows that reality may not be immediately definable, but this possibility does not faze his confidence. He is mentally equipped to meet all contingencies. Even if the world is insane or unlikely, work provides control, and Hank knows how to put work to work.

The Yankee's practicality initiates behavior that appears to be paradoxical at first. He has what he calls "the circus side of my nature"—a love for making every accomplishment look as sensational as possible. It seems that he loves meaningless displays more than a job properly done. When he opens the well and restores the holy fountain, he accompanies the first gush from his pump with great ceremony, magic words, choirs, and fireworks. It is impossible, he says, to put too much style into a miracle. But this show is not a frill designed merely to satisfy the Yankee's ego (although it does do that); it has the very practical purpose of shaping the appearance of the accomplishment to the belief of his audience. It makes The Boss appear to be supernaturally powerful. He believes that the people would not comprehend a simple plumbing trick—indeed, might be hostile to it—but would be won by a magical triumph over the powers of evil. Earlier Hank had thought that he was in a circus when he saw a knight riding down upon him. As he ascends in power, he utilizes to the utmost the circus side of his nature. In short, he counters the circus of Arthurian England with a virtuoso presentation of his own: a display of the circus acts made possible by nineteenth-century technology.

Hank's virtuosity is a function of his knowledge that people see what they want to see. Many of the jokes in the book occur when this awareness confronts some character's peculiar point of view. The story of Sandy's pigsty-castle is a definitive case. Sandy sees fair damsels held captive by an ogre. Hank sees a pig farm. Sandy is distressed at this confusion: " 'It was not enchanted aforetime. . . . And how strange is this marvel, and how awful—that to the one perception it is enchanted and dight in a base and shameful aspect; yet to the perception of the other it is not enchanted, hath suffered no change, but stands firm and stately still. . . .' " To humor her, Hank "rescues" the pigs by buying them, driving them home, and housing them in the manner to which Sandy believes they are accustomed. Sandy is now delighted, but Hank's view remains realistic and uncomfortable: "Of course, the whole drove was housed in the house, and, great guns!—well, I never saw anything like it. Nor ever heard anything like it. And never smelt anything like it. It was like an insurrection in a gasometer."[26]

Sandy's automatic transformation of raw fact into medieval romance is a source of pure fun and is absurd creation in its own right. But when a character's view distorts his behavior in such a way that great injustices are perpetrated, then the joke becomes serious. Morgan le Fay thinks nothing of stabbing the page who bumps her knee by accident. Hank cannot understand, at first, why she is unconcerned about this and a number of other atrocities she commits. He calls the page's murder a crime. "'Crime!'" she exclaims; "'How thou talkest! Crime, forsooth! Man, I am going to *pay* for him!'" This leads Hank into his famous disquisition on predestination and original sin:

> Oh, it was no use to waste sense on her. Training—training is everything; training is all there is *to* a person. We speak of nature; it is folly; there is no such thing as nature; what we call by that misleading name is merely heredity and training. We have no thoughts of our own, no opinions of our own; they are transmitted to us, trained into us. All that is original in us, and therefore fairly creditable or discreditable to us, can be covered up and hidden by the point of a cambric needle, all the rest being atoms contributed by, and inherited from, a procession of ancestors that stretches back a billion years to the Adam-clam or grasshopper or monkey from whom our race has been so tediously and ostentatiously and unprofitably developed.

Out of all this, Hank hopes to save "that one microscopic atom in me that is truly *me*" (that statement would leave a shred of hope in the book were Hank able to prove that it could be done). He continues: "No, confound her, her intellect was good, she had brains enough, but her training made her an ass—that is, from a many-centuries-later point of view. To kill the page was no crime—it was her right; and upon her right she stood, serenely and unconscious of offense."[27]

This concept of contextual determination of morality is illustrated everywhere in the book and is at last one of the things that causes Hank to fail. The King, who, it must be admitted, makes a valiant effort to see things from new angles by joining Hank in peasant disguise for a tour of the nation, is nonetheless crippled by a view that gives all prerogatives to the nobility. The people themselves are strictly confined to the view driven into them by the nobility and the church. As Hank learns to his regret when the interdict is passed, they will all revert to superstition and loyalty to the class structure, even those who appeared to have accepted his pragmatic outlook. The boys who stay with Hank and go down fighting do not revert to the medieval view only because they have been trained from infancy in Hank's own factories and schools. They stick by him for the same reason the people revert to medievalism. They have been trained to hold what Hank considers a better point of view, but they have been trained nonetheless.

Hank's view and his methods fail at last, and it is important to see why. There are, of course, simple weaknesses in Hank's character stemming from that lack of sentiment he mentions at the beginning. He is quite capable of wishing Sir Dinadan dead for telling a moldy joke and giving Morgan le Fay permission to hang a whole band for playing badly. But these instances are jokes designed simply for laughs, well within the tradition of rough humor, providing no firm clue about Hank's character faults. However, when the Yankee coolly shoots a knight from his saddle (albeit in self-defense) and proves himself capable of constructing devices for mass execution of his enemies, we recognize that it is beyond the limits of his imagination to solve the dilemma of man's shortsightedness by any means other than annihilation of those he considers shortsighted.

It may be, of course, that Twain was on Hank's side all the way, believing seriously that reform follows only after the old order dies. Hank's story would then be a tragedy because he lets his pragmatism slip. He loses his battle to wipe out ignorance and superstition simply because he forgets for one instant his own methodology. He has, all the way through the book, tested every appearance to determine its underlying reality, leaving nothing to chance. He knows that anyone can be fooled; he is himself the best maker of appearances, and he has confidence in his knowledge of the difference between fact and sham. At the end of the book, when the interdict has turned all of knighthood against him, the Yankee stands without faltering because he puts his confidence entirely in his machinery. The electric fences and the Gatling guns wipe out twenty-five thousand attacking knights. But with victory in sight, the Yankee makes, or finds he has made, three errors of logic and reason. The first is that, in response to human feeling, he decides to turn off the fence and help those knights who are only wounded. As he bends over Sir Meliagraunce, the knight treacherously stabs him. Then, wounded and no longer alert, Hank allows the simple old peasant woman to enter the cave. She is really Merlin, who administers the potion which puts Hank out of the sixth-century action. Hank would not have allowed himself to perform these two acts of unthinking kindness if he had stuck to a purely practical view. The third error is a mistake of planning, a lapse in his scientific method. If the treacherous knight and Merlin had not gotten to Hank, the stench of the rotting bodies of twenty-five thousand knights would have. Had he been a perfect prag-matist, an infallible technician, Hank would have figured out some instantaneous disposal method.

This interpretation has dark absurd implications. Hank's solution, the Franklinian method, the perfect practicality of the machine age, is a good problem-solving process but, while too complicated to be controlled by any mortal, it is still not compli-cated enough to anticipate all the follies of mortals. As good as he is, Hank cannot think of all the ways in which he might fail and thus cannot invent a program that will cover all contingen-cies. A mechanical structure is no better than the fallible man who makes it.

But that is not the worst thing wrong with the totally mechan-istic view. It is dehumanizing. It requires that its maker and user be completely without feeling. Any scrap of emotion Hank shows ruins the program. That in itself makes Hank's nineteenth-century values—whether he himself succeeds or fails—potentially as dangerous as those of the sixth century. On the other hand, a man of sentiment and feeling cannot control a world that needs scientific answers. Twain offered no third alternative. He may or may not have believed a balance could be struck—but he gave neither Huck nor Hank the imagination to create meaning and order in an absurd world.[28]

4 · Tragedy Traps

His later writings demonstrate that Twain continued, with increasing pessimism and decreasing humorous spirit, to believe that the imagination to create meaning in a meaningless universe was not one of man's gifts. The answer to the question of *What is Man?* is that man is no more than a creature defined by the things he is related to; he struggles for existence in the same way any organism without a mind would do. He is unable to expand his vision to find a solution that will yield a harmonious human community. His mind simply makes him aware of his own absurdity. The man who corrupts Hadleyburg—one of the splendid con men of American literature—does so simply because he knows exactly how men are programed. All he has to do is excite certain motives, which is the same as pushing the right buttons, and he gets from the people of Hadleyburg absolutely predictable behavior. One might in this instance see The Man as a creator—or at least an exposer—of the absurd; he would then be one of those few characters who momentarily escape the trap (a list that would include Huck and Hank until their defeats). Twain's darkest absurd books are *The Mysterious Stranger,* for which he wrote a tentative and ambiguous ending which resolves nothing, and "The Great Dark," which is one of several beginnings for a story based directly on a view of the universe as totally self-contradictory and therefore absurd in the hopeless sense. "The Great Dark" is almost devoid of humor, although it is based on a joke about man. Another tale, "Three Thousand Years Among the Microbes," has the same thematic base but does achieve some great moments of laughter and is Twain's last perfectly balanced effort in serious humor. These stories are unfinished or without resolution partly because they grew so directly from Twain's own disastrous reality in his later years, but also partly because they are unfinishable stories. They represent a final vision of ambivalence. The total absurd view includes the awareness that endings are arbitrarily and illogically happy or sad. At any given point in an absurd story, the action can go towards comedy or tragedy with perfectly equal motivations in the plot and structure for doing either.

This awareness of the duality of everything shows up in Twain's choice of pseudonym, in his love of stories about confused identities—*The Prince and the Pauper* and *Pudd'nhead Wilson*, for example—and most vividly in the stories of "The Great Dark" group, two versions of which carried the titles "Which Was the Dream?" and "Which Was It?" These fragments were all composed between 1896 and 1905, after Twain's bankruptcy in the publishing business, the failure of the Paige typesetter, and the death of Susy. The stories share a single plot device. A man who in "this" life is near the peak of success falls asleep and dreams that his success turns abruptly into disaster. Twain's intention was to make the dream the substantial part of the story, showing the man's fortunes worsening and his family dying until all that sustains him is the thought that these events must be part of a bad dream. This is not, however, a knowledge that he is in a dream; it is simply and ironically the feeling—half wishful—that any man has when his fortunes turn incredibly bad. As Twain outlined the ending for this story, the man was to awake after what had seemed to be years to find that he had dreamed everything and was actually, after just a few minutes of sleep, back with his family.[29] The point of the story line is to show that the dream and the reality are indistinguishable.

As John S. Tuckey pointed out in introducing the recent edition of these fragmentary writings, Twain was at the time of their composition reading, among other discussions of the interrelationship between dreams and the mind's idea of reality, the arguments of Georg Christoph Lichtenberg, who regarded dreams as real events which might seem to last for years. Dreams were "a life and a world," and "a man can really never know whether he isn't sitting in a madhouse."[30] Twain, in his working notes, recorded his intention to use Lichtenberg's arguments as part of the narrator's attempt to convince his wife of the possibility of confusing reality and dreams.

Apparently Twain seriously believed that life was dreamlike; certainly there were times when he found his own reality ambiguous and elusive. Once in 1893 he wrote, "I dreamed I was born, and grew up, and was a pilot on the Mississippi, and a miner and journalist . . . and had a wife and children . . . and this dream goes on and on and on, and sometimes seems so real that I almost believe it *is* real. I wonder if it is?"[31] There are throughout his notebooks, letters, and autobiography tantalizing references to his dream self, his double, the other person inside of him. Every man had a dark side which no one else ever saw.[32] At any time, the dream world and the real world could become indistinguishable. Upon entering his old house in Hartford after many years' absence, he wrote these impressions to his wife, still in Paris: "[I]t seemed as if I had burst awake out of a hellish dream, & had never been away, & that you would come drifting down out of those dainty upper regions with the little children tagging after you."[33] By the time he came to write his darkest books, Twain was convinced that there is no test for reality, that not only is what man sees absurd but the position from which he sees is also absurd, unfixed, and not definable. The man who had for years consciously equated absurdity with distortion was by now convinced that reality was the absurd.

The first of the dream stories, which now carries the title "Which Was the Dream?" is a dreary tale of ruin and shame. At one point the narrator makes a comment revealing his belief that some dreams can substitute a happier existence than that provided by reality. He has been reading to his children when he is abruptly interrupted: "For ten minutes I had been wandering with these two in a land far from this world; in the golden land of Romance, where all things are beautiful, and existence is a splendid dream, and care cannot come. Then came that bray of the brazen horns, and the vision vanished away; we were prisoners in this dull planet again."[34] Twain abandoned this version of the story for another, slightly humorous one, which now bears the title added by Bernard DeVoto, "The Great Dark." Of this change in plans, Twain wrote:

A week ago I examined that MS—10,000 words—& saw that the plan was a totally impossible one—for *me*; but a new plan suggested itself, & straightway the tale began to slide from the pen with ease & confidence. I think I've struck the right one this time. I have already put 12,000 words of it on paper. . . . I feel sure that all of the first half of the story—& I hope three-fourths—will be comedy; but by the former plan the whole of it (except the first 3 chapters) would have been tragedy & unendurable, almost. I think I can carry the reader a long way before he suspects that I am laying a tragedy-trap.[35]

Mark Twain here assessed his own intentions better than anyone else ever could. "The Great Dark" does exactly what Twain said it would do. It shows that the joke of life is that a man can walk without abruptly shifting his direction from a happy freedom into a tragedy trap.

The story begins with the protagonist, Henry Edwards, romping with his children on the occasion of the birthday of one of them.[36] In the midst of play, Henry takes the two little girls into a room to show them the grandest of the birthday presents—a microscope. The slides that came with the microscope provide a very exciting time for everyone, but the best is one they prepare themselves from a drop of pond water. They have some trouble focusing, and the drop is not visible until the lens is screwed down tight against the slide. Then huge monsters are seen swimming in an endless sea.

Later, after the party has quieted down, Henry lies down on a sofa for a nap. He has been profoundly impressed by the "ocean in a drop of water"; it is "unknown, uncharted, unexplored by man." As he falls asleep, the "Superintendent of Dreams" appears, and they talk over the ways and means of exploring that microworld in a dream.[37] What Henry actually does as he falls asleep, then, is start the dream himself, ordering it up to satisfy his curiosity. The Superintendent provides a ship and crew, and Henry finds himself on the microscopic sea. Now, of course, the sea appears to be huge; everything is in the perspective Henry is familiar with. Very soon, what he had planned as an adventure in a dream proves strange in ways he had not anticipated. The members of the crew act as if they had been transported from the outside world without knowledge of what happened. They have good bearings, and their navigational computations demonstrate quite firmly that they should have raised Greenland, but obviously they are in the open sea. Their instruments provide the appalling information that they have run right over Greenland. Then elephant-sized caterpillars and gigantic wood lice (the microbe-monsters) begin to appear, and several sailors take the pledge. Henry begins to suspect that he is in an actual world, one in which a real ship sails eternally on a real sea looking for a lost land. The microbe-monsters have assaulted the ship and may do so again at any time. What he had once thought to be the circle of light from the microscope reflector is now an inaccessible white-hot region that the ship must avoid.

This microscopic world is a perfect metaphor for Twain's personal world and for his America. The ship tosses forever between storm and calm looking for an idyllic and peaceful country its passengers believe they have lost. Henry Edwards and the Superintendent of Dreams—who resembles in many ways the Satan of *The Mysterious Stranger*—discuss the situation in relativistic terms, showing that the worlds under and outside the microscope are alike in an essential way. The Superintendent explains that the thin edge of shadow outside the light is several thousand miles wide, the glass slide "bottom" of the ocean is thirty thousand miles long, and the length of the microscope barrel is a hundred and twenty thousand. Henry says, " 'It gives me the head-ache. Are these the fictitious proportions which we and our surroundings and belongings have acquired by being reduced to microscopic objects? ' " The Superintendent replies, " 'They are the proportions, yes—but they are not fictitious. You do not notice that you yourself are in any way diminished in size, do you? ' " Henry must answer that he does not; the ship and the men aboard it are also " 'all natural.' " The Superintendent continues, " 'Very good; nothing but the laws and conditions have undergone a change. You came from a small and very insignificant world. The one you are in now is proportioned according to microscopic standards—that is to say, it is inconceivably stupendous and imposing. ' "[38] The point is clear: to the man standing on the ship in the drop-of-water sea, the drop-of-water world is huge enough. But it would not be huge to a large consciousness, and the world outside the microscope is just as insignificant when viewed in relation to the cosmos.

Henry is surprised to find his family on board as well as himself. His wife shows no sign at first of any knowledge about the world outside the microscope. Henry is also surprised to find that others on the ship expect him to know everything about their shared experiences and common surroundings. He realizes that what he had taken to be the real world outside the microscope is the dream world of this one, and he is shocked to find that memories of the waterdrop world do begin to return to him. He discovers that he has a past in which the waterdrop world was the real world. After awhile, with a little mental exercise, his wife and children are able to remember dreams they have had, and these dreams are also of the world outside the microscope. Henry at last finds that he knows two worlds without being able to test the reality of either.

As Twain's notes for the ending to "The Great Dark" indicate, Henry and his wife find themselves caught in the region of the disastrous white light, suffering terribly from the glare and heat. The ship fends off attacks from the monsters, who have been driven crazy by a drop of Scotch placed on the slide by the wife of the outside world. The sea dries up; the captain and Henry stumble across the desert—formerly the ocean's floor—in search of another ship which disappeared earlier with Henry's infant son and Lucy, the captain's daughter, aboard. They find the ship, all aboard mummified from the heat. Upon returning, they discover that the ship's crew has fought among themselves, a stray shot killing Jessie. Two days later, everyone is dead from heat and despair except the captain and Henry who are left sitting with the corpses of their families. At this point, Henry was to wake up to be with his family as he had been in the beginning. He was to look up in shock at seeing them coming to say goodnight; his hair would have turned snow white.[39]

There is in the fragment one note of hope based on a character's ability to create something out of nothing. It occurs at the point Twain broke off the manuscript proper. The captain is trying to quell the crew's thoughts of mutiny. " 'Are we rational men,' " he asks, " 'manly men, men who can stand up and face hard luck and a big difficulty that has been brought about by nobody's fault, and say live or die, survive or perish, we are in for it, for good or bad, and we'll stand by the ship if she goes to hell!' " He calls upon them to put their trust in God and not be cowardly. They cheer—as heartily as they can—and he concludes, " 'There—that's the kind. And so I'll tell you how the thing stands. *I* don't know where this ship is, but she's in the hands of God, and that's enough for me, it's enough for you, and it's enough for anybody. . . . If it is God's will that we pull through, we pull through—

otherwise not. We haven't had an observation for four months, but we are going ahead, and do our best to fetch up somewhere.' "[40] There is the courage of Sisyphus in this cry; in the vast waste, the dislocated man who wants to save himself must bravely do his best to fetch up somewhere.

The parallels between these late fragmentary variations on the dream story and *The Mysterious Stranger* are apparent. Professor Tuckey has traced the composition of *The Mysterious Stranger* through at least three versions spanning 1897-1908, dates which include the composition of the dream variations. William M. Gibson has edited the manuscripts, presenting for the first time the versions and fragments of the tale as Twain wrote them, the 1916 edition (and all reprints since) having contained extensive alterations and strange additions by Albert Bigelow Paine and Frederick A. Duneka.[41] In a revealing letter written July 28, 1904, Twain spelled out the vision that takes form in *The Mysterious Stranger*. He stated that some part of every day or night for the last seven years had appeared to him to be "NON-EXISTENT." He continued, "That is, [it appears] that there is *nothing*. That there is no God and no universe; that there is only empty space, and in it a lost and homeless and wandering and companionless and indestructible *Thought*. And that I am that thought. And God, and the Universe, and Time, and Life, and Death, and Joy and Sorrow and Pain only a grotesque and brutal *dream*, evolved from the frantic imagination of that insane Thought." He then added a precise ironic definition of his own absurd sense: "By this light, the absurdities that govern life and the universe lose their absurdity and become natural, and a thing to be expected."[42]

The fragment Twain labeled "Conclusion of the Book" (which Gibson places at the end of the version titled "No. 44, The Mysterious Stranger" and which stands as the ending in all other editions) represents a perfectly ambivalent view of nihilism. The character called "44" (Satan) delivers to August (Ted) a speech emphasizing a creative principle which could counter nihilism: " 'I am but a dream—your dream, creature of your imagination. . . . I am perishing already. . . . In a little while you will be alone in shoreless space . . . for you will remain a *Thought*, the only existent Thought, and by your nature inextinguishable, indestructible. But I your poor servant have revealed you to yourself and set you free.'" Here the mysterious stranger is asserting a principle analogous to absurd creation: August is forever alone and miserable, but at least his mind is free and in control of his own version of reality. "44" goes on to advise August to "'Dream other dreams, and better!'" Then, however, he calls August a "'useless Thought, a homeless Thought.'" August is "appalled."[43] The ending of this story is not a resolution; it offers both despair and absurd creation as equally possible reactions following the awakening to nihilism.

Since Twain himself did not attach the "Conclusion of the Book" to a finished manuscript, the reader conceivably could seek a resolution elsewhere in the story. The best one lies in Satan's admonition to the human race to laugh until its humbugs are blown to atoms. This advice is the same Twain gave himself when he set his course as humorist; the reader wishes he could take the admonition to laugh as Satan's last words. The history of Twain's composition of the various mysterious stranger stories is the history of a struggle to find a creative alternative to the conclusion, "there is nothing." As Twain worked out a formula for nihilism in *The Mysterious Stranger* variants, he revealed his discovery that responses to nihilism are arbitrary. One can despair in loneliness, one can affirm the creative principle, one can laugh. Twain experienced lonely despair but combined the last two choices in his work: he made laughter creative.

In the final analysis, *The Mysterious Stranger* itself can be taken as an act of absurd creation. Twain knew that all he could do was to keep on writing, just as Huck keeps on running. Tuckey concluded his study of Twain's struggle to produce the book with "Mark Twain was the mysterious stranger. And he played his role wonderfully to the last."[44] That this role was exceedingly difficult and dangerous is demonstrated by the fact that *The Mysterious Stranger* never was composed as a whole; Mark Twain's last major absurd creation almost failed to be created.

"Three Thousand Years Among the Microbes" is not Twain's last work by any means—it was written in 1905—and is incomplete just as are his other late stories. It is, however, whole and finally definitive in the sense that in it the absurd is seen and recreated in a perfect balance between serious and comic that is missing from most of his late stories. The narrator, a man who has been reduced to a cholera germ by a capricious magician, is introduced by that Godlike wizard into the blood of "a hoary and mouldering bald-headed tramp" named Blitzowski. Microbe time is lengthened in proportion to the reduction of the narrator's size, so that three thousand years in the bloodstream are nothing more than three weeks of human time. The device alone is funny; here dwells our hero among the millions of inhabitants of the United Organs of Blitzowski. As a metaphor for the world, the diseased and grotesque geography of the tramp is completely appropriate to Twain's vision.

The satirical highlights of the story are a number of mock answers to universal questions. The questions themselves are satirized. The solution to the mystery of man's purpose in the universe is made quite clear: his mission is to feed and house the microbes. In turn, the microbes define man as well as inhabit him:

When I became a microbe, the transformation was so complete that I felt at home at once. This is not surprising, for men and germs are not widely different from each other. Of germs there are many nationalities, and there are many languages, just as it is with mankind. The germs think the man they are occupying is the only world there is. To them it is a vast and wonderful world, and they are as proud of it as if they had made it themselves. It seems a pity that this poor forlorn old tramp will never know that, for compliments are scarce with him.[45]

Furthermore, the human transformed into microbe can experience what any Transcendentalist would long for: a clear view of the perfect organic unity of all nature. The limited human eye, when aided, might be able to see only a speck, but

with my microbe-eye I could see *every individual* of the whirling billions of *atoms* that com*pose* the speck. *Nothing is ever at rest*—wood, iron, water, everything is alive, everything is raging, whirling, whizzing, day and night and night and day, nothing is dead, *there is no such thing as death*, everything is full of bristling life, tremendous life, even the bones of the crusader that perished before Jerusalem eight centuries ago. There are no vegetables, *all things are* ANIMAL; each electron is an animal, each molecule is a collection of animals, and each has an appointed duty to perform and a soul to be saved.[46]

The stylistic ambivalence of this passage is astonishing. The vision of life in everything is joyfully celebrated. The vision of life in everything is hilariously satirized.

Life in the bloodstream, with this kind of vision upon which to found a personal philosophy, is always bright. The narrator shows that the landscape concurs, for the light there never diminishes. The final irony, comic and deeply serious, is that optimism can be enjoyed by any man willing to forget that he sees only what he can see and that what he can see is always a joke. "In Blitzowski," reports the microscopic narrator blissfully, "there is no night."[47] Twain's transcendental germ has based his cheerful faith upon the beautiful and true appearances of a diseased bloodstream. His hope is automatically as absurd as Blitzowski himself. No author ever told a joke simultaneously more hilarious and nihilistic than this one.

VI

The Prime Maniacal Risibility: William Faulkner

It is as though upon a face carved
by a savage caricaturist a monstrous
burlesque of all bereavement flowed.

DARL, OF ANSE

1 · INVENTING ENOUGH STUFF

AN UNDERGRADUATE English student once asked William Faulkner if he thought his humor was serious. Faulkner replied: "it's a part of man too, it's a part of life . . . there's not too fine a distinction between humor and tragedy, that even tragedy is in a way walking a tightrope between the ridiculous—between the bizarre and the terrible."[1] There are moments in his books when that traditionally thin line between the bizarre and the terrible evaporates entirely, for William

Faulkner was a master of deliberately ambivalent serious humor. It is, in fact, often difficult to determine any qualitative difference in Faulkner's work between one grotesque event which is funny and another grotesque event which is terrifying. How is the reader to react, for example, to Temple Drake's desperate cry as the sadistic, impotent Popeye moves towards her, his depraved intent to rape her with a corncob just beginning to become clear? " 'Something is happening to me!' " she screams. This evaluation of the situation has to be the understatement of the century. Only a strange or sick mind would appreciate this as a joke, but irony and surprise have combined with the understatement to provide the ingredients for a comic scene. The understatement might be funny if we did not automatically judge the event brutal as well as grotesque. Our cultural aversion, not some qualitative technical difference between humor and horror, prevents laughter. There are, however, equally brutal grotesques in *As I Lay Dying*: Addie's bubbling corpse, rotting upside down in the coffin; Cash spread-eagled on top of it, his broken leg cemented to the lid; the rest of the family, each crazy in his own way, riding the cart or walking alongside; buzzards wheeling overhead; townspeople scattering as the putrid caravan rolls down their main street. Yet the Bundrens' experience, surely as dangerous and painful as Temple's, is hilarious as well as grim. Temple's disaster does not appeal to our love of ambivalence; the Bundrens' odyssey does. The style of the Bundrens' story helps make the difference, but the crucial distinction between the two events is our culturally determined willingness to accept the humorous side of the burlesque funeral journey while refusing to acknowledge any potential humor in depravity's threat to womanhood.

Temple's disaster may or may not have been intended to resemble humor; at any rate, no one laughs at it. The Bundrens' journey, however, is certainly designed to be funny, even though some readers may not initially find it so.[2] The best of Faulkner's truly comic passages are ambivalently funny in the way *As I Lay Dying* is, and the humor in them cannot be appreciated until the reader is willing to assume some peculiar moral stance. This is because Faulkner's comedy is the result of his awareness that attitudes are contextual and arbitrary. His humor is founded on a perfectly lucid moral relativism. His characters live in a world that is never stable, even when it is the carefully defined world of Yoknapatawpha County. In this fictional world, as in the real world it reflects, the only values in existence are those accepted or created by the characters themselves. The endless process of defining and trying to stabilize values, of testing them against the perceptions of the intellect and the elusive dictates of the heart, is the struggle Faulkner thought worth portraying both seriously and humorously. He did not propose that the values in conflict be familiar ones. His protagonists seldom appear to be heroic in the usual sense. They become heroic only when we abandon the common standards by which heroes are judged and accept a different moral framework. (Initially, when reading a Faulkner book, we may laugh because we perceive the difference between our common moral framework and that in which a hero's struggle takes place, but our standard must at least temporarily be suspended for us to see the heroism as well as the incongruity.) Joe Christmas, Mink Snopes, and Darl Bundren are heroes, but the morality of their motivations and ends would be judged by the usual standards as criminal. Furthermore, the character who best articulates the common values of the educated readers of Faulkner, Gavin Stevens, is a hopeless failure when it comes to evaluating situations and deciding on courses of action that will with any certainty prove "moral." Faulkner's relativistic manipulations produced stories in which conflict can occur between or among any values at all.

Thus the conflict in a Faulkner story is often quite startling. If the values on both sides of a conflict do not completely offend our absolute standards, then ambivalent humor results when we complement our sense of the difference with a sense of the resemblance between some startling conflict and one we regard as "normal." The constant which is found in "normal" literary conflicts and in startling Faulknerian conflicts is the struggle of a man to fulfill or escape his fate.

Usually, it seems impossible for a Faulkner protagonist to perform an act of will which effects an outcome he desired or predicted. Faulkner's characters are cast in the shadow of the passive voice. They are moved. They work out a fate in its entirely, but the end of their inevitable journey is not theirs to determine. The heroic pattern occurs when a character accepts his fate and makes it the choice of his will. This is a contradiction in terms. Faulkner accepted the contradiction. He said of one of his favorite characters: "I would say that Lena Grove in *Light in August* coped pretty well with [her fate]. It didn't really matter to her in her destiny whether her man was Lucas Burch or not. It was her destiny to have a husband and children and she knew it, and so she went out and attended to it without asking help from anyone. She was the captain of her soul. One of the calmest, sanest speeches I ever heard was when she said to Byron Bunch at the very instant of repulsing his final desperate and despairing attempt at rape, 'Ain't you ashamed? You might have woke the baby.' "[3] Lena is not helpless in the face of what we call terrors and indignities. She simply creates an alternative world in which there are no terrors or indignities. Where any woman might be expected to despair at having to search over miles of Alabama and Tennessee to find a husband, Lena is always happy to find herself one step further on. Like Sisyphus, she accepts her fate and makes it her will, rejoicing in the creation of something out of nothing.

This is affirmative comedy of the absurd. Analogous to Lena is Anse Bundren, unmoved by Addie's death, focusing instead on getting them teeth and a new wife. Also related is the paranoid Mink Snopes, who overcomes all obstacles in his quest to murder Flem, reminding himself along the way that "Old Moster jest punishes; He dont play jokes." But the question of determinism is not always posed humorously by Faulkner, and, when it isn't, the deep seriousness which underlies the humor found elsewhere is revealed without ambivalence. In the final chase scene of *Light in August*, Percy Grimm relentlessly pursues Joe Christmas to an absolutely irrevocable end. Faulkner refers to the pursuer and the pursued as players on a game board. Each makes his move in turn. Each believes he knows what move the other is about to make. They see each move of the game with perfect clarity. But the great question of the game remains forever insolvable: "[Grimm] was moving again almost before he had stopped, with that lean, swift, blind obedience to whatever Player moved him on the Board."[4] Equally enigmatic is the final picture of the Sartoris family: "the dusk was peopled with ghosts of glamorous and old disastrous things. And if they were just glamorous enough, there was sure to be a Sartoris in them, and then they were sure to be disastrous. Pawns. But the Player, and the game He plays . . . He must have a name for His pawns, though. But perhaps Sartoris is the game itself—a game outmoded and played with pawns shaped too late and to an old dead pattern, and of which the Player Himself is a little wearied."[5] What Player moves the players? Whatever unknown Player it is that moves players. More often than not in Faulkner, He has no name, and, sometimes, the players are moved but there is no Player.

In the Nobel Prize acceptance speech, Faulkner said the proper subject for fiction is the heart in conflict with itself. That statement is a condensed relativistic theory of art. It means that the conflict can be any conflict. It also means that the focus will not be on the conflict between the man and whatever Player there is. Since the Player is unknown, the man who survives will be the man who creates and endures his own struggle. The meaning of the pattern of motion is built into the pattern of motion itself.[6] A man endures and prevails because he can talk and the talking can lead to something more than talk. The soul, Faulkner said, will try to exercise compassion and sacrifice and endurance. These values are inextricably wed to man's puny voice; man can just talk—or he can talk creatively, making values and meaning as he does so.[7] Faulkner saw that even the making of a novel was absurd, that its meaning was its own, that its value lay in the author's and reader's ability to join in a single creative moment: "The only mistake with any novel is if it fails to create pleasure. That it is not true is irrelevant: a novel is to be enjoyed. A book that fails to create enjoyment is not a good one."[8] This intention reveals a strong purpose behind his complex style and his startling relativism. The reader is always asked to participate in and enjoy the act of creation.

"I don't hold with the myth of Sisyphus," Faulkner once said. This appears to contradict his pronouncements on creation. But the context of this statement shows that Faulkner was referring to another element in the myth, not the question of creation. "Man . . . is free and he is responsible, terribly responsible. His

tragedy is the impossibility—or at least the tremendous difficulty—of communication. But man keeps on trying endlessly
to express himself and to make contact with other human
beings. Man comes from God. I don't hold with the myth of
Sisyphus. Man is important because he possesses a moral sense.
I have tremendous faith in man, in spite of all his faults and his
limitations. Man will overcome all the horrors of an atomic war;
he will never destroy mankind."[9] What Faulkner didn't "hold
with" in the myth was the implication that man's motion was
meaningless because he had been condemned and alienated by
the gods. Curiously, Faulkner reacted to the myth in essentially
the same way Camus did, though the form of their reaction is
different: Camus imposed upon the myth the idea that Sisyphus
created his own meaning; Faulkner rejected the meaninglessness
of Sisyphus's toil and said that men do create meaning, through
their "moral sense." Faulkner defined this sense as the ability
man displays to express himself, to make contact with others like
himself, and to overcome all horrors. In this way man shows
that he came from God.

In a class discussion at Virginia, Faulkner declared an intention that is strikingly analogous to Sisyphus's absurd creativity:
"But that was what I was trying to say—that man will prevail,
will endure because he is capable of compassion and honor
and pride and endurance."[10] This is not quite the same statement as the similar lines from the Nobel Prize speech. The
stress here is on a capacity which is inseparable from performance. The statement is circular: man will endure because he
has endurance; man has endurance because he endures. Supernatural ideals do not apply; honor, pride, and endurance are
products of man's creativity. To Loïc Bouvard, Faulkner said,
" 'The most important thing is that man continues to create, just
as woman continues to give birth. Man will keep writing on pieces
of paper, on scraps, on stones, as long as he lives. Man is noble.
I believe in man in spite of everything.' "[11]

The motivations for man's creative processes are not logical:

I—what I meant, to write from the heart is—it's the heart that
has the desire to be better than man is, the up here can know
the distinction between good and evil, but it's the heat that
makes you want to be better than you are. That's what I mean

by to write from the heart. That it's the heart that makes you want to be brave when you are afraid that you might be a coward, that wants you to be generous, or wants you to be compassionate when you think that maybe you won't. I think that the intellect, it might say, Well, which is the most profitable—shall I be compassionate or shall I be uncompassionate? Which is most profitable? Which is the most profitable—shall I be brave or not? But the heart wants always to be better than man is.[12]

Reason yields survival. Creation from the heart yields values in a universe that is absolutely neutral. This creativity differentiates man as man. The process is absurd and may be absolutely hilarious. When hilarious, its humor is in itself an alternative to resignation in the face of meaninglessness.[13]

Deeply aware of how this creativity works, Faulkner invented his own microcosm of the world, named it Yoknapatawpha County, and equated it with the universe: "I like the idea of the world I created being a kind of keystone in the universe. Feel that if I ever took it away the universe around that keystone would crumble away. . . ." When he said this, he added a joke: "If they believed in my world in America the way they do abroad, I could probably run one of my characters for President . . . maybe Lem [Flem] Snopes."[14] And again, he said, "Beginning with *Sartoris* I discovered that my own little postage stamp of native soil was worth writing about and that I would never live long enough to exhaust it, and by sublimating the actual into apocryphal I would have complete liberty to use whatever talent I might have to its absolute top. It opened up a gold mine of other peoples, so I created a cosmos of my own. I can move these people around like God, not only in space but in time too."[15] Faulkner dedicated himself to the continuing construction and manipulation of that cosmos in spite of his belief that the artist's social role is always marked by futility: " 'The artist is the one who is able to communicate his message. In doing this, he has no intention of saving mankind. On the contrary, the artist speaks only for himself. Personally I find it impossible to communicate with the outside world. Maybe I will end up in some kind of self-communion—a silence—faced with the certainty that I can no longer be understood. The artist must create his own language. This is not only his right but his duty . . . . I will certainly keep on writing as long as I live.' "[16] In short, Faulkner practiced the absurd creation he recommended: he continued to write on pieces of paper.

Chaotic Yoknapatawpha County is the background of the adventures and struggles of characters who either try to impose some order upon the disintegrating environment or find themselves inseparable from it. And Yoknapatawpha County is in a state of advanced disintegration, especially after the Civil War. In coping with such an environment Faulkner's characters —usually unconsciously—construct value systems appropriate to the chaotic conditions. Those who cope the best may well be ruthless and amoral: Jason Lycurgus Compson, for example, who creates the Compson domain by trading a little mare against Ikkemotubbe's ignorance; or Thomas Sutpen, who builds a dynasty out of a compulsion to beat the rich by getting rich; or Flem Snopes, who sees everything, almost never speaks, and proves himself to be the perfect opportunist.

The disintegration in Yoknapatawpha County began when a man (specifically, Chief Ikkemotubbe, as told in the appendix to *The Sound and the Fury*) decided for the first time that land was man's to sell. This is a fall from innocence. It is a shift from the primitive ideal state of "I-Thou" (so described by Martin Buber), in which man and nature are in mutual relation, to the state of "I-It," in which man has broken the mutuality and regards nature as a set of definable objects which are his to use. This is a romantic theory of why things are chaotic. It ought to imply a direct solution: a man can save his soul by re-establishing mutual relation with wild nature. But Faulkner's attitude towards the wilderness as a source of moral knowledge was not exactly idealistic. His books indicate that he believed the gap between man and nature to be permanent, and occasionally he revealed a suspicion of the entire theory itself.

In *Go Down, Moses*, for example, Faulkner directly contrasted the materialism and flimsy civilized conventions of the white man in the late nineteenth and early twentieth centuries with the natural and intuitive knowledge of Sam Fathers, the last of the noble savages. The stories are for the most part set in a wilderness that is rapidly being eroded by suburbs and highways.

There is no possibility for man and the wilderness to return to a state of innocence. Ike McCaslin repudiates his heritage, gives up ownership of land, and has had in his youth a revelatory contact with the bear. He believes that his conduct forever must "become"—do honor to—the spirit of any animal he slays. Ike has, in short, performed the rituals and assumed the attitudes that are the prerequisites for a return to mutual relation. But in spite of this he is never shown to have achieved a reconciliation with nature. Furthermore, the code of morality he discovers in the woods turns out to be merely personal, unusable, ineffective, and misunderstood in the town. All that he learns in the wilderness turns ludicrous when he tries to transform his knowledge from ideal into action. The ideal of purity and nonownership is distorted in his experience into marriage with a viciously virginal woman and life in a tiny rented room on a back street in Jefferson.

The events in the woods themselves are suspicious because they border on the hilarious. Is the reader expected to take seriously the confrontation between innocent boy and wise bear? How should he regard the statement that something runs in the veins of Sam Fathers which flows in the veins of the deer, too?[17] Sam knows exactly where all the animals in the forest are at any given time and where they will run. He is in constant mystical communion with nature. In a scene apparently intended seriously to prove Sam's natural nobility, Sam and Ike stand in the stillness watching a giant mythic buck glide past in all its regal majesty. Sam raises his right arm, palm outward, and speaks in the old language. " 'Oleh, Chief,' " he says; " 'Grandfather.' "[18] It is difficult to take Sam Fathers's salutation to his reincarnated grandfather seriously (especially since "Oleh" is a slightly altered form of "hello" spelled backwards), but that is precisely the point of Faulkner's ironic primitivism. The ideas of mutual relation and natural innocence can only be seen as ludicrous in a fallen world. Sam's greeting to his grandfather is not funny when regarded simply as dark myth derived from the misty swamp of Mississippi story. The fall from harmony is the base of tragedy also.

But pure tragedy is not finally appropriate to Faulkner's vision of the absurd. He saw an absurd universe peopled by absurd men whose reactions to absurdity must be automatically ironic. This is nowhere more clear than in the case of the Christ figures in his books. For instance, Jewel and Cash may appear to be Christ figures in *As I Lay Dying*, since Jewel saves Addie from fire and water, and Cash, a carpenter, lies cruciform on a casket. (Taken together, their initials are J. C.) But these characters help perpetrate vengeance, and one of them, Jewel, betrays his brother. The resemblance between these two and Christ is deliberately made to look silly. Benjy in *The Sound and the Fury* resembles Christ because he bears the burden of a family's sins the way Christ bears mankind's. But the implications of this are that Christ in the Compson chaos is an idiot.

Faulkner made a very intriguing remark about his most deliberate effort to imitate the Christ story, that monumental failure, *A Fable.* "What got you into the *Fable?*" asked a student. "That was *tour de force.* The notion occurred to me one day in 1942 shortly after Pearl Harbor . . . who might that unknown soldier be? Suppose that had been Christ again, under that fine big cenotaph with the eternal flame burning on it? That He would naturally have got crucified again, and I had to—then it became *tour de force*, because I had to invent enough stuff to carry this notion." The next question was, "You were writing from an idea then?" To this Faulkner replied, "That's right, that was an idea and a hope, an unexpressed thought that Christ had appeared twice, had been crucified twice, and maybe we'd have only one more chance. . . ."[19] His attitude is clear: the ludicrousness and the hope together require the invention of enough stuff to carry the ambiguity. Writing stories about Christ figures in the twentieth-century chaos is a joke in itself. It is, however, a joke of hope, a joke of absurd creation.

Joe Christmas in *Light in August* is the prime example of the ambivalent Christ-figure joke in Faulkner.[20] If Joe Christmas is Christlike, then the implication is that Christ in Yoknapatawpha County would be lynched as a rapist and murderer. A potential Christ figure born in this time and place would automatically never take the form of Christ. Faulkner points up the joke by assigning his character a whole list of superficial elements from the Christ story: Christmas has the initials J. C.; he dies at thirty-three; his parentage is ambiguous; he "ascends" into the memory of his killers when he dies; five bullets stitch a quincunx on his chest. Having materialized ambiguously, Christmas remains unidentified as to color, parentage, or philosophy. He tries to refuse a firmly defined "place," but, since he has been shunned from birth as a half-caste exile and renegade, he is convinced that he is nothing but a half-caste exile and renegade. There are no possibilities for a revelation of divinity. He cannot become the Christlike absurd creator because he never sees that anyone could be. The ultimate irony of the story is that a modern Christ would be damned. Joe Christmas is Johanna's lover, her murderer, and a fugitive. Unlike the original Christ, Christmas has no way to discover or supply any meaning for his random existence.

Faulkner did draw characters who solve the absurd dilemma, although they do so unconsciously. The best examples are Dilsey in *The Sound and the Fury*, Lena Grove in *Light in August*, and Cash in *As I Lay Dying*. Cash has a ready answer to death: he manufactures the best possible coffin. Lena Grove quietly and with unflagging patience walks down the road carrying her baby, seeking its father, never deviating, never questioning. Dilsey endures because, through her basic compassion and primitive faith, she creates some semblance of order in the Compson household. "The good people, Dilsey, the Negro woman, she was a good human being," Faulkner said; "That she held that family together for not the hope of reward but just because it was the decent and proper thing to do."[21]

Faulkner's humor is rightly called absurd humor when it arises from the heroic and comic struggle of a creative character like Dilsey. In some of his books the struggle to create is not comic, although it may be absurd. Quentin Compson's struggle, culminating in suicide, is a tragic absurd conflict. The major actions of *Sartoris, Intruder in the Dust, A Fable, Absalom, Absalom!* and the central plot of *Light in August* are not funny, although these books have their comic strains. Some of Faulkner's short fiction and his last major book, *The Reivers*, are comic but not in the absurd sense.

There are, of course, absurdly funny moments everywhere

in his fiction. The incredible Ned in *The Reivers* is a comic creator, swapping Grandfather Priest's Winton Flyer for a race horse which wins when tempted by sardines. The scene in which Boon Hogganbeck gets gypped by a man who runs an improved mudhole designed to trap hapless motorists is reminiscent of the strong tradition of con men and their victims.[22] Old Man Falls in *Sartoris* has a comic speech with absurd moral implications, and an unlikely coincidence proves him right. Old Bayard has suffered for a long time from a cancerous wen on his face. Bayard believes the lesion to be one that modern doctors would have to treat with complicated and hopeless procedures. Jenny harasses Bayard mercilessly to get to a doctor and have it taken care of "right." Bayard has it treated instead by Old Man Falls, who says, " 'I reckon them doctors air still a-tellin' you hit's gwine to kill you, ain't they? . . . Ever' now and then a feller has to walk up and spit in deestruction's face, sort of, fer his own good. He has to kind of put a aidge on hisself, like he'd hold his ax to the grindstone. . . . Ef a feller'll show his face to deestruction ever' now and then, deestruction'll leave 'im be twell his time comes.' "[23] The humor of this creative philosophy turns on the circularity of that final statement. Old Man Falls is right, however. He puts a salve on the wen and predicts a cure date. Miss Jenny later forces Bayard to go to the doctor. The doctor touches the wen, and it falls off. The date is the one predicted by Old Man Falls. The whole event defines in miniature Faulkner's love of absurd creation as a comic device.

It is this unexpected creative pattern in the face of continual failure and "deestruction" that most often characterizes Faulkner's absurd humor. In the Snopes trilogy, meaning emerges from situations not likely to generate meaning, and characters create actions and values that the reader outside the cosmos of the books would judge as criminal, perverted, stupid, or ludicrous. And once, in what must have been a furiously brilliant six weeks, Faulkner wrote a perfectly balanced serious comedy, *As I Lay Dying*. In it, the unconscious creativity of the Bundrens is offset by the tragic total awareness of Darl. *As I Lay Dying* is the definitive absurd book of the most distinctive humorous moralist of twentieth-century America.

2 · SNOPES WAS HERE

What the writer wants, speculated Faulkner, is not necessarily success but something to offset his own inevitable dissolution. The author knows "he has a short span of life, that the day will come when he must pass through the wall of oblivion, and he wants to leave a scratch on that wall—Kilroy was here—that somebody a hundred, a thousand years later will see."[24] Flem Snopes, says Charles Mallison, one of the interpreters of the Snopes phenomenon in Jefferson, left something like a monument. The monument was the water tower where all the copper and brass fittings that Flem filched from the power plant were deposited by Tom Tom and Tomey's Turl. Flem had originally tricked the two Negroes into helping him steal the fittings, and they hid them in the tower in retaliation and for their own protection. Only it wasn't a monument at all, the town realized. It was Flem's footprint.[25] Faulkner's statement on the motivation of the artist is not a joke; the story of Flem's footprint is. Yet the product of creation—leaving a mark—is the same in both. Flem's footprint is a joke because the creative process has been shifted from the world of high idealistic purpose to a morally ludicrous world where rascals operate best. "The good and the shining angel ain't very interesting . . . ," Faulkner said, and the good and shining angel wouldn't be very funny, either.[26]

Faulkner told several stories in the Snopes trilogy about characters leaving footprints. The characters are all drawn as creators of absurdity in an absurd county. The pattern of invention is the same for each character. It is a struggle for creativity in a place, time, and society which automatically counter all invention by intrinsic negating forces. Some unseen fragment of the chaos inevitably renders any newly invented solution meaningless. Finally, since the solutions are the work of people who are inseparable from the county, the solutions are at the moment of their conception part of the general absurdity. The meaning of the struggle lies in the struggle itself, not its success or failure.[27] That meaning is also absurd, but it is generative because the struggle yields values which transcend their context: heroism (no matter what the hero's goal), steadfastness (no matter what the motive), and cleverness (no matter who is taken advantage of). The struggles are then differentiated by tone. Flem's story is consistently comic and grotesque. Eula's story moves from pastoral comedy to an ironic tragedy of fate in which her surprisingly great inner resources are displayed. Gavin Stevens's story is that of the keen perceiver whose perception is not matched by his ability to solve problems; he is the bumbling solution inventor whose solutions never quite work. The tone of his story is that of quixotic comedy. The story of Ike, the idiot Snopes, and his beloved cow is an exercise in the transformation of a conventionally ludicrous situation into a story of high comic beauty. Linda Snopes shares something with the vengeful heroines of Greek tragedy as she determines Flem's death by releasing Mink into his journey of retribution. Mink's story is in turn the most startling of all: in spite of motivations that we must call mean and depraved, Mink forges at his own level a curious integrity, determination, faith, and courage. His objective and motive are immoral in our view, of course: he is going to murder Flem because Flem failed to save him from being jailed for killing Houston. Our view of Mink might or might not be mitigated by our belief that his victim is an evil grotesque, depending upon whether we believe that justice belongs to law or that justice can be poetic. In any case, Faulkner, who narrates the last chapter of *The Mansion* in the authorial voice, tells us that Mink has through his struggle become equal with all heroes.

The Hamlet is a collection of revised stories and fragments of earlier pieces, but it is, of course, anything but casual; it is a whole unified by themes as well as overlapping story lines. Its setting is perfectly appropriate to the absurd. Frenchman's Bend is a metaphor for disintegrated southern hopes. Before the Civil War, it was the site of a large plantation, and the ruins of the Old Frenchman's palatial house are still evident. Everything is residual and fragmentary. (The book takes place during the first decade of the twentieth century; Faulkner thought 1907 would be about the right date.[28]) The Old Frenchman might not even have been a Frenchman, since the people who had succeeded him "had almost obliterated all trace of his sojourn," and anyone speaking with a foreign accent was automatically dubbed a Frenchman in these parts anyway. His broad acres have been "parcelled out now into small shiftless mortgaged farms for the directors of Jefferson banks to squabble over before selling finally to Will Varner. . . ." The house has been pulled to pieces, priceless walnut trimmings, oak floors, and all the siding that could be reached without effort having gone into the fireplaces of the Frenchman's "heirs-at-large."

The Varners themselves, especially Will and his son Jody, are appropriate to this scene of "fallen baronial splendor." Will sits on the porch of the Frenchman's broken-down house chewing and spitting, a large, rapacious, wily, Rabelaisian fountainhead of advice, more powerful than law. His son, "a prime bulging man, slightly thyroidic," is drawn as a frantic and avaricious opportunist with all his father's lust for power and wealth but with none of Will's cleverness or talent.[29] The career of the Snopes family in Frenchman's Bend begins when Jody plans to cheat Ab Snopes by renting him a farm and then driving him out just before the crop is made. Jody hears that Ab might once have burned a barn. It is possible that Ab could burn the Varners' barn if he ever became dissatisfied with anything. Jody decides to turn this frightening possibility to his own advantage: at just the right time, he will remind Ab that he has the reputation of being a barn burner, and Ab will have to quit the country. The trick turns against Jody, not because Ab moves first or retaliates afterward, but because Jody becomes obsessed by the thought of fire. To keep Ab and Flem placated, he makes one concession after another, even though the Snopeses have asked for nothing. Jody's imagination cripples him completely, and, as he grows more frantic and ineffective, Flem assumes Jody's place in the hierarchy of Frenchman's Bend.

Olga Vickery described such "economic activity" in Frenchman's Bend as a perversion: "It assumes this obsessive quality only when it ceases to answer an actual human need and introduces its own standards and values. At its best it provides an opportunity for exercising an intellectual skill against a worthy opponent for the sake of honor or even for the sheer pleasure of the game. At its worst the same skill is used ruthlessly and efficiently to amass wealth and to acquire power over other men. In both cases, the result is a destruction of human relationships as based on mutual trust. . . ."[30] In other words, the economic conflicts between the Snopeses and the natives of the Bend consist of the fraudulent and deceptive practices of absurd men fighting to survive in a fallen world, to con their way through the Yoknapatawpha maze. But Faulkner has given this traditional pattern a twist. Most of the characters who are fooled in *The Hamlet* are not deceived by an opponent's ploy. They are almost invariably deceived in the way Jody is: by the machinations of their own imagination.

Jody is frightened by rumor only; he has absolutely no concrete evidence that Ab is really a barn burner. The irony of his decline in the face of imagined catastrophe is that he acted originally in the full confidence that he knew how to use appearances regardless of the truth. To his dismay, he discovers that he cannot operate without knowing the hidden facts. Eventually he becomes immersed in speculation about trivia, until he finds that he can make no move at all against the encroachment of Snopes: " 'Hell fire. He's been here three days now and he aint even set the gate up. And I dont even dare to mention it to him. I dont even dare to act like I knowed there was even a fence to hang it to.' He twitched the reins savagely. 'Come up!' he said to the horse. 'You hang around here very long standing still and you'll be a-fire too.' "[31] When Jody tries to get Flem on his side, he talks and talks about " 'that fellow' " (meaning Ab) who shouldn't be thinking of burning things and running off because his landlord (meaning Jody) would see to it that a benefit would accrue for " 'that fellow' " if he were to stay " 'quiet and peaceable.' " To all of this frantic speculation, Flem replies only with short questions and a blank face: " 'What benefit?' " Jody at this point talks so much that Flem sees his opportunity to become clerk of the Varner store by letting Jody believe that giving him the job will be the guarantee of the Snopes's good will. Jody keeps on weakening his position by elusive and allusive talk. He assumes that Flem knows exactly what he is referring to: " 'All right,' he said. 'Next week then. You'll give me that long, won't you? But you got to guarantee it.' " Flem pretends ignorance still (it is equally possible that he really is ignorant of specifically what is bothering Jody, but we doubt it). " 'Guarantee what?' " says Flem.[32] Ironically, the Snopeses themselves can be sold, and they sell one another. Ab probably learned the trick of letting people deceive themselves the day he bought back a tired horse he had sold earlier. He failed to recognize it because it had been painted and its skin blown up like a tire to made it look fat.[33]

Early in the book, the Snopeses take on mythical aspects. These aspects are not given in the authorial voice; we cannot know whether Faulkner intended us to believe that the Snopeses inherently possess these attributes or if he meant to show their myth being built up by only the townspeople themselves. What we do observe is the townspeople's mythmaking. The sympathetic hero, observer, and comment-maker of the book, Ratliff, is responsible for much of the invention of the myth. He and the other citizens of the Bend speculate endlessly on what the Snopeses will do next. The speculation itself prepares the way for what the Snopeses will do and helps them do it. Faulkner carried this theme throughout all the books in the trilogy, and in the later two it becomes Jefferson which sees the Snopeses in mythic terms. When Charles Mallison begins to narrate *The Town*, he says, "So when I say 'we' and 'we thought' what I mean is Jefferson and what Jefferson thought."[34]

Ratliff is a clever man, a peddler out of the comic tradition, a wheeler-dealer who knows better than anyone else how to make those endlessly complicated series of trades which finally end in a dollar or two profit and a good deal of fun for the trader. He of all the characters in *The Hamlet* ought to be able to avoid getting nicked by the Snopeses. But Flem sells Ratliff because he does not seem to try to trick him. He knows how to use Ratliff's own love of deception and half-truth against him. He simply channels Ratliff's energies, talents, and love of con games in a way that allows Ratliff to con himself. Flem has taken as part of his business-deal marriage the Old Frenchman's place. Ratliff wonders why Flem would want it, and the moment Ratliff raises this question he has already taken the bait. Flem makes absolutely no overt effort to sell the place to anyone. Old stories have been told about money buried many years ago on the Frenchman's place. Ratliff observes that Flem is digging in the garden at night. Ratliff, always the cautious man, takes in two partners and hires a local wizard to go over the ground with a witching stick. They readily discover three bags of coins and are convinced. Ratliff and his partners buy the place at Flem's price. After a great deal of further, fruitless digging Ratliff suspects that they have been sold. Finally he looks at the coins they dug up before the purchase; some bear recent dates. He has been fooled by an old trick—salting the mine—and he has neglected to make the simplest check of all, which would be to look directly at the immediate evidence, the dates of the coins.

One of Ratliff's partners is Henry Armstid, who previously took a beating at Flem's Texas horse sale. He continues insanely to dig in the garden in spite of his knowledge that he has been conned. Passersby come to gawk. One says, " 'Anybody might have fooled Henry Armstid. But couldn't nobody but Flem Snopes have fooled Ratliff.' "[35] Everyone agrees, but the joke is that what Flem has done has been to let Ratliff fool himself. All Flem had to do was salt the mine with appearances and let Ratliff's confidence in his ability to make whole truths out of little indicators do the job of conning.

The same process makes Flem's horse sale successful. When he and his Texan acquaintance drive the horses into the center of the hamlet, everyone makes sly comments on what a wild and useless lot they are. But Ratliff, for one, already knows that the men will buy: " 'So Flem has come home again. . . . Well, well, well. Will Varner paid to get him to Texas, so I reckon it aint no more than fair for you fellows to pay the freight on him back.' "[36] Ratliff is right. When the Texan holds the auction, every onlooker appears to be indifferent, or hostile to the possibility of being conned. Yet every supposedly disinterested bystander has brought money in his pocket, some, like Henry Armstid, having raided their wife's sugar bowl for the family's last five dollars.

A juxtaposition of activities during the wild horse sale provides a contrast between absurd activity and stabilizing constructivity. The men and boys stand dickering for the horses, exchanging insults with the Texan, knowing all the while that the game will end with each man owning a useless and dangerous horse. Each will have rationalized himself into believing he can tame the horse and put it to work or ride it for pleasure. While all this is going on, Mrs. Littlejohn emerges in the background, carrying a hogshead of water, and begins to do her washing. While the men play their senseless game, Mrs. Littlejohn makes dirty clothes clean. No detail is left out; she works and creates cleanliness. From time to time she stares at the horse lot in disbelief at how far men will go to achieve freedom from their women regardless of the outcome. But Faulkner makes no moral judgment about the different activities. Mrs. Littlejohn's washing seems sensible in terms of immediate human needs. On the other hand, the absurd game of horse trading fulfills another need, the need for competition, exercise of wit, and fun. Both activities are generative, and what is generated is not judged in moral terms. One activity is stable, the other volatile.

The game of Snopeses versus Frenchman's Bend and Frenchman's Bend versus Snopeses usually elicits delightful laughter. In Faulkner's picture of the universe, Snopeses and Frenchman's Bend will inevitably come together—they are complementary forces, and they deserve each other. But the humor turns darker at times when, from the reader's point of view, real damage occurs. Ratliff's defeat is no disaster; he loses his share of the lunch counter, but he takes it with a grain of good humor, and we know that he has the wherewithal to continue practicing survival. Henry Armstid is a pitiful case, however, and the picture of his wife pleading for the return of her last five dollars is pathetic as well as comic. When Flem takes over the Varner fortune by marrying Eula, who is pregnant by Hoake McCarron, Ratliff feels (and the reader may well feel) a deep sense of waste. She has been pictured as Helen, as the earth mother, as the essence of ripeness and sexuality; she is the life-force, the pastoral queen. But her doom is inseparable from that of her geography; she is beautiful, lazy, and decadent. To Ratliff, she symbolizes a primitive and natural beauty gone corrupt and stagnant. In the waste of Eula, he sees the waste of a world in which creative activity has degenerated into absurd circlings.

The characters in *The Hamlet* are haunted by the feeling that the Snopeses are not the only jokesters they have to contend with. They sense that the Snopeses are only part of some universal joke created by some unknown jokester. When Ratliff sees

Ike Snopes for the first time, an idiotic creature with thick thighs bursting from his overalls dragging a block on a string behind him, he says, " 'And yet they tell us we was all made in His image.' " Bookwright responds, " 'From some of the things I see here and there, maybe he was.' " Ratliff says that he would never believe that God was an idiot, even if he knew it were true.[37] To Jack Houston, who is stranded a mile from his horse while chasing Ike and the cow, the joke appears to have been quite deliberately conceived: "it seemed to him that once more he had been victim of a useless and elaborate practical joke at the hands of the prime maniacal Risibility, the sole purpose of which had been to leave him with a mile's walk in darkness."[38] This practical joke of circumstances grows more and more ominous for Houston as he gets deeper into his tangle with Mink Snopes until it ends in a most ludicrous reversal. The tenacious and fiery pursuer, Houston, is slain from ambush by his desperate and paranoid quarry, Mink.

Faulkner's ability to derive a moral statement from absurd comedy is best displayed in *The Hamlet* by his consecutive telling of two love stories. The first is the story of Eula and Flem, as interpreted by Ratliff. That Flem should marry Eula is a horror to Ratliff, who recalls a certain grotesque picture of Flem. On the floor behind the counter in the store, Flem copulates with "this here black brute from the field with the field sweat still drying on her that she dont know it's sweat she smells because she aint never smelled nothing else. . . ." She lies there, Ratliff imagines, looking up past Flem's bobbing head at the rows of canned delicacies which she could never afford, and asks, " 'Mr. Snopes, whut you ax fer dem sardines?' "[39] Ratliff's vision of grotesqueness, supposedly based on correct assumptions (Flem's impotence not being a barrier to copulation but a part of its ludicrousness), is contrasted directly to the beauty of Ike's love story.

Ike's lover is described in rich romantic imagery and moving poetic rhythms: "It would not be after one hour, two hours, three; the dawn would be empty, the moment and she would not be, then he would hear her and he would lie drenched in the wet grass, serene and one and indivisible in joy, listening to her approach. He would smell her; the whole mist reeked with her;

the same malleate hands of mist which drew along his prone drenched flanks played her pearled barrel too and shaped them both somewhere in immediate time, already married."[40] From this point on, the reader is led through sequences of description which show that Ike believes he is pursuing a beautiful object and that his motives arise from the wellsprings of human affection. Little by little, the reader becomes aware that Ike's love is a cow. The author's purpose is then clear. He has revealed the awful ludicrousness of the Snopes version of love and, by assuming a radical viewpoint, has measured the beauty of a love that ought to appear depraved but does not. By telling a story of sodomy in the traditional language of love, Faulkner created something affirmative out of something grotesque. By reversing our expectations about two kinds of love—marriage and sodomy—he illustrated the perils of making judgments from conventional viewpoints. In Faulkner's cosmos, what we take to be natural is often grotesque; what we take as grotesque is often made harmonious. The morality of an action lies in the pattern of the action: true love is true love, and the objects of love are unimportant. The style in which the action is presented reflects the beauty of the action and transcends our limited opinions of the performers. The morality in the pattern of action is re-created by the storyteller, Faulkner himself.

The second book of the Snopes trilogy, *The Town*, is scarcely about the Snopeses; it contains the story of Gavin Stevens's resistance to the Snopeses and his ever-expanding interpretation of what he calls Snopeslore. Gavin's story extends into *The Mansion* and overlaps with the main absurd plot of that book, Mink's quest to murder Flem. In both novels, Gavin's resistance to the Snopeses is complicated by his emotional involvement with Eula and Linda. His behavior in respect to Eula and Linda is motivated by the highest ideals as well as by simple natural drives which he understands and accepts. Such a perceptive man ought to be able to effect successful action. But Gavin cannot; he thinks he can predict and move towards specific ends but is always waylaid by something unforeseen. Gavin is one of three characters through whom the story of *The Town* is told. Charles Mallison tells part as a storyteller would, injecting his own prejudices and irrational responses. Ratliff has a broad view and tells the story from the position of observer and deliberate analyzer of character motives. He comments extensively on Gavin. Gavin himself is not usually presented as a storyteller but as a mind open for examination. Gavin can be seen perceiving and analyzing all events and impressions, attempting to draw conclusions, and succeeding only in carving out his own tragicomedy.

Gavin is an absurd actor with an intense awareness of his, the town's, and mankind's dilemma. He knows that the Snopes phenomenon is partly a function of his and the town's imagination: "Yes . . . that was a part of our folklore, or Snopeslore, if you like. . . ."[41] It is Gavin who sees the events and geography around him in terms of cosmic metaphor. Standing on a ridge at night overlooking Jefferson, he records his expansive vision:

> First is Jefferson, the center, radiating weekly its puny glow into space; beyond it, enclosing it, spreads the County, tied by the diverging roads to that center as is the rim to the hub by its spokes, yourself detached as God Himself for this moment above the cradle of your nativity and of the men and women who made you, the record and chronicle of your native land proffered for your perusal in ring by concentric ring like the ripples on living water above the dreamless slumber of your past; you to preside unanguished and immune above this miniature of man's passions and hopes and disasters—ambition and fear and lust and courage and abnegation and pity and honor and sin and pride—all bound, precarious and ramshackle, held together by the web, the iron-thin warp and woof of his rapacity but withal yet dedicated to his dreams.

This vision characterizes the way Gavin Stevens thinks, and his ability to see meaning, or to make it (sometimes one or the other, sometimes both), is the source of the pathos and comedy of his bumbling efforts to maintain order and morality around him. It is also the source of the moral courage that keeps him trying to do so. He knows exactly what his Sisyphuslike position is: "Because the tragedy of life is, it must be premature, inconclusive and inconcludable, in order to be life; it must be before itself, in advance of itself, to have been at all."[42] It is his lucidity that makes his failures painful.

Once while preparing to leave Jefferson on a trip, Gavin Stevens asks Ratliff if he can " 'hold the fort' " and " 'tote the load.'" "'What fort?'" says Ratliff; "'What load?'" "'Jefferson,'" says the lawyer. "'Snopeses. Think you can handle them till I get back?'" Ratliff replies, "'Not me nor a hundred of me. . . . The only thing to do is get completely shut of them, abolish them.'" Gavin says no to that: "'Say a herd of tigers suddenly appears in Yoknapatawpha County; wouldn't it be a heap better to have them shut up in a mule-pen where we could at least watch them, keep up with them, even if you do lose a arm or leg ever time you get within ten feet of the wire . . .?'" Gavin sees himself and Ratliff fighting inevitability, staying the tide of change and the onflow of Snopeses only when they are lucky or exceedingly clever. He is fatalistic: "'No, we got them now; they're ourn now; I dont know jest what Jefferson could a committed back there whenever it was, to have won this punishment, gained this right, earned this privilege. But we did. So it's for us to cope, to resist; us to endure, and (if we can) survive.'"[43] (Gavin's irony echoes Faulkner's words in the Nobel speech—a Faulknerian joke.) Gavin's is a vision of an unknown communal original sin. Man's punishment is ironic and darkly funny; he is to be forever plagued by Snopeses and afflicted by the sense that he will never even know what the original sin was.

Gavin's relationship to Eula in *The Town* is at first embarrassing to him not because she is married to Flem but because Manfred de Spain, her lover, continually taunts Gavin for his failure to initiate a sexual affair with Eula. The taunts take the form of comic racket: de Spain roars his car past the house where Stevens lives with his sister, opening his exhaust cutout and letting the explosive chatter act as his derisive laughter. All of Gavin's attempts to make contact with Eula comically disintegrate. Once he sends her a corsage to wear to the cotillion. His sister, social arbiter of the town, insists that this will cause a public scandal. Thinking he is creating a humorous solution, he sends one to every lady invited to the dance. Manfred de Spain, not to be outdone, extends his running jokes on Gavin by doing the same thing. The town wallows in flowers, and Mrs. Rouncewell, the florist, enjoys a boom. Charles Mallison's father calls it the great Rouncewell panic. An important point is made about Gavin's failure to win the game of jokes and to see the humor in his own ludicrous position. Charles Mallison recalls that his father thought the corsage deluge funny, but Gavin didn't: " 'I had to make that one [the joke on the term "Rounce-well panic"] myself,' Father said. 'It was Gavin's by right; he should have done it but right now he aint even as faintly close to humor as that one was.' "[44] De Spain tops off the jokes by sending Gavin a corsage made of a rake head and two flowers bound together by a used condom.

Gavin's affair with Linda, Eula's daughter by Hoake McCarron, has its inception in Gavin's determination to "save" her while she is still in high school. She is literate, sensitive, intelligent; he buys books and meets her in the drugstore fountain area to give them to her. His endless machinations to make himself look like an interested tutor and not a middle-aged lecher are funny. He helps her gain entrance to the university at Oxford, Missis-sippi, and later encourages her to leave Jefferson and live in Greenwich Village.

Eula's and Linda's stories end in tragedy in spite of and partly because of Gavin's attempts to save them from the Snopeses. There is very little he can do to save Eula. He does make contact with her; they discuss Linda's future. Eula tells Gavin how to save himself and her daughter; all he need do is marry Linda. (Ratliff later seconds that advice.) On that score, Gavin suffers a Hamletlike indecision, weighing the appearances of things against his own mixed desires until he cannot take that step. When Eula kills herself, Gavin sees her death as a monumental waste, the deepest footprint Snopes has made so far. In trying to save Linda, he tries to prevent her being crushed in the Snopes footprint too. According to Charles, Gavin is appalled when Rat-liff convincingly suggests that Eula's motivation for suicide was boredom. " 'To waste all that, when it was not hers to waste, not hers to destroy because it is too valuable, belonged to too many. . . . Why?' " asks Gavin in anguish. Then he answers his own question, awakening to the truth of Ratliff's suggestion: " 'Bored. . . . She was bored. She loved, had a capacity to love, for love, to give and accept love. Only she tried twice and failed twice to find somebody not just strong enough to deserve, earn it, match it, but even brave enough to accept it. Yes . . . of course she was bored.' "[45]

Charles observes in the beginning of *The Town* that nothing ever happened in Jefferson until Snopes came. Throughout the book, Charles watches as Gavin experiences the tragedy of nothing multiplied by itself. Flem Snopes stirs up the nothing and parasitically makes his wealth out of it. Gavin tries to save something—Eula—from that whirlpool of corruption and then has to watch as it comes back to nothing after all. Gavin is capable of metaphorizing Eula as Helen, but he is not able to create the love to fill the vacuum he perceives around her. His is a failure of absurd creation.

The story of Linda continues into *The Mansion*. After being sent to Greenwich Village by Gavin, she takes up residence with Kohl, an idealistic intellectual and practicing sculptor. Kohl and Linda go to Spain to fight on the Loyalist side. Kohl is killed and Linda deafened by a mine explosion. When Linda returns to Jefferson, Gavin and she begin a passionate and intense relationship. Charles imagines the two of them making love like teen-agers, in a car, but their affair is actually sterile, complicated by Linda's frigidity, an apparent result of the trauma of the blast. Gavin's machinations in Linda's favor reach the danger point when he helps her obtain an early release for Mink Snopes, who has served thirty-eight of a forty years' prison sentence. He does not realize that Mink will kill Flem Snopes; it dawns on him too late that Linda knows he will. Gavin warns Flem and sets up protection for him, but it fails. The last absurdity of his well-intentioned machinations is that he unwittingly becomes accessory to Linda's plan to free herself by making it possible for Mink to murder Flem. The ambivalence of Gavin's position is classic: the first thing on his mind was to free Linda, the last was to help commit murder.

At least Gavin does aspire towards solution. He even enjoys some success in creating a tangible good when he helps save Lucas Beauchamp from being lynched and teaches Charles Mallison the nature of man's dilemma (in *Intruder in the Dust*). Man is not always right, Gavin says, but he can at times become " 'again conceptible of pity and justice and conscience even if only in the recollection of his long painful aspiration towards them, toward that something anyway of one serene universal light.' "[46] But even here, Gavin leaves the stage in the echo of laughter at his expense. At the end of the book, Lucas politely pretends to insist that his engagement of Gavin as lawyer is a business deal and must be settled. The standard response would be for Gavin to refuse payment, and Lucas probably expects this. Instead, Gavin surprises Lucas by agreeing and charging two dollars. Lucas retaliates by slowly counting out a ragged dollar and some odd coins. With infinite patience, he places a bag of pennies on the table, declaring the count to be fifty. Stubbornly extending the joke, Gavin insists Lucas count them out, since this is business. Lucas does so, very slowly. Then he waits. " 'What are you waiting for now?' " asks Gavin, hoping to conclude the joke with his own triumph. " 'My receipt,' " Lucas says.[47] That is the last line of the book.

Mink Snopes is the one character in *The Mansion* who does endure and prevail even though he appears to be the least likely hero of all. Mink endures and prevails by matching his will to his fate and his fate to his will. He thinks that the barriers which fate throws in the way of his quest are indications that he is on the right track. Any logical mind would assume barriers to be barriers. But Mink is absurdly creative; he makes the universe conform to his idea of justice. He is one of those interesting rascals of whom Faulkner said "only an individualist can be a first-rate artist."[48] Mink's tenacity, endurance, and simple faith in inevitability make his quest a virtuoso performance.

Mink's story begins in *The Hamlet*. He owns a cow which wanders into Jack Houston's pasture. He leaves it there, thinking to bring it home after it has fattened on Houston's grass awhile. When Mink tries to collect the animal, Houston demands money for pasturage, having a legal right to compensation. After a bitter and funny squabble in court, the destitute Mink pays by working on Houston's farm for fifty cents a day credit towards the price of the pasturage. When Mink finishes, Houston surprises him by demanding a pound fee, a legal nicety that allows him one dollar for housing the cow in the first place. Houston has waited to ask for the fee just to insult and harass Mink. Mink bears this stoically. He works the fee out, too—one dollar, two days. When Mink is finished, he takes his cow and goes home. He gets his shotgun, sets up an ambush, and shoots Houston off his horse. As he pulls the trigger, he thinks, " 'I aint shooting you because of them thirty-seven and a half four-bit days. That's all right; I done long ago forgot and forgive that. . . . That aint why I shot you. I killed you because of that-ere extry one-dollar pound fee.' "⁴⁹ (This recollection appears in *The Mansion*.) Mink's journey thus begins with a bizarre joke. The joke grows more grotesque as Mink tries to hide Houston's rotting body, which keeps falling apart. Finally he is caught.

Mink envisions God as a determining force whose objectives are unknown but who will make everything right in the end. The way Mink conceptualizes this philosophy, which seems conventional enough in terms of the Presbyterianism of Yoknapatawpha County, is comic. Mink believes God will make things right by helping him endure jail until he can carry out his revenge against Flem for not saving him from being convicted of Houston's murder. Mink says he does not believe in Old Moster in the same way most folks do. His view is of an ultimate, predestined balance and justice, a general equalization:

> He meant, simply, that *them—they—it*, whichever and whatever you wanted to call it, who represented a simple fundamental justice and equity in human affairs, or else a man might just as well quit; the *they, them, it*, call them what you like, which simply would not, could not harass and harry a man forever without some day, at some moment, letting him get his own just and equal licks back in return. They could harass and worry him, or they could even just sit back and watch everything go against him right along without missing a lick, almost like there was a pattern to it; just sit back and watch and . . . enjoy it too; maybe in fact They were even testing him. . . . But at least that moment would come when it was his turn. . . .⁵⁰

The astonishing thing about Mink's absurd faith in inevitable compensation is that in his world it is continually justified. Flem arranges for Mink to escape and then tips off the warden. This insures him twenty additional years of freedom from Mink's revenge, which is the amount of time added to Mink's sentence when he is caught. Mink's resolve is merely affirmed by this; he says, " 'If I had made it out then, maybe I would a changed. But I reckon I wont now. I reckon I'll jest wait.' "⁵¹ Later Mink is forced by his cellmates to choose between escaping with them (and likely being caught again) and being killed to prevent his informing on them. He starts a fight in the dark, rolls under the bed to escape their knives, and is taken to the warden just in time. The instigator of the plot, a murderer named Stillwell, escapes later anyway. Thereafter, on every holiday, he sends Mink a note threatening to kill him when he is released. Mink simply says that Stillwell will be taken care of. Mink is right. In San Diego, a ramshackle, unused church falls in on Stillwell. When he hears of this, Mink draws a breath and says " 'I can go now . . . I can be free.' "[52] Old Moster takes care of everything.

Sustained by this comic faith, Mink endures thirty-eight years in the penitentiary at Parchman. Upon his release, he undertakes an arduous journey through a world that has altered completely since he was imprisoned. He has never encountered so many cars, has never seen an airplane or neon lights. The roads have all changed, but he finds his way to Memphis. There he buys a revolver just before the Memphis police broadcast a bulletin on him. Gavin, having guessed Mink's intentions, has informed them, but too late. Mink painfully makes his way back to Jefferson and slips past the sleeping bodyguard into Flem's room in the mansion. There his first round misfires, but the second does not, and his mission is completed.

Mink begins to run, and after awhile he lies down exhausted in the woods. He knows that this is dangerous; he believes that when a tired man sleeps on the ground, the earth tries to pull him into itself. But now at last he can risk that, his part of the pattern of equalization having been fulfilled. As he loses consciousness, the book ends:

it seemed to him he could feel the Mink Snopes that had had to spend so much of his life just having unnecessary bother and trouble, beginning to creep, seep, flow easy as sleeping; he could almost watch it, following all the little grass blades and tiny roots, the little holes the worms made, down and down into the ground already full of the folks that had the trouble but were free now, so that it was just the ground and the dirt that had to bother and worry and anguish with the passions and hopes and skeers, the justice and the injustice and the griefs, leaving the folks themselves easy now, all mixed and jumbled up comfortable and easy so wouldn't nobody even know or even care who was which any more, himself among them, equal to any, good as any, brave as any, being inextricable from, anonymous with all of them: the beautiful, the splendid, the proud and the brave, right on up to the very top itself among the shining phantoms and dreams which are the milestones of the long human recording—Helen and the bishops, the kings and the unhomed angels, the scornful and graceless seraphim.[53]

This astonishing image of organic unity in death raises a number of problems. Mink's meanness, his basic paranoia, and the fact that his quest for justice has as its aim murder make this equalizing seem bitterly ironic and not comic. Our respect for life seems negated in favor of justification and compensation. On the other hand, Flem is a villain, and Mink is like the vengeful Greek hero, sacrificing his life to eradicate disorder. Moreover, as one of the reversals built into the Yoknapatawpha cosmos, Mink's act of negation is really an act of creation. The passage also makes equalization in death ambivalent: is Mink equal to all because he is equally heroic or because he is equally dead? The ultimate morality of the Yoknapatawpha cosmos— and the universe itself—is hidden. But Faulkner has framed a morality. Mink did all a man can do in Faulkner's cosmos: he put his faith in Old Moster's mathematics and proceeded with his enduring and prevailing. We cannot finally judge Mink except to observe that he has been "equal to any, good as any, brave as any . . . anonymous with all of them. . . ." Mink's absurd quest is appropriate to the absolute paradoxes of the Yoknapatawpha chaos.

3 · THE SAVAGE CARICATURIST

Describing Flem Snopes's face as he arrives for the first time to clerk in Varner's store, Faulkner wrote: "It was as though the original nose had been left off by the original designer or craftsman and the unfinished job taken over by someone of a radically different school or perhaps by some viciously maniacal humorist or perhaps by one who had had only time to clap into the center of the face a frantic and desperate warning."[54] An analogous line describes Anse Bundren in *As I Lay Dying*: "Pa looks at [Cash], his face streaming slowly. It is as though upon a face

(195

carved by a savage caricaturist a monstrous burlesque of all bereavement flowed."[55] These are marvelously elusive similes which could initiate endless disquisitions on the nature of the comic absurd. Who is the craftsman? Who is the viciously maniacal humorist? Who is the savage caricaturist? Is it God? Is it Faulkner? Is it what Houston called the prime maniacal Risibility of the universe? Or is it no one at all, since, as simile, the comparison is literally comparison and as such remains ambiguous. The face is a caricature, but it was not necessarily carved by a savage caricaturist; it looks "as though" it were, but this does not say for certain that there is a carver. The passages do imply that it cannot be known whether or not there is a caricaturist or craftsman. The second quotation describes *As I Lay Dying* itself; the book is a "monstrous burlesque of all bereavement." The creator of the burlesque is just as elusive as the savage caricaturist. One thing about the second quotation is certain, however: the judgments about Anse's face are made by Darl Bundren. When the reader judges the funeral journey in *As I Lay Dying* as burlesque, he does so from a point of view he shares with Darl, the moral perceiver of the book.

Each chapter in *As I Lay Dying* is assigned to one character and told from his view almost as if he were telling a part of the story. More is told in some of the chapters than the character can know, however, so it is more accurate to say that the implied author tells the story through the different voices of his characters. Vardaman is not acting as storyteller when he says, "My mother is a fish"; the phrase's implications are a matter of agreement between author and reader. Vardaman makes metaphors unconsciously and automatically; they are not metaphors which express moral knowledge but which formulate incomprehensible experience. His equation of his mother with a fish encapsulates all his inexpressible feelings, putting them into a form he can live with. Addie believes that forcing Anse into the funeral journey will metaphorically yield vengeance. Cash, the most consciously perceptive character in the book besides Darl, speaks the language of facts and figures. Jewel's metaphors are expressed in passionate and violent action. Darl is the only one who makes metaphors from the position of a moral evaluator. He alone has a sense of irony. It is only he who sees the funeral journey as grotesque, and only he tries to stop it. He sees that burying Addie is incidental to the real desires of Vardaman, Dewey Dell, and Anse. What everyone else takes to be Addie's sentimental deathbed wish he knows to be a twisted desire for revenge. Darl and Addie are the only ones who make judgments about abstractions like vengeance in the first place. The darkly humorous tragedy of this book is that Darl can formulate the simile about the savage caricaturist but has no way to answer the question it poses.

Faulkner himself believed that the family's journey is the full expression of the theme of man's surviving even when this means surviving absurdly: "The Bundren family . . . pretty well coped with [their fate]. The Father having lost his wife would naturally need another one, so he got one. At one blow he not only replaced the family cook, he acquired a gramophone to give them all pleasure while they were resting. The pregnant daughter failed this time to undo her condition, but she was not discouraged. She intended to try again and even if they all failed right up to the last, it wasn't anything but just another baby."[56] Anse survives the crisis by accepting whatever compensation lies at hand. Dewey Dell keeps on trying to solve a developing problem, and if she fails she will simply stop thinking of it as a problem. These characters can't go wrong. If they were able to judge their plight as absurd, terrible, or grotesque, their story would be tragic. But they do not have a tragic awareness. Their psychology is as comic as their dilemmas: the reader cannot tell whether they have an ability to negate problems or an inability to see problems. Darl has neither gift, and the great irony of this book is that the most perceptive character is the one least able to cope with fate.

Darl's doomed attempts to create a solution to the journey's absurdity are complicated by his being too much unalone. A large factor in his insanity is his consciousness of everybody else's consciousness. Other characters are isolated, and some try to break out of themselves. In the past, Addie tried violently beating her pupils to make them know her. When she does become unalone, ironically, it is when she is tricked by Anse's first words of love and by Whitfield disguised as sin. Dewey Dell becomes terribly unalone when she believes that Lafe is waiting for her in the barn. It would seem that the objective of human activity ought to be communication. But Darl knows the irony of these moments of contact: Dewey Dell is pregnant and Lafe won't marry her; Whitfield is Jewel's father and a ludicrous hypocrite. Darl knows that Anse wants teeth and a new wife and Vardaman wants to see the train. Whereas Jewel and Cash might seem to be Addie's saviors, Darl sees that their efforts to save her from fire and water have two results quite different from salvation: the extension of her vengeance and his own betrayal. Darl sees and thinks too much to be able to compensate for the insanities of the journey. He sees it as a travesty of love, honor, salvation, and bereavement. To survive the journey requires a firm point of view that excludes such judgments. The characters who survive are committed to points of view which cancel the problems of the absurd.

Cash, for instance, is the perfect pragmatist. One could argue that Anse and Dewey Dell survive because they are stupid, but this could never be said of Cash. Cash is, in fact, nearly as perceptive as Darl. He is the only character who sympathizes with Darl's final insanity; he makes a relativist's moral statement by recognizing that insanity may be a matter of contextual definition: "This world is not his world; this life his life."[57] But Cash's perception does not cripple his mind, even though the journey cripples his leg. Like Franklin, Cash creates structures that can be judged by immediate, tangible criteria. When he broke his leg the first time, he did not speculate as to why he fell but measured the distance of the drop. While others in the family stand around waiting for Addie to die, Cash carefully bevels the boards for her coffin so that it will fit neatly together and be watertight. In contrast to Darl, who burns a barn, Cash builds barns and evaluates them as being among those things man makes good by his sweat and time. Cash does not laugh at absurdity; of Darl's laughter, he says, "I be durn if I could see anything to laugh at."[58] Cash is the conscious absurd creator without humor. He sets aside the metaphysical difficulty for the physical possibility. In the face of life, Darl laughs; in the face of death, Cash builds a coffin.

Darl's moral vision involves traditional Christian concepts. He thinks that Addie's desire for vengeance will damn her and doom the family. He believes that she should have been buried promptly, that her soul is in limbo as long as the journey continues. Listening to Addie's body steaming and festering in the coffin, Darl and Vardaman discuss the motives for burial:

> "What is she saying, Darl?" I say. "Who is she talking to?"
> "She's talking to God," Darl says. "She is calling on Him to help her."
> "What does she want Him to do?" I say.
> "She wants Him to hide her away from the sight of man," Darl says.
> "Why does she want to hide her away from the sight of man, Darl?"
> "So she can lay down her life," Darl says.
> "Why does she want to lay down her life, Darl?"
> "Listen," Darl says. We hear her. We hear her turn over on her side. "Listen," Darl says.[59]

To Vardaman's last question, Darl has no answer. He is convinced only that it is wrong to let Addie rot above ground. To Darl, the log in the river (which he says surges up "like Christ"), the current, the buzzards, the heat, the processes of natural decay —all the forces of nature—seem to be trying to bring the travesty to an end. When Darl tries to "hide her away from the sight of man" by burning the barn, he is executing his moral judgment.

Darl's laughter as he is carried off to Jackson is the result of his knowledge that he and his family are the leading characters in a comedy of horrors. But the main irony of the book surpasses in horror and hilarity Addie's bubbling corpse, Cash's broken leg, Dewey Dell's sex-metaphor bananas, Jewel's obsessions, Vardaman's confusion, and Anse's incredible luck. Not only do Darl's efforts to prevent vengeance fail, but, as he finally realizes, they are based on a misconception in the first place. No one is affected by Addie's vengeance except Darl himself. Jewel lost his horse, but he'll get another. Vardaman remains confused, but he was simple to start with. Besides, he got to go to town, where his father found a duck-shaped woman to replace his fish-shaped mother. Dewey Dell lost her money and kept her baby, but it wasn't much money and it's just another baby. Even Cash, who broke his leg, managed to break the same one as before. Cash also looks forward to comfortable winter evenings with a new record from the mail-order catalogue spinning on that graphophone. Anse, the target of the vengeance, is richer than he ever was: he has a new Mrs. Bundren and those long-awaited store teeth. In short, Darl's frantic attempts to execute the dictates of his moral perception come to exactly nothing. He sees the absurdity of the journey, but he does not realize until too late that his efforts to correct it are doomed to be absurd, too. A final irony is that his own objective—to get rid of the corpse—is accomplished by the family, who simply bumble along until they get Addie buried.

Darl laughs because the universe is always ambiguous, always the reverse of what even he, the perceiver, can see. The universe is like the three images of doubleness Darl remembers as he watches himself being carried off:

> They pulled two seats together so Darl could sit by the window to laugh. One of them sat beside him, the other sat on the seat facing him, riding backward. One of them had to ride backward because the state's money has a face to each backside and a backside to each face, and they are riding on the state's money which is incest. A nickel has a woman on one side and a buffalo on the other; two faces and no back. I dont know what that is. Darl had a little spy-glass he got in France at the war. In it it had a woman and a pig with two backs and no face. I know what that is. "Is that why you are laughing, Darl?"
> "Yes yes yes yes yes yes."[60]

Darl laughs because the universe as he has learned to envision it is a beast with two backs. Everything has two sides inextricably linked and indistinguishable. When he thinks he sees the face of things, he sees the reverse; when he sees the reverse, he cannot see the face. His is the laughter of the initiate who has caught and is caught by the cosmic joke.

VII

These Fruitful Fruitless Odysseys: John Barth

"One must needs make and seize his soul. . . ."

BURLINGAME

I · ODYSSEY IN THE FUNHOUSE

WHEN ASKED if the discussion of suicide in *The Myth of Sisyphus* had colored his characterization of Todd Andrews in *The Floating Opera,* John Barth replied, "There certainly may be similarities between them, but it didn't color my work because I haven't read *The Myth of Sisyphus.* I believe Camus says the first question that a thoughtful man has to ask himself is why he is going to go on, then make up his mind whether to blow his brains out or not; at the end of *The Floating Opera* my man decides he won't commit suicide because there's no more reason to stop living than to persist in it."[1] Thus Barth showed that thoughtful men ask similar questions and arrive at similar answers without having to read each other's books. Barth's character formulates one simple and direct response to the absurd dilemma: "there's no more reason to stop living than to persist in it." Having arbitrarily decided to live, Andrews simply continues to live and to invent action. One of his actions is the writing of *The Floating Opera,* his own history. John Barth himself seems to have transcended the dilemma by writing stories. "There is a Hindu thing that I've always wanted to go clear through," he said. "It's called *The Ocean of Story.* . . . Four feet long. Wouldn't it be wonderful to have written that? "[2] The basic motivation for writing stories is the "impulse to imagine alternatives to the world. . . ." What the writer really wants to do, Barth said, is to "re-invent philosophy and the rest—make up your own whole history of the world." The motivation for absurd creation is, then, the recognition that the universe has meaning only when a man assigns it meaning. The man who controls the meaning best is the highly inventive man—the artist.

The motivation for comic absurd creation is the recognition of the fun to be had revealing the inseparability of the real and the fictional world. The comic novelist is not a serious historian because he believes that it is impossible to record a truth without changing it into a new truth. The question of being a "realist" in fiction is a question that can be made to look silly because reality and fiction are already indistinguishable. A book, whether its technique is "realistic," "surrealistic," "romantic," or whatever, always has life as its subject and is itself one of the facts of life, with its own reality. Furthermore, life outside books can be just as fabulous as fables. A work of history is a selection and interpretation of events and is, therefore, a story. Even what men take to be reality is a story: "God wasn't too bad a novelist, except he was a Realist. Some of the things he did are right nice: the idea that ontogeny recapitulates phylogeny is a master stroke; if you thought that up you'd be proud of yourself." Any model of reality is a story about reality's story, just as a mathematical model of a phenomenon represents the plot of that phenomenon. What is hilarious is the way men accept models of reality as reality and forget that the model has a story reality of its own. Immediately observable information, in fact, becomes a story the moment it is perceived and can then be seen as simultaneously real and unreal: "Robert Louis Stevenson could never get used to the fact that people had two ears, funny-looking things, and eye-balls in their heads; he said it's enough to make you scream. I agree."[3] Barth is not too interested in trying to write "realistic" fiction: "One ought to know a lot about Reality before one writes realistic novels. Since I don't know much about Reality, it will have to be abolished. What the hell, reality is a nice place to visit but you wouldn't want to live there, and literature never did, very long. . . . Reality is a drag."[4]

The storyteller who transfers the simultaneous reality and unreality of the world to his own cosmos does not decide which is which; he re-creates the phenomenon as a dilemma or joke. The title of Barth's *Lost in the Funhouse* is a metaphor for the artist's ambiguous position. This book is a "sequence" of related short stories, some previously published, but the whole arranged loosely as an exercise in the problems the absurd creator as storyteller faces. Appropriately, some of the stories are quasi-autobiographical. A few are designed for conventional printing, with a narrator speaking in the third person or with a first-person narrator telling his own story. Other pieces are composed for oral recitation by the author or live voices other than the author's. One piece, titled "Autobiography," is from a tape designed to be played while the author sits quietly in view of an audience. Several of the stories are told in such a way that the difference between author and narrator is deliberately reduced until the two are indistinguishable.

These devices create frames in which the processes of storytelling in the world of the book and the processes of John Barth's telling of the story before the reader's eyes are constantly being examined at the same time. Thus there are stories within stories within stories and narrators quoting narrators quoting narrators. In "Menelaiad," for example, Barth (or the implied author— Barth writing in his persona as writer) retells the story in the words of a modernized Menelaus who in turn quotes others and recalls his own earlier tellings:

> " ' "Nothing for it but to do as Eidothea'd bid me," ' " I say to myself I told Telemachus I sighed to Helen.[5]

The narrative levels continue to accumulate. There is even a storytelling Menelaus whom Menelaus imagines:

" ' " ' " 'By Zeus out of Leda,' I commenced, as though I weren't Menelaus, Helen Helen, 'egg-born Helen was a beauty desired by all men on earth. . . .' " ' " ' " "⁶

The storytellers involved in these passages are John Barth, professor at Buffalo and writer at large; John Barth, implied author of the story; Menelaus, the "I" of the story but also Barth's re-creation of an ancient literary figure; the Menelaus of the past who told his story before; and a storytelling Menelaus who is a figment of Menelaus's imagination. Little wonder this story begins "Menelaus here, more or less."⁷

The stories in *Lost in the Funhouse* are arranged to encompass various stages in the life of the artist from his conception through his late years of deepening involvement with unanswerable questions. The first piece in the book is a preface to this arrangement and is a metaphor for the endless activity to which the author in and of the book commits himself: the infinite creation of story. It is printed on a vertical strip running from bottom to top on both sides of a single sheet. Instructions are included for cutting out the strip, twisting it once, and joining the ends together. The result is a Möbius strip, a continuous one-sided surface upon which one can now read the words, for as long as he lives if he so desires, "ONCE UPON A TIME THERE WAS A STORY THAT BEGAN ONCE UPON A TIME THERE WAS A STORY THAT BEGAN ONCE UPON A TIME THERE WAS A STORY THAT BEGAN. . . ."

The next story, the first portrait of the artist, is called "Night-Sea Journey" and is a satirical allegory of man's absurd quest for the meaning of his existence. The satire begins as the story opens:

> "One way or another, no matter which theory of our journey is correct, it's myself I address; to whom I rehearse as to a stranger our history and condition, and will disclose my secret hope though I sink for it."
> "Is the journey my invention? Do the night, the sea, exist at all, I ask myself, apart from my experience of them? Do I myself exist, or is this a dream? Sometimes I wonder. And if I am, who am I? The Heritage I supposedly transport? But how can

These Fruitful Fruitless Odysseys: John Barth

I be both vessel and contents? Such are the questions that beset my intervals of rest."

The tone of the passage and the clichés the narrator uses suggest that Barth is making the questions into a joke. The disturbing factor in the joke is that these questions are, in spite of their absolute familiarity, man's most basic ones—and they are unanswerable. Therefore, the joke is not only on the narrator but on everybody, author and reader included. The serious joke grows as the reader learns that the narrator's familiar questions have to do with the purpose of mankind's commonest experience, the journey of life. The narrator swims with millions of his companions through dark seas towards an unknown destination. The goal of the journey is a personified female entity whose warmth can be sensed by some of the travelers. The existence of the quest's objective cannot be proved by anyone, and many fear that the joy of union with "Her" spells oblivion as well as ecstasy. These doubts and uncertainties are the conflicts embodied in all theologies. The ultimate joke of the story hinges on the reader's discovery that the narrator and his companions are spermatozoa.

To the reader's delight, the sperm-narrator talks about his dilemma in the terminology of the absurd:

"If at times, in certain humors—stroking in unison, say, with my neighbors and chanting with them 'Onward! Upward!'—I have supposed that we have after all a common Maker, Whose nature and motives we may not know, but Who engendered us in some mysterious wise and launched us forth toward some end known but to Him—if (for a moodslength only) I have been able to entertain such notions, very popular in certain quarters, it is because our night-sea journey partakes of their absurdity. One might even say: I can believe them *because* they are absurd.

"Has that been said before?"

The spermatozoa swim bravely upstream for two measures, flailing their tails, then must rest, sliding backwards one measure. During these periods of inactivity, the narrator ponders and soliloquizes. Thousands of his companions drown every instant, while the survivors sustain one another by singing "Love! Love!" The narrator recalls that some, including himself in his nihilistic moments, have speculated that the journey is without meaning. He answers the question of suicide in a way that echoes Todd Andrews's arbitrary logic: " 'Indeed, if I have yet to join the hosts of the suicides, it is because (fatigue apart) I find it no meaning-fuller to drown myself than to go on swimming.' " He has heard some say, " ' "The night-sea journey may be absurd, but here we swim, will-we nill-we, against the flood, onward and upward, toward a Shore that may not exist and couldn't be reached if it did." ' " The choice for the thoughtful swimmer is, then, "give over thrashing and go under for good, or embrace the absurdity; affirm in and for itself the night-sea journey; swim on with neither motive nor destination, for the sake of swimming, and compassionate moreover with your fellow swimmer, we being all at sea and equally in the dark."

The narrator tries to insist that he does not find the embracing of absurdity acceptable: "If not even the hypothetical Shore can justify a sea-full of drownèd comrades, to speak of the swim-in-itself as somehow doing so strikes me as obscene. I continue to swim—but only because blind habit, blind instinct, blind fear of drowning are still more strong than the horror of our journey." With this, the joke seems genuinely nihilistic: if the swimmers cannot elect to like their condition, then nothing moves them but meaningless chemical processes. The narrator admires swim-mers who strike off in their own directions, asserting their independence even though it costs them their lives, and he en-vies the hedonists. But he rejects both blatant nonconformity and egoism as being "more dramatically absurd, in our senseless circumstances, than tailing along in conventional fashion. Sui-cides, rebels, affirmers of the paradox—nay-sayers and yea-sayers alike to our fatal journey—I finally shake my head at them." But even as he rejects these alternatives, he is dedicating himself to the more intrinsically absurd, if not the more dramatically ab-surd, solution: swimming on in full awareness of the absurdity of swimming on. He does not reject the absurd mode after all; where others say *nay* or *yea*, he says both at once.

Being perfectly lucid, the narrator acknowledges the absurdity of his choice to remain in the intrinsically absurd situation: " 'A poor irony: that I, who find abhorrent and tautological the doc-trine of survival of the fittest . . . may be the sole remaining swimmer! . . . Chance drowns the worthy with the unworthy . . . and makes the night-sea journey essentially *haphazard* as well as murderous and unjustified.' "⁸ Ironically, his guess is correct. His attempts to reject an absurd solution and his philosophical discourse itself are terminated by his being the spermatozoon who unites with "Her." The union is an ambiguous event, just as traditional mystical union with the godhead is ambiguous: it is ecstasy but it is also intellectual annihilation. The hero protests his flood of joy: " 'I am not deceived. This new emotion is Her doing; the desire that possesses me is Her bewitchment. Lucidity passes from me; in a moment I'll cry "Love!" bury myself in Her side, and be "transfigured." Which is to say, I die already; this fellow transported by passion is not I; *I am he who abjures and rejects the night-sea journey!* . . . I am all love. "Come!" She whispers, and I have no will.' "⁹ His last effort to defy love fades as he broadcasts a warning to the fluid, a message to those who may come behind him: " 'Stop Your hearing against Her song!' " He disappears into the warm globule shouting, " 'Love! Love! Love!' " The final twist of the joke is that the ecstatic union produces a new life but the consciousness that went into the union is gone and will never know that new consciousness is born. The conception is both rebirth and death, and this ambivalence is the basic truth of cyclical life.

Three of the stories in the collection are about a boy named Ambrose, who may or may not be the issue of the union depicted at the end of the "Night-Sea Journey" (by inference, of course, he is). The stories are deliberately Joycean portraits of the artist as a young man, and Barth may have intended Ambrose to resemble Barth. The reader is invited to make these comparisons because Barth has deliberately built the parallels between himself, Ambrose, and Joyce into the stories. To compound the joke, he has drawn Ambrose as a budding author who is deliberately imitating Joyce's conscious literary apprenticeship.

Ambrose is thirteen, and he thinks of himself as being at the awkward age. In the first of his stories, "Ambrose His Mark," Ambrose does the telling—in the first person. In the second two stories, the author uses third person, but we have the impression —probably because the first story was told by an "I"—that Ambrose is still telling his own story. Thus in "Lost in the Funhouse" it is impossible not to equate the author's speculations with Ambrose's. "Is it likely," says the storyteller, whoever he is, "does it violate the principle of verisimilitude, that a thirteen-year-old boy could make such a sophisticated observation?"[10] A third possibility is that Barth lets Ambrose tell his own story in retrospect. This blending of narrator identities makes "Lost in the Funhouse" structurally tight in spite of constant interjections about the difficulties of writing a story. "There is no *texture of rendered sensory detail*," the teller complains about his story, and he feels that it lacks the conventional diagrammatic rise and fall described by Freitag's Triangle.[11] He constantly worries about using clichés and italicizes them to show that he is conscious of them. The subject of the story is storywriting, and its satire centers on the conventional things people talk about when they talk about storywriting.

The interjections complement the story's plot. Ambrose, trying to impress a girl friend, hopes to act sophisticated and nonchalant when he accompanies her through the funhouse at a carnival. He actually fears that he will get lost in there and imagines what might happen if he does. His imaginings are directly related to the subject of storywriting. As the teller (Barth or the older Ambrose) talks about writing the story, young Ambrose of the plot is imagining how the story of being lost in the funhouse would be written. In turn, being lost in the funhouse itself is a storytelling situation, because, when lost, one has nothing left to do but sit down in some corner to await rescue or death, telling stories to oneself to avoid going insane. One ending Ambrose imagines for the story is "He died telling stories to himself in the dark; years later, when that vast unsuspected area of the funhouse came to light, the first expedition found his skeleton in one of its labyrinthine corridors and mistook it for part of the entertainment."[12] This sentence is a condensation of Barth's and Ambrose's idea of the curious status of the storyteller.

At points in this book, Barth appears to be more than cynical about the process of absurd creation, even as he accepts it as inevitable. In a piece called "Title," he rambles across various stock problems of composition, having begun with an axiom: "Everything leads to nothing: future tense; past tense; present tense. Perfect. The final question is, Can nothing be made meaningful? . . . If not, the end is at hand. Literally, as it were."[13] Later, he seems bitter but resigned: "There's only one direction to go in. Ugh. We must make something out of nothing. Impossible. Mystics do. Not only turn contradiction into paradox, but *employ* it, to go on living and working. Don't bet on it. I'm betting my cliché on it, yours too. What is that supposed to mean? On with the refutation; every denial is another breath, every word brings us closer to the end." Following this, he recognizes that the alternative to having no hope is to supply some alternative, making something out of nothing after all. Still, "That's no alternative. Unless I make it one. Just try; quit talking about it, quit talking, quit!" And finally, he plunges into the ludicrous, noting that writing is a matter of filling sentence-structure boxes: adjective into adjective slot, noun into noun, verb into verb. What the writer and his story are doing is creating each other—an absurd notion complicated by the possibility that in "Title" the story itself may be telling its own story: "that's what I'm leading up to, me and my bloody anticlimactic noun, we're pushing each other to fill in the blank."[14]

The author's condition may thus be wretched; John Barth —whoever he is—says in this book that he believes it is. The teller's proper point of view is "first person anonymous," and we must accept this as a description of whoever it is that speaks here.[15] The problem and its solution are inseparable, completely reversible, one and the same: "To be moved to art instead of to action by one's wretchedness may preserve one's life and sanity; at the same time, it may leave one wretcheder yet."[16] The writer finally can do nothing but stay on his Möbius strip, telling stories ever onward and upward and downward and backward. "Lost in the Funhouse" ends with the simultaneous problem and solution neatly stated: "He wishes he had never entered the funhouse. But he has. Then he wishes he were dead. But he's not. Therefore he will construct funhouses for others and be their secret operator—though he would rather be among the lovers for whom funhouses are designed."[17]

As readers, we are constrained to doubt the story's last claim. As we look into Barth's funhouses, we must declare that we who are outside looking in cannot help but envy the builder just as he envies lovers and readers. Is there really, after all, a difference between doers in the world, lovers in the funhouse, readers in their chairs, and authors in their books? And whether we are lost or found, we are still in the house of fun. In Barth's own terms, the only way to transcend the absurd is to put our sense of it to work, realizing that creating absurd alternatives is a high and difficult variety of fun. It is fun to write stories. It is fun to read stories. It is even fun to read and write about reading and writing stories.

2 · MYTHOTHERAPY

It is also fun to rewrite stories. John Barth's first two novels, *The Floating Opera* and *The End of the Road,* pose the question: If all values are relative, how does a man ultimately justify anything? The response of the main character in each book to the question is not the same, and the response of Todd Andrews in the first edition of *The Floating Opera* is not the same as that of Todd Andrews in the revised edition. (Barth has revised his first three novels; all were republished in 1967. The revised editions are used here. Only *The Floating Opera* underwent drastic revisions in plot.) Andrews's answer in the first edition is an act of absurd creation; he chooses to manufacture meaning. In the second edition, which apparently represents Barth's intention before he was encouraged to soften the ending, Andrews simply fails to commit suicide and decides thereafter that the absence of motives for living is exactly matched by the absence of motives for suicide. In *The End of the Road,* Jake Horner, who posits relativism just as Andrews does, cannot create answers, find an identity, or assume a workable mask. He discovers that all alternatives are qualitatively equal and as a result is unable to choose. Several times he freezes into immobility, and at the end of the book he simply places himself under the control of someone else. He finds that every situation is multiply ambiguous because it can be evaluated in as many ways as there are perspectives applying to it. Any single action which might be chosen to solve a problem opens new sets of ambiguous questions.

Todd Andrews is an explorer in the absurd, and he narrates his discoveries in *The Floating Opera.* (The book is his—he is writing it, and he explains various themes in it as he goes along.) He enjoys philosophical game-playing. He theorizes that the universe may be meaningless, attempts to disprove the thesis, and fails. He raises the question of suicide and seeks an unambiguous motive for either living or dying. Todd is also an introvert and a hypochondriac. Much of what he does and thinks is influenced by his belief that his heart is flawed and could quit at any moment. It has not failed since he learned of the flaw, thirty-five years prior to the time of the narrative, but he continues to weigh his decisions and evaluate his actions against the fact that it could fail in the next second. The effect of this obsession is obvious: any speculations Todd makes are shaped by the recognition that the question of meaning is ludicrous to one whose definition processes are always on the brink of annihilation. The fact that Todd's long survival has already proved him quite healthy makes his speculations comic. But the final point is not to be taken so lightly. Any man could be annihilated in the next second, and thus the question is ludicrous any time it is raised. Every man raises the question nonetheless.

Todd attempts to approach the question of meaning logically and consistently, just as he says he approaches all questions. He proclaims at the beginning of his narration that "although my principles might change now and then—this book, remember, concerns one such change—nevertheless I always have them a-plenty, more than I can handily use, and they usually hang all in a piece, so that my life is never less logical simply for its being unorthodox. Also, I get things done, as a rule."[18] But in spite of this claim to consistent principles, he continually reveals that he knows that actions are seldom based on principle and that apparent principles always change. "Getting things done" means spending some time practicing law, which he believes to be a game. He recalls several examples of cases which were not settled as matters of morality or even of clearly defined law. One very funny example involved a minor collision of two cars owned by rich and politically influential men of his town. He and the opposition's lawyer decided to see exactly how long the case could be disputed and how much it could cost. Todd applies the term "game" to their manipulation of the case, which is still going on at the time of narration, several years after the accident.[19] Naturally, it is not difficult within a complicated legal structure, the kind that any system has in its maturity, to extend such a game ad infinitum, and Todd and his colleague have done just that. Often Todd makes love to the wife of his friend, Harrison Mack. Jane and Harrison are very open-minded people; she initiated the relationship and Harrison, at least outwardly, approves. Clearly, Todd Andrews has instead of a sense of principle an awareness of how morality is subject to whim.

He also has an artist's sense of the problem of vision. He knows that a man sees only fragments of events and that, in narrating his own story about an event that changed his life, he risks presenting his "case" partially. He offers at the outset of his narrative to explain what the title means. The *Floating Opera* is a showboat that was tied up at Long Wharf during the period of his earlier life when the event occurred that changed his thinking, and that event occurred partly on the boat. The title has another significance, having to do with the problem of vision and interpretation:

> It always seemed a fine idea to me to build a showboat with just one big flat open deck on it, and to keep a play going continuously. The boat wouldn't be moored, but would drift up and down the river on the tide, and the audience would sit along both banks. They could catch whatever part of the plot happened to unfold as the boat floated past, and then they'd have to wait until the tide ran back again to catch another snatch of it, if they still happened to be sitting there. To fill in the gaps they'd have to use their imaginations, or ask more attentive neighbors, or hear the word passed along from upriver or downriver. Most times they wouldn't understand what was going on at all, or they'd think they knew, when actually they didn't.[20]

He points out that this is the way men inevitably see life. He asks his reader's strict attention: we must be alert to catch each nuance of the plot as it drifts in and out. Thankfully, however, Todd Andrews can organize experience; his narrative is easier to understand than his floating opera would be.

Initially, it seems that Andrews is not bothered by paradoxes. " 'An act of will is the easiest thing there is,' " he says to Harrison, who has just complained that his own weakness causes a certain ennui. In turn, Harrison asserts that " 'You can't discount psychology. . . .' " Todd says, " 'Psychology doesn't interest me. We act as if we could choose, and so we can, in effect.' "[21] This remark does not indicate that Todd believes in free will (he obviously considers the free will-determinism question another joke), but it does tell us that he thinks he believes that choices can be invented. He is fond of outlining sequences and determining their logical ends. When patterns have no logical ends, he dismisses them as he does the determinism circle. He figures out exactly what lies behind the love triangle and what constitutes its several possible final effects. Half in jest, half seriously, he advises old Mr. Haecker to kill himself, demonstrating syllogistically that suicide is the decision most appropriate to the circumstances. He begins his argument with an axiom: if a man has no abstract faith, then the question of suicide is the first he must answer. Mr. Haecker admits that he is not a religious man. The next step, then, is to determine whether or not one is happy. Mr. Haecker is old, ill, unproductive, and lonely. He concludes that he is not happy. Then the thing to do is commit suicide, Todd offers. But, responds Haecker, " 'If death is the absolute end, then you're better off alive under any circumstances.' " Andrews delivers the logical product of the syllogism: " 'That doesn't follow. If death is the end, then it's neutral. Which is better. to be unhappy or to be neutral?' "[22] Todd later learns that Haecker has taken him quite seriously, although his attempt at suicide has failed (a later attempt does not fail). This arouses Todd's curiosity but no feeling of responsibility.

The chain of events that Todd refers to as the change in principle began one morning when he awoke believing that somehow he had arrived at the logical resolution of his early exploration of the absurd. His resolution, which he attempted to carry out on or about June 21, 1937 (he can't quite remember the date) was to do what he had recommended to Haecker —commit suicide. Some of his reasons were the same as those he had used in his syllogism. The other details of his rationale are summarized neatly in his journal, which he calls his "Inquiry." There are also psychological motives for suicide which Todd unconsciously displays as he tells his story. His father committed suicide for reasons that seem trivial to him, so he is predisposed to an obsession with the motives for suicide. He had a nicely traumatic experience during World War I: he ruthlessly murdered a German soldier after spending a night embracing him in a human spasm of mutual fear and love. But these motives are not the ones that Todd can examine with logic. At first, the suicide plan seems nothing more than the simplest solution to the dilemma of his bad heart. He lives from day to day, paying his hotel bill every morning, beginning each day with this "gesture of cynicism" and ending it with a "gesture of faith": making another entry in his "Inquiry."[23] Suicide at least would mean that he chooses death and the manner of death instead of waiting for it.

But his plunge into the absurd is a more important motive than the concern about choice versus chance. From the beginning, he has liked displacing his point of view to see the joke in things. He notes that nature is a "heavy-handed symbolizer": wherever he walks, he finds silly coincidences, living clichés, ludicrous juxtapositions of things that seem to have meaning because men have made meaning out of so many juxtaposed things:

> One is constantly being confronted with a sun that bursts from behind the clouds just as the home team takes the ball; ominous rumblings of thunder when one is brooding desultorily at home; magnificent dawns on days when one has resolved to mend one's ways; hurricanes that demolish a bad man's house and leave his good neighbor's untouched, or vice-versa; Race Streets marked SLOW: Cemetery Avenues marked ONE WAY. The man whose perceptions are not so rudimentary, whose palate is attuned to subtler dishes, can only smile uncomfortably and walk away, reminding himself that good taste is a human invention.[24]

Even making love has extreme risks, he tells us; it will not do to put mirrors in our bedrooms where we can watch ourselves. "Nothing, to me, is so consistently, profoundly, earth-shakingly funny as we animals in the act of mating. . . . a mirror can reflect only what it sees, and what it sees is funny."[25]

In telling of his college days, he says he knows that his story, which is true, sounds like a lampoon of student life.[26] His is a mind already disposed to the kind of absurd perception which sees the joke in everything.

His ability to see the joke is related to his discovery that the value of everything is assigned from the outside by people, and *"nothing* is intrinsically valuable. . . ."[27] He next finds evidence that people have no logical motives for attributing values to things. Jane's little girl, Jeannine, asks him a series of basic child's questions which he tries to answer directly: "'Why?'" she asks when he takes her to see the showboat. In return, he asks, "'Why what? . . . Why do the actors act funny or why do the people like to watch them?'" She asks, "'Why do the people?'" Todd answers, "'The people like to go to the show because it makes them laugh.'" She responds, again, "'Why?'" Eventually Todd says it is because people like to be happy, and when Jeannine asks "'Why?'" to that, he says, "'Why do they like being happy? That's the end of the line.'" When she asks why people eat, he says, "'to stay alive.'" When she asks why they want to stay alive, he says, "'That's the end of the line again.'" In spite of having given this response, Todd refuses to accept as a final answer the possibility that people want to live because they want to live. Later, Jeannine the questioner puts that answer into basic terms. She asks for an ice cream cone; Todd, reversing their usual roles, asks her why she wants one. She keeps answering, "'I want one'"; he keeps asking why. Her final answer remains, "'I want one,'" and Todd, giving in, buys it for her.[28] He loves these games. Finally, he records his conclusions in his "Inquiry," intending them as his last notes. The first three are "Nothing has intrinsic value," "The reasons for which people attribute value to things are always ultimately irrational," and "There is, therefore, no ultimate 'reason' for valuing anything." After further rationalizing, he believes he has discovered the end of his masks, and adds two statements to his first three: "Living is action. There's no final reason for action," and "There's no final reason for living."[29] Since he seemingly believes that life should have a rationale, he elects suicide. His investigation is, he says, closed.

It is after this that Barth's two versions differ radically. In the first edition, Todd decides not to kill himself because he is interrupted by an event which moves him emotionally. He has turned on the gas in the galley of the *Floating Opera* and has sat down to await death while the show goes on overhead. First a crewman walks into the galley and shuts off the gas, not quite realizing what is going on. Next, an emergency develops: Jeannine has a convulsion while watching the show upstairs and is brought down to the dining room by a frantic group of people. Todd awakens from his stupor, and, as he emerges from the galley, he begins to experience fright himself. This is a feeling, a spontaneous evaluation of a situation. It breaks the hold of his logic trap. He recognizes that he has spontaneously believed that Jeannine's life has intrinsic value, but later he continues to rationalize, apparently unable to accept the possibility that values are generated by fear, beauty, and love. He declares that suicide is as arbitrary an act as living. He ecstatically announces that, while there are no absolute values, there are relative values, and these are no less real. He calls his accidental reprieve a narrow escape.[30]

In a prefatory note to the 1967 edition, Barth claims that the revised version is actually the older, original form of the story. Apparently he was asked to soften the ending or to make it more palatable. The ending of the 1967 edition makes Todd's absurd view consistent. In it, Todd is so firmly convinced that nothing matters that he plans to blow up the entire *Floating Opera,* killing himself and the audience, which includes Jane, Harrison, Jeannine, and the rest of the cast of characters in his story. To accomplish this, he opens the gas jets in the galley, lights one stove burner, and returns to his seat at the show upstairs. Something happens to prevent the explosion; perhaps an unseen draft has caused the gas to escape. Todd does not care about why it did not explode or that his suicide-mass murder plan has failed. A new thought has occurred to him. Having asked himself the question, " 'Why not blow up the Floating Opera?' " and having once answered " 'Why not,' " he now answers " 'On the other hand, why bother?' " He amends his "Inquiry" to read, "There's no final reason for living (or for suicide)" and that is the end of the matter.[31] He resumes his life, his games, and his masks.

A basic similarity between the plot of *The Floating Opera* and that of *The End of the Road* is that the protagonist of each book spends time in bed with his best friend's wife. In both cases, the husband knows of the affair and responds to it in what he considers an "objective" manner. In *The End of the Road*, however, the husband, Joe Morgan, does not approve of the relationship. His objectivity is displayed as a ludicrous obsession, a hypocrisy, and a contradiction in terms. He uses the adultery to justify prying into the mind and soul of his wife, Rennie. Joe and Jake, who is the narrator, are opposing characters in terms of theme as well as plot. Jake acts on instinct more often than not, believing it is the only guide he has that does not constantly contradict itself. His intellectual maneuverings —his rationalizations—always lead him to no decision at all. But the intuitive actions upon which he relies yield nothing but pain and trouble. Joe believes that he lives a perfectly rational life. He is sure that probing, questioning, and analysis can reveal the true self and its motives. He is certain that events have causes and thinks he can find out what the causes are. Both of these characters, one confident about reason and the other a conscientious skeptic, wreak havoc whenever they do act.

It is characteristic of Jake that he is not able to explain why he goes to bed with Rennie. He thinks there might be some reasons—he is attracted by her clumsy force, her maternal lushness, her simple desire for what she thinks is intellectual conversation, and her natural ability to handle horses—but these are silly. Their adultery has its immediate apparent causes: Rennie has discovered that Joe, whom she has idolized, can look ridiculous; Jake and Rennie have taken long horseback rides and have had long talks together; Joe has left town and deliberately invited the two to spend evenings together. They tumble into bed impulsively: "I think a slow-motion camera would not have shown who moved first—and it happened further (but I would not say *consequently*) that our separate ways led to the same bed."[32] This spontaneous act eventually leads to agony and death. Joe, learning of the affair, probes Rennie's mind mercilessly, seeking the "genuine" self beneath the exterior, searching out the "true" motives. Jake participates in this to a certain extent but generally argues against Joe's rationalizations by reiterating his belief that people are what they are and do what they do. Joe and Jake thus play the determinism game while Rennie is gradually led deeper into confusion and despair. She gets pregnant, is not sure whether Jake or Joe is the father, and decides to get an abortion. She dies on the abortionist's table.

Jake is not the villain of the piece. Joe's rigorously applied moral absolutism proves more vicious than Jake's amorality, and it is Joe who inadvertently and ironically proves that even serious men are absurd. The event that reveals his ludicrousness to Rennie defines his absurdity. Joe believes himself to be the ultimate logician; he is certain that he is serious, that values are serious, that the universe is serious. In a conversation with Jake, Rennie defends Joe's seriousness and his theory that people ought to be authentic. Jake argues that nobody is ever authentic and decides to prove that Joe is no exception. As they talk, they stand outside the Morgans' living room window. The blinds are pulled except for a crack of light at the bottom. Jake leads Rennie to the window, and they peer in to observe Joe marching about in his boy scout uniform, making faces in the mirror, and burbling nonsense syllables. Shortly, Joe sits down in a chair, hums a tune, picks his nose, and masturbates. Rennie is destroyed.[33] Clearly, Joe is just as absurd as anyone else; all that is required is that he be viewed from the right angle. He has made himself ludicrous as well because he professes not to be absurd. Joe's absurdity is also terrible because his serious purposefulness contributes its share of the factors leading to Rennie's death.

Jake sees the conflict between himself and Joe in terms of metaphor: "when at length I carried Rennie to the bed . . . I was able to do so only because, for better or worse, enough of my alertness was gone to permit me to dramatize the situation as part of a romantic contest between symbols. Joe was The Reason, or Being (I was using Rennie's cosmos); I was The Unreason, or Not-Being; and the two of us were fighting without quarter for possession of Rennie, like God and Satan for the soul of Man." This "pretty ontological Manichaeism" stands no close examination, he points out, and, therefore, it has the virtue of excusing him "from having to assign to Rennie any essence more specific than The Human Personality, further of allowing me to fornicate with a Mephistophelean relish, and finally of making it possible for me not to question my motives, since what I was doing was of the essence of my essence."[34] That any alert speculation would have frozen Jake into immobility is one side of his basic dilemma. The other side is shown when he realizes that his unthinking actions yield visibly negative results. If he thinks, he cannot act; if he acts in response to unanalyzed metaphors or impulses, he creates tragedies. At the end of the book, Jake exits desiring responsibility but unable to assume it.

Mythotherapy could be the solution to Jake's problem. Mythotherapy is a method developed by a doctor who runs a clinic for mental patients. The doctor's credentials are ambiguous, but his therapy is practical. Jake met the doctor at a point when his problem was at one of its critical peaks. He had just passed his master's oral and had discovered that he had no "self-convincing reason" to continue doing what he was doing. He decided to take a trip on his last thirty dollars. He did not know where he would like to go, so he asked the ticket agent where thirty dollars would take him. This should have been a simple solution to the problem of not being able to decide. But the agent gave him a list of four cities in Ohio to which thirty dollars would buy a ticket. After a brief examination of possible motives, which he quickly rejected, Jake discovered that there were no good reasons for going to Cincinnati or Crestline or Dayton or Lima. "There was," he finally decided, "no reason to do anything." He sat down on a bench and remained there, frozen, sightless, without sense or thought. Jake calls his malady *cosmopsis*—the vision of cosmic neutrality.[35] It is the sense of the meaninglessness of everything. Approximately twenty-four hours later the strange doctor, who had been observing him, diagnosed the cosmopsis. He snapped him out of his fit and took him into mythotherapy.

Mythotherapy is absurd creation based on immediate needs. The doctor's theories resemble Ben Franklin's. He is not infallible; he is also the doctor who performs Rennie's fatal abortion. But he fails this primarily because he does not know that Rennie has just eaten a large dinner of wieners and sauer-kraut (she strangles in her own vomit). Properly applied, mythotherapy is simply a game of reestablishing an identity, a process popular psychology blithely calls role-playing. The theory assumes that no one innately has an identity but ac-quires it through environmental shaping. If a man should lose it through a cerebral accident or mental illness—or by being afflicted with cosmopsis—then he must acquire a new identity. The difficulty is that when one has cosmopsis he resists all identities; he is not, as an infant is, an organism innately ready to be shaped by outside forces. He has to re-create a role as does an actor in a drama. The doctor says, " 'Here's the point: an immobility such as you experienced that time in Penn Sta-tion is possible only to a person who for some reason or other has ceased to participate in Mythotherapy. At that time on the bench you were neither a major nor a minor character: you were no character at all.' " He adds that Jake will have to be taught an identity just as a recovered paralytic has to be taught to walk. Jake will have to assume a new mask. This is not hypocrisy, insists the doctor: " 'All questions of integrity involve this consideration, because a man's integrity consists in being faithful to the script he's written for himself.' "

Mythotherapy is forcing oneself to choose simple, arbitrary reasons for making more complicated choices. To the extent that one does not exercise choice, the doctor theorizes, one does not exist. One must somehow be conscious of motion, the stream of action and reaction that defines the existence of a man in his environment. The doctor advises Jake to take up choice-making exercises: " 'Above all, act impulsively: don't let your-self get stuck between alternatives, or you're lost. You're not that strong. If the alternatives are side by side, choose the one on the left; if they're consecutive in time, choose the earlier. If neither of these applies, choose the alternative whose name begins with the earlier letter of the alphabet. These are the principles of Sinistrality, Antecedence, and Alphabetical Pri-ority—there are others, and they're arbitrary, but useful.' "[36]

The doctor warns against love affairs, which involve end-lessly complicated decisions. He prescribes masturbation as sexual therapy. This would be the simplest kind of satisfactory action, having an immediate and easily defined goal separate from complicating contexts. If Jake were to take this advice seriously, he would be deliberately selecting as one of his early therapeutic choices an absurd activity involving no risks to himself or anyone else. Joe's theories do not recognize absurd activity, and this is why his masturbation contradicts the context he has constructed around himself and with which he has enmeshed Rennie. It is Joe's obsession with "genuineness" that gives his action its devastating meaning. The doctor is trying to say that harmless actions do not have to be assigned any meaning and would be good things for Jake to start with.

But cosmopsis is a deadly disease which assimilates all cures. The script Jake writes for himself is ill-conceived. He tries to act essentially but has no essence. His impulsive actions contribute directly to tragedy. When at last he says that he craves responsibility in Rennie's death, he cannot convince himself that he has actually had a role in anything, even though he obviously has. He sees his responsibility but remains detached, unable to feel it or know it. On the phone several days after Rennie dies, Jake and Joe commiserate. Joe asks Jake what he plans to do next. Jake ignores the question. Joe asks again, " 'Well, what's on your mind, Jake? What do you think about things?' " Jake hesitates, "entirely nonplused." He answers, " 'God, Joe—I don't know where to start or what to do!' " The next day Jake does manage one action. He quits his job to return to the mythotherapy clinic (which has moved to another state to escape close official scrutiny). He leaves his statue of the Laocoön in his apartment, believing that he leaves his dilemma behind. He is going to commit himself totally to the doctor's care.[37]

In a moment of intensity and crisis, Todd Andrews discovers responsibility and feeling. He continues to rationalize in retrospect, but at least his rationalizations lead him to create arbitrary reasons for working, deciding, and living. Jake Horner also experiences a moment of intensity and crisis. He desires but does not get responsibility; he looks for but does not find some permanent feeling upon which to base a moral commitment. Unable to create an alternative to despair, Jake commits

(2 2 1

himself to the therapy of arbitrariness. The only shred of hope at the end of Barth's second book is the possibility that Jake's commitment to the mythotherapist's control can be taken as a choice.

3 · EPIC CIRCLES

In all his work, John Barth displays an acute awareness of the tendency of story to become cyclical, of the potential infinitude of "Once upon a time. . . ." The existence of a thousand and one stories is what gratifies him, and writing the one-thousand-and-second story is the thing to do next. Barth knows and uses all the oldest tricks of storytelling, the oldest of which is to tell the story straight. (To call him avant-garde would be an insult.) Telling the story can in itself be a long process. The distance from the beginning of any event to its end is usually far, and each event contains many events and is part of some larger event. To tell a story is to face the problem of defining beginnings and endings. All lives begin at birth and end at death. To trace lives from birth to death is one way to define a story's limits. Some stories can begin with the birth of an idea or action and stop with the death of the idea or the end of action. But life is cyclic as well as linear; old ideas and old people die while new ideas and new people are being born. The very moment in which we live, the constant present, is itself ambivalent: a given instant in time dies as the new instant is born. If one is to be happy, he chooses to rejoice at the birth of the new moment. If he is inclined to sorrow, he chooses to contemplate the death of the past moment. John Barth has deliberately re-created the cyclic nature of everything by inventing worlds within worlds, illuminating both story worlds and real worlds. He has stated his intention to re-create as much of the world of worlds as possible. His last two novels are thus gigantic and remarkable re-creations of history and myth.

The Sot-Weed Factor is a novel in the spirit of Fielding's comic epic, and it even resembles *Tom Jones* in some specific ways. It also has affinities with Sterne's study in the absurd,

Tristram Shandy. But Barth's "eighteenth-century novel" is structured in the twentieth-century manner. Every incident is accounted for; everything that happens contributes directly to the mainstream of events. In *Tom Jones* and *Tristram Shandy*, digressions in plot occur which do contribute to the themes, but in *The Sot-Weed Factor* there are no digressions in plot or theme. *Giles Goat-Boy* is a comic epic, too, and in addition displays the more salient features of the traditional mythic epic: it encompasses all of the basic metaphysical questions of the culture from which it sprang; it recounts events which appear to be supernatural; it has a dominant allegorical structure which has various interpretations; its hero undertakes a quest to assume a place as a people's savior. What is common to both books is the pervading sense of the absurdity of everything. Their protagonists—Ebenezer Cooke and Goat-Boy—labor towards certain goals, creating values around their goals and assuming at first that these values are not arbitrary. They gradually discover that all things are not as they seem, and eventually they are convinced that men operate in a vacuum, the Establisher of Ultimate Value being either nonexistent or unavailable. They end in ambiguity, unable to tell the difference between plus and minus, good and bad, saved and lost. Both protagonists, however, remain committed to the search, which may take the form of nothing more than a continuation of activity and a perseverance in life's struggles.

The Sot-Weed Factor is Barth's re-creation of history. The poet in the novel who writes the satiric poem "The Sot-Weed Factor" has an historical counterpart in Ebenezer Cooke, Maryland's earliest poet, who actually wrote a poem by the same title and published it in 1708. Serious antiquarians have found the historical Ebenezer Cooke an elusive personality; it is not quite possible to pin down his identity (no one seems sure if his name is a pseudonym or not), his origin, or the details of his career. Barth's Cooke has an even more elusive identity; counterfeit Cookes constantly appear aboard ships between England and America, in other towns in Maryland, or in an inn down the road just ahead of the "real" Cooke. Ebenezer himself never knows quite who is portraying whom. Barth uses other information about Cooke straight from the records: the historical Ebenezer Cooke did have a sister named Anna; the plantation he inherited from his father was called Malden and was located on Cooke's Point at the mouth of the Choptank; one of Henry Burlingame's avatars in the book is Nicholas Lowe, and this is the name of an actual person about whom the historical Cooke wrote an elegy; and the original Cooke also called himself Maryland's laureate. In addition, Barth's book portrays historical political figures (most of whom are Burlingame in disguise), actual Indians, and existing places. Accounts written by John Smith are constantly being discovered by various characters; most of these are Barthian rewrites. The book has all the earmarks of an historical novel based closely on facts. The difference is that these are only earmarks; Barth actually invented the important parts of the story himself—the character of the characters, the majority of the events, and all the thematic devices.[38] History has no themes, no subjects; these are supplied by the historian. Barth has simply done the historian's job twice: he has taken a story out of history and made an expanded story out of it, re-creating and inventing truths while pretending to relate the truth about Cooke, Maryland, and "The Sot-Weed Factor."

As the book's protagonist, Ebenezer learns that truth is a matter of layers within layers, circles within circles. Barth has deliberately made Ebenezer's development as a poet a reversal of the historical Cooke's career. In the last part of the book, Barth's character is seen writing the 1708 version of "The Sot-Weed Factor." The historical Cooke published a later version of his "The Sot-Weed Factor" in which he eradicated most of the bitterness and vicious satire of the first. This and his other late work tended to romanticize life in the colony.[39] Barth's Cooke, however, begins his career by declaring himself Maryland's laureate while he is still in England and proceeding to write idealistic and sentimental drivel based on his daydreams about the voyage to come, the Maryland countryside and towns he has never seen, and the heroic pioneers he expects to meet. Rapidly disillusioned as he encounters the real Maryland scene, a newly aware Cooke throws away his old style and cranks out the biting satire of "The Sot-Weed Factor"—1708 version. Ebenezer's disillusionment is developing so rapidly at the time he writes his poem that he becomes capable of forgetting about it once it's finished. He is mildly gratified when he learns that it has found its way into the hands of a publisher. (It is printed a year after its completion, 1709.)

Although Ebenezer is the protagonist of Barth's book, he is not the primary vehicle of the deception motif. Henry Burlingame is the man who knows everything about appearances, and it is he who is the manipulator of deception. Ebenezer is always one of the deceived. As Ebenezer and Anna's childhood tutor, Henry introduces his version of the problems of Platonic theory (both to the children and to the reader). He is, we gradually learn, the ultimate confidence man, a man of many identities, a man whose own real identity remains ambiguous even at the end when, traditionally, the reader would expect it to be revealed. Burlingame is a definitive absurd creator. He even manipulates history, creating and solving vast political and social upheavals in the colony of Maryland. As a man of disguises, he appears to Ebenezer, whose point of view we are usually confined to, in an extraordinary number of roles: the children's tutor, Henry Burlingame, a wiry young scholar whose background is shadowy and whose failure to earn a baccalaureate is unexplained; Peter Sayer, who saves Ebenezer from a beating at the hands of a shopkeeper and who warns him that "especially in Maryland . . . friends may change their colors like tree frogs"; Ebenezer's servant Bertrand (Bertrand poses often as Ebenezer); Ebenezer, while Ebenezer finds himself mistaken for Burlingame; Tim Mitchell, a man who loves all the world so intensely he tries to have intercourse with all living things; Nicholas Lowe of Talbot, a role that for a while appears to be his "real" one; Lord Baltimore, who tells Ebenezer a biased story of the history of his concerns in Maryland and who awards him an appointment as Maryland laureate; John Coode, the shadowy leader of forces opposing Baltimore; Monsieur Casteene, former governor of Canada and supporter of the Jesuit interests in Maryland; and, finally, son of an Indian chief, Chicamec, who is leader of an army of displaced Indians and runaway slaves in rebellion against all white intruders in the territory. His roles include the leaders of all the warring political factions in Maryland!

At the personal level, Burlingame has spent much of his busy life seeking his parentage—clues are to be found in all the various

John Smith manuscripts—and it does seem certain that he is Chicamec's son. In the end of the book, he returns to Chicamec, ostensibly to try to persuade the renegades to settle with the whites peacefully, but he then disappears once and for all. His final role in the story is unknown. The only clue to his whereabouts at the last is that his tribe, the Ahatchwhoops, do not precipitate massacres in Maryland, although it is supposed that they migrate northward to Pennsylvania and join the Five Nations, which in turn participate with the French in the massacres at Schenectady and Albany. Barth's implication is that the "real" history of the historical figures and events which he used for his book is no less shadowy than the history of his invented characters and events.

Burlingame is most creative in his roles as leaders of the factions struggling for control of Maryland. He declares that he assumes disguises "for sundry reasons stemming from my work," but he never defines his work. Apparently his work—besides seeking his parentage and "real" identity—is the absurd work of making absurd events occur in an absurd world.[40] "The world's a happy climate for imposture," he says with a smile.[41] And Burlingame is an excellent impostor. As Ebenezer is often forced to recognize, Burlingame is a better Baltimore than Baltimore, a better Coode than Coode. In fact, Ebenezer has virtually no concrete evidence that any other Baltimore or Coode exists. Burlingame's "true" motives are not decipherable; this enhances his creative nature. He acts, so he says, from a love of all the world. He repeatedly points out that for every *yea* there is a *nay*; it is he who, as Baltimore, Sayer, Mitchell, Lowe, and several other figures, educates Ebenezer to the ambiguity of all situations. One of the reasons for this book's length is the great pains Barth has taken to show Ebenezer learning (and to indicate to us) that there is always an endless number of different opinions and interests at work in any single historical event at any single instant. That viewpoints and facts conflict confuses Ebenezer, but to Burlingame multiplicity is beautiful. All roads are fine roads—Burlingame is nonjudgmental. Ebenezer was, too, in his idealistic youth. Before he decided to become the Virgin Poet Laureate of Maryland, he was almost frozen into indecision by all the charming possibilities for action in the world. But Ebenezer never achieves a true love for multiplicity, while Burlingame seems always to have had it.

Burlingame's creativity does have its Satanic side—he says so himself. His character appropriately reflects the universe's ambivalence. He is a mythic figure in this respect, creating states, stirring crises, moving Maryland into motion. He advises Ebenezer to teach. Teach what? Anything. Learn each aspect of the subject one hour before the pupil arrives. He also urges Ebenezer to seize the moment: "'My dear fellow . . . we sit here on a blind rock careening through space; we are all of us rushing headlong to the grave. Think you the worms will care, when anon they make a meal of you, whether you spent your moment sighing wigless in your chamber, or sacked the golden towns of Montezuma? Lookee, the day's nigh spent; 'tis gone careening into time forever. Not a tale's length past we lined our bowels with dinner, and already they growl for more. We are dying men, Ebenezer: i'faith, there's time for naught but bold resolves!'"[42] This is a perfect relativist theory: it matters not what a man does as long as he moves until he can move no longer. The implications of such a creed (or noncreed) are harrowing; a Burlingame can justify anything, great or terrible. Ironically and ambivalently, Burlingame's force depends upon his sexual impotence. The fact of his impotence makes his desire to swive the whole world a metaphor for a drive to re-create and to possess what he cannot have: the whole universe and its whole history. But one thing is clear: if Burlingame does not move, history stops.

Ebenezer is not impotent—sexually. He commits himself to an ideal of virginity, saving himself for true love. By this commitment he denies himself any possibility of all-inclusiveness; he defines himself narrowly. Towards the end of the book, he gives his virginity to his true love—the whore Joan Toast, who first moved his sensibilities in London and then appeared in Maryland, diseased and decaying from months of hardship at sea and in the colony. Joan has been raped by a gigantic black pirate in the rigging of the ship on which she crossed; it is he who transmits the pox to her. The rape, which Ebenezer witnesses, is compared to a spider's pouncing on a fly in a web and is deliberately presented as a key image for haphazard and neutral universal determinism. Ebenezer's yielding of virginity to Joan does not cancel

(227

but extends his self-definition. Joan is dying of the pox. She holds the title to Malden as a result of a string of ludicrous legal maneuvers and accidents, one of which involved her marriage to Ebenezer. She decides to give the property to Ebenezer, who had earlier foolishly and unknowingly signed it away, if he will culminate their marriage before she dies. He wishes to show her his love and to make amends for her agonies; he does not care whether he gets Malden or not. He yields his virginity for a reason he thinks noble, gets his inheritance anyway, acquires the pox (which he keeps in check with herbs recommended by Burlingame), and takes his place as the official Laureate of Maryland.

Thus it is Ebenezer's adventure which resembles and parodies the shape of the traditional quest story: static situation—fall—rise—new higher static situation. Tom Jones leaves his childhood home and innocence to quest for "something" and ends by acquiring his rightful moral and social status. But Ebenezer's quest is ironic, since it is clear that when he is sexually innocent, he is really morally fallen. His virginity is kept at a dire price to everyone around him; others invariably get hurt whenever he acts to preserve it. His journey does not teach him a moral view but simply reveals continually that no firm moral view can be assumed. What he acquires at last is not stability but a situation as owner of Malden which continues to be nerve-racking, painful, and ambiguous. This, of course, is more lifelike than Tom Jones's happy stasis. In short, his quest goes backward as well as forward, down as well as up. Barth proves that a stable moral status is impossible by giving us an overview of Ebenezer's continuing dilemmas after he assumes his inheritance—the place where the story would traditionally end. Ebenezer dies confused. Nobody gets out of this book alive. Nobody gets out of this world alive.

"Things are not as they seem" could be the motto of *The Sot-Weed Factor;* it is a line delivered to Ebenezer and to us by Burlingame, McEvoy, Joan Toast, Anna—everybody. This repetition makes a joke out of the absurd theme itself; nonetheless it is what Ebenezer has to learn. This line is made finally ironic because nothing ever is as it seems even when appearances are stripped away. There is no final fact. Burlingame says, " 'Whoever saw an odyssey bear fruit?' "[43] This is the key to his absurd creativity. " ' 'Tis our fate to search,' " he declares, and " 'seek our soul,' " though all we will find "'is a piece of that same black Cosmos whence we sprang and through which we fall. . . .'" A man, he adds, "'must needs make and seize his soul, and then cleave fast to't, or go babbling in the corner; one must choose his gods and devils on the run, quill his own name upon the universe, and declare, "'Tis I, and the world stands such-a-way!" One must *assert, assert, assert,* or go screaming mad. What other course remains?'"[44]

Burlingame says his philosophy grows from a "hilarious view" of the world, and Ebenezer learns this view from him. One of the best absurd metaphors in the book, a dream Ebenezer has, comes after he discovers that the hilarious view is, like the pox, a disease—once contracted, it can never be cured. The realization of this vision occurs simultaneously with the loss of innocence and the acquisition of knowledge. The hilarious view and the dream it produces precedes Ebenezer's literary breakthrough; he is afterwards able to sit down and churn out the final version of "The Sot-Weed Factor." Ebenezer's dream is induced by opium administered by Burlingame; like a twentieth-century acidhead, he has a vision of the cosmic joke.

In his dream, Ebenezer walks towards twin mountains of polished alabaster. One, he believes, ought to be Parnassus. He asks passers-by which it is and gets conflicting answers. Everyone knows it is the mountain on the right, but no one knows from which side a seeker should approach before choosing the one on the right. The mountains look exactly alike as far as Ebenezer can tell. Multitudes of people are trying to climb both mountains, meeting all kinds of grotesque barriers on the way up. At the first ring of each mountain, monsters mash the climbers' fingers; most give up at this point. Similar clubbings take place in some of the higher rings. On one level groups of women seduce the climbers and distract them permanently from their mission. Others near the summit are felled either by the deafening applause of those below them, which causes them to backslide, or by stones thrown from the summit. This is an allegory on the position of the nearly successful artist who is either knocked off by those whose status he threatens or is drowned in the applause of lesser men and stops short of achievement. Ebenezer chooses a mountain arbitrarily and begins to climb. Suddenly, to his surprise, he is whisked to the top. There is no visible reason for his instantaneous success. A ludicrous dialogue occurs between him and one of the ancient climbers already encamped on the summit. The altitude is too great for them to hear the applause below. The view is pleasant—they can see almost the whole picture—but it all looks alike. There is, the old man says, " 'naught here to climb for . . . nor aught anywhere else, either. They'd as well climb mountains as sit still and die.' " Ebenezer decides to jump off. " 'No reason why you oughtn't, nor any why ye ought,' " says the old man. Ebenezer stops, sighs, and says that it all looks frightfully empty. The reply is " 'Empty indeed . . . but there's naught o' good or bad in that. Why sigh?' " " 'Why not?' " asks Ebenezer, and that begins another of those circular interchanges on the theme of "Why?"[45]

The theme of the book—that the universe is always ambivalent —is expanded in countless ways. One of the most important is that Ebenezer and Anna are twins, a fact which leads Burlingame into long rhetorical exercises on the mythic symbolism of twin-ship and its implications of universal polarity. Which pole is which is not a thing that man can know. Burlingame demonstrates to Ebenezer that all assertions, even the existence of *thee* and *me,* are acts of faith, impossible to verify empirically. Ebenezer grudgingly admits this and says in anguish, " 'Marry, your discourse hath robbed me of similes: I know of naught immutable and sure!' " Burlingame answers, " ' 'Tis the first step on the road to Heaven. . . .' " Ebenezer replies, " 'or haply 'tis the road to Hell.' " Burlingame cocks his eyebrows and says, " ' 'Tis the same road, or good Dante is a liar.' "[46] This primary ambivalence is the problem that Goat-Boy faces, and his mission is nothing less than to save the world.

Giles Goat-Boy is Barth's monumental re-creation of myth. All of the allegorical elements in it have exact counterparts in the real world, which is, first of all, represented in the allegory as being divided into East Campus and West Campus. Each of the campuses is controlled by a huge computer complex that symbolizes the twentieth-century military-industrial-political-educational-social monolith. The western computer is WESCAC (West Campus Automatic Computer). That Barth should choose a gigantic computer as the metaphor for the twentieth-century monolith is natural precisely because this monolith is becoming computerized. Thus Barth's metaphor is not fabulous; it is a matter of constantly increasing factuality in the real world. WESCAC has assumed the role of the God of Biblical text. The book itself is a readout from the computer; its subtitle is "The Revised New Syllabus."

Goat-Boy is led to believe that he is born of a virgin mother and fathered by the computer, and it is the computer which issues his enigmatic mission along with a list of impossible subassignments "*To Be Done At Once, In No Time.*" The subassignments include "*End the Boundary Dispute*" (solve the conflicts between East and West) and "*Overcome Your Infirmity*" (cure your goatlike gimpiness and/or your inherent fallibility). His ultimate mission is spelled out on a circular device divided into quarters, each quarter containing one of the words of the phrase "PASS ALL FAIL ALL."[47] It could also read, of course, "ALL PASS ALL FAIL," "FAIL ALL PASS ALL," or "ALL FAIL ALL PASS." Robert Scholes has made a suggestive allusion in praising the book: "we have got our sacred book now. In the midst of our tribulations *Giles Goat-Boy* has slouched toward Buffalo to be born. Hallelujah!"[48] With this, Scholes has hinted that the figure of Goat-Boy is ambiguous in the traditional way, just as is Yeats's anti-Christ and, as well, the New Testament Christ who taught that only faith, not evidence, proves God. Goat-Boy's problem is not only to find the tests for truth and justice but to find the tests which will prove that he is what he believes he is: the new Grand Tutor, the savior of the world. Goat-Boy's quest for his identity begins when he is still the famous Ag-Hill Goat-Boy—he has been raised with the goats on the Campus farm. Barth has thus given his protagonist a point from which to view the real world—or the book's metaphorically real world—in all its absurdities (a traditional satiric device). Goat-Boy at first does not suspect that he might be the Grand Tutor, but things keep happening to suggest his uniqueness. It is Max, his foster father, who finally decides that the legendary indicators point to Goat-Boy as a savior. When Goat-Boy himself becomes convinced that he may be the Grand Tutor, he leaves the farm and begins his quest.

What Goat-Boy learns in his long and arduous journey of exposure to the world is that things cannot be differentiated, even by him who may be the Grand Tutor. He learns, very rapidly, that all those who would guide him along the way are either deliberately misleading, blind, or ignorant. Harold Bray, apparently the anti-Grand Tutor, is the most enigmatic of these guides. Maurice Stoker is another whose ambiguity confuses what ought to be for Goat-Boy an easy definition process. Stoker appears to be Satanic; he is in charge of the Inferno underneath the Campus and leads a pack of Hell's Angels on motorcycles. Goat-Boy no sooner decides that Stoker, at least, is one who can be passed or failed than he discovers that Stoker has his good side. There are mitigating circumstances in even the devil's case.

Goat-Boy is not the first Grand-Tutorlike personage to walk the Campus; the earliest was Enos Enoch, who is allegorically parallel to the first Christ (Christians are Enochists). Goat-Boy has heard of or read about others. Max is Jewish and could be the foster father of a Grand Tutor or, because he is eventually shafted (crucified) by being burned on a phalluslike shaft, could be a Grand Tutor himself. (He is also an exile, having been repudiated by the scientific community for his unorthodox studies.) That the pattern of Christ's life can be figured over and over without the world's ever being able to recognize the true Christ (as it cannot recognize any immutable abstract morality) is the book's basic joke. The crucifixion occurs continually; the Messiah is never realized. When Harold Bray appears, his imitation of Grand Tutorship is indistinguishable to the world from one that would indicate the true Grand Tutor. As in traditional Christian allegory, Harold Bray is an instrument for assuring through his opposition that Goat-Boy will function as a savior. Also as in tradition, it is impossible to tell if the anti-Grand Tutor is on Stoker's side or is an emissary from the Founder (God). But it works the other way, too; Harold Bray depends for recognition as Grand Tutor upon the possibility that Goat-Boy can appear to be the anti-Grand Tutor. Goat-Boy's faith in his own genuineness is shaken by contradictory events. First Harold Bray works against him, then appears to help him through difficult stages in his quest, such as his passage through the computer and rebirth out of it—a journey never accomplished by mortal and reserved by legend for the real Grand Tutor. Finally, Goat-Boy, Harold Bray, the Campus, and the reader are all left in the dark as to the identity of the true

Grand Tutor. If the reader decides it is Goat-Boy, then he has achieved an act of pure Goat-Boyian faith.

Max is the first character in the book to introduce the concept of a world in which differentiation is impossible. Max's synthesis of his notorious studies (which comprehend all fields) has yielded a cyclic-organic-relativistic view of the cosmos. Not only by analogy but in reality, all things are part of and reflections of the primary cycle of the universe. Even if the primary cycle is not observable, the secondary cycles always are, and they in turn suggest symbolically and analogically that the primary cycle does exist. Max's view levels all distinctions and fuses the cycles into one set of motions which is in turn one motion. His conclusion is not simply "ontogeny recapitulates phylogeny," although the lives of men do resemble in microcosm the life of man. This is just one cycle in the set and in turn encompasses as one of its own set the Grand Tutor cycle. Max sees an even broader law: "ontogeny recapitulates cosmogeny"—the cycles in any event reflect The Cosmic Cycle. Max is also the world's only scholar of Mathematical-Psycho-Proctology. A variation of his law of Cyclology reads "proctoscopy repeats hagiography"—the study of the processes visible through the anus is one and the same as the study of the lives of saints.[49] All cycles, small and large, specific and general, anatomical and mythic, are the same. To say that the life of ascension to salvation is inseparable as process from an exploration of the rectum is a grand joke. That it is a joke does not reduce the theme of cyclic unity to insignificance. Ours is creative laughter as well as ironic. Max's view is simple transcendental organicism, and the notion that all life is one life, when fully recognized, is funny as well as awesome. Barth both satirizes and supports it. Walt Whitman said that a mouse is miracle enough, and he kept his parts as clean as his mouth. Henry David Thoreau saw one Law in the rank dead horse, the melting sandbanks, and the strong and beautiful bug gnawing its way out of an applewood table. Fishing, he caught the universe in a horned pout. To say both *yea* and *nay* is what the ambivalence of the universe demands of the creative mind.

Thus Goat-Boy's earliest education, received at Max's knee, points towards fusion and not differentiation. But, as he seeks

(2 3 3

his status as Grand Tutor, he is introduced to more and more methodology for differentiation. He acquires a walking stick equipped with lenses for reflection and magnification; it is not very helpful in determining who will pass and who will fail. He talks with all the great minds of his society to find that all are narrowly obsessed with a single point of view. In one scene, Goat-Boy watches a play—*Taliped Decanus*—which exposes him for the first time to the dilemma of the fall. (The play is, incidentally, not only a splendid parody of *Oedipus* but a remarkably complete satire on the way everyone reads *Oedipus*.) One of his highly educated friends points out to him that " 'We all flunked with the first two students in the Botanical Garden . . . we're committed to Knowledge of the Campus. . . .' "50 It is certain revelation from somewhere beyond the Campus that Goat-Boy needs, and all that he gets from WESCAC is ambiguity.

The language, the metaphors, and the sheer bulk of the allegorical patterns of this book are in themselves hilarious. Goat-Boy's quest is inextricably woven into all the ludicrous motions of any individual life and the whole life of man. His experience is cyclic. Philosophical searching, symbolic mastering of the steps to Graduation, social and sexual intercourse—all are displayed in their seriousness and their hilarity, but above all in their endless circularity. Ultimately, since Goat-Boy's mission and his identity remain ambiguous, the book must end ambiguously. On the one hand, it ends tragically because Goat-Boy does not succeed in reprograming WESCAC to make a better Campus or in proving himself to be the Grand Tutor. On the other, it ends comically because, with a grim smile, he gimps bravely forward to meet his persecutors and leaves behind the record of his adventures as a message to the world. He exits at age thirty-three and a third (naturally), remarking as he closes, "Passed, but not forgotten, I shall rest."51 The joke of that line lies in its style, its punning allusiveness, and its expansive significance: the cycle continues forever.

One of the manifestations of the polarity expressed by the theme of *Giles Goat-Boy* is the two major attempts Goat-Boy makes during his quest to solve the mystery of his assignment. If he could do it, of course, he would actually be the Grand Tutor, the One who can judge the difference between the Passed and the

Failed. Barth is implying throughout that the question of salvation has always been a mystery to Christendom precisely because causes and effects cannot be traced in all their indefiniteness and circularity, and because men inside a situation cannot tell where that situation is placed on some supernatural scale of justice. Goat-Boy's first effort is an attempt to be logical and categorical about who shall fail and who shall pass. He first tries to divide humanity into elect and damned, basing his choices on the evidence of behavior and immediately perceivable results. He finds that men and events are so complicated he will never be able to make such decisions. What he sees as results are only appearances and beneath these appearances he finds continuing contradictions, all of which are further appearances hiding further contradictions.

His second try takes the form of a modern variety of benevolent and all-forgiving Christianity (or Enochism) extended to its logical end. The satire against this benevolence is the darkest of all, since it works against Max's cosmic view as well. Having discovered that morality is relative, Goat-Boy decides to pass all and fail none. This is the ultimate absurd equalization founded on an arbitrary logic: all things are equal and compensatory and all processes level out to a simple neutral *is;* therefore, nothing can be bad; therefore, whatever is, is good. The result of this decision is both terrible and funny. The Chancellor (president) of West Campus takes Goat-Boy's new philosophy to heart and puts it into action. An amnesty frees all criminals and psychopaths. The result of the activation of Goat-Boy's organic-cosmic-cyclic-relativistic view is chaos. Ultimately, Goat-Boy's comedy and his tragedy are that he fails to discover in all of mankind's knowledge and in his own inner resources any way to know absolute moral truth or to decide that a relativistic view can yield a goodness to substitute for salvation.

Neither is there any middle way. Goat-Boy sees the cosmic joke. Of the ambiguous Pass-Fail message he says: "That circular device on my Assignment-sheet—beginningless, endless, infinite equivalence—constricted my reason like a torture-tool from the Age of Faith. Passage *was* Failure, and Failure Passage; yet Passage was Passage, Failure Failure! Equally true, none was the Answer; the two were not different, neither were they the same;

and *true* and *false,* and *same* and *different*—Unspeakable! Unnamable! Unimaginable! Surely my mind must crack!"[52] As long as there is continuation—as long as the world revolves in its cosmological cycles—there is no way to differentiate what is well and what is ill. All Goat-Boy can do is recognize that some knowledge not available to us may resolve the question; when the cycles end, when Commencement Day arrives, then the distinctions will be made known. On the other hand, that resolution will also be the end. There is no way out of the bind except cheerfully and nihilistically to say both *yea* and *nay.* In her senility, Goat-Boy's gentle and funny mother mixes old aphorisms and delivers beautiful paradoxical prophecies. In one such splendid combination, she unwittingly defines the only possible ultimate answer to the absurd dilemma. This is her favorite axiom, her quiet statement of faith, her reassurance to her son that everything will balance out. Goat-Boy records: " 'All's fair that ends well,' Mother murmured to the air."[53]

VIII

A Heritage of Corpses

> *" 'Son,' my father said to me, 'some-*
> *day this will all be yours.' "*
>
> PHILIP CASTLE

I · CREATION ON THE RUN

THE QUESTION of whether or not arbitrary creation can counter an awareness of the absurd is continuously raised in both comic and serious American literature. On the one hand, logic and experience dictate withdrawal; on the other, an inner strength of spirit or a deep sense of humor demands an affirmation of life. Nihilism and cheerfulness ought not to co-exist but do. In many American books, humor cancels nihilism. But in others which are still essentially funny—Pynchon's *V* or Vonnegut's *Slaughterhouse Five*, for example—humor sharpens the grimness without canceling it. Still others leave the reader dangling, incapable of defining his own response. Such books escape total nihilism only because they are funny and are thus an affirmative act by the author himself.

The emphasis in the age of Melville was on positive creation rather than nihilism, comic or serious. Novels from that age commonly end with a protagonist still creating alternatives to resignation or suicide. Melville's stories are often dominated by comic nihilism (as is *Billy Budd*) or total ambiguity (as is *The Confidence-Man*), but there is, especially in the early books and in the theme of Queequeg's and Ishmael's creativity, a deep insistence on some stable and eternal truth. Ishmael clearly recognizes the comedy of the absurd: "There are certain queer times and occasions in this strange mixed affair we call life when a man takes this whole universe for a vast practical joke, though the wit thereof he but dimly discerns, and more than suspects that the joke is at nobody's expense but his own."[1] But Ishmael also believes in an insular Tahiti, a center of calm within himself.

Melville's contemporaries were less inclined than he was to see the cosmic joke in all its implications and were more consistently and seriously hopeful about positive creation. Emerson defined the comic as that which deviated from the ideal. The ideal was true, and Man Thinking would be able to tap the ideal, discovering and avoiding the comedy of half-truth. Thoreau was more ironic; under those inspiring rhythms of *A Week* and *Walden* one senses an awareness that the river, the woods, and the pond just possibly would not yield meaning unless one labeled them meaningful. Nature had no questions—she was herself an answer —so why endeavor in vain for any other explanation? He went instead to his morning work. This was brilliant comic logic of the same cut as Franklin's codfish rationale. But Thoreau was not a humorist, and he challenges his readers directly and seriously.

Hawthorne worked in both the serious and comic modes to demonstrate the efficacy of creative action. Hester Prynne's resolution is to be taken seriously, and Dimmesdale's failure is tragic (in spite of the modern reader's inclination to laugh when Dimmesdale opens his coat to display whatever it is underneath). When Hester declares that her adultery has a consecration of its own, when she calls for action instead of resignation, and when she labors to make the letter symbolize what she wants it to symbolize, she is being absurdly creative but not comic. Hers is the victory of work, which Hawthorne seriously offers as the solution to uncertainty. The instances of absurd humor which appear in Hawthorne occur most often in stories about creators whose attempts to create fail ludicrously or yield a grotesque result. These distortions are functions of a ludicrousness or grotesqueness which characterizes the creator's heart and mind. Rappaccini is comic as well as horrifying, fighting evil with evil. His is a noble effort in its way, but Hawthorne magnifies the inherent paradox of the attempt: fighting poison with poison makes Rappaccini the poisoner. Aylmer's meddling is of the same sort; in trying to create perfection he annihilates a nearly perfect reality. The humor of "Rappaccini's Daughter" and "The Birthmark" is a humor of the grotesque. The comedy of *The Blithedale Romance* is the comedy of ludicrous failure. The people who gather at Blithedale are supposedly creative, perceptive, and capable of love. They comically and miserably fail at the most essential task of all, the creation of community. But Hawthorne was not an absurd comedian, even though his sense of the absurd shows clearly. His point of view is comparable to Jonathan Edwards's: what is absurd in the world is that which deviates from our knowledge of rightness. The comedy of *The Blithedale Romance* is Emersonian; its satire is corrective. It focuses on the failure to achieve the true; its characters achieve what Emerson called in "The Comic" that "well-intended halfness."

Walt Whitman was a total absurdist or a total comedian, but his comedy does not arise out of nihilism. The opposite is true; to Whitman, the whole universe was an exhilarating joke. If its grotesques are reflections of the cosmic joke, the cosmic joke is in turn the same thing as the cosmic hope. Whitman, whose life and works exemplify free creation on the run, saw the universe as both beautifully funny and perfectly complete: confronted by anger and death, he would "let up again to feel the puzzle of puzzles, / And that we call Being" (*Song of Myself*, section 26).

After Melville, the next great master of the ambiguous style is Henry James. There is deep humor in James, the character of which is so elusive that terms like "tragicomic" or "serious humor" do not approach descriptiveness. It has properly been called a strange alloy, an interdependence of tragedy and comedy.[2] Some exceptionally brave and perceptive characters—Maggie Verver, Christopher Newman, Lambert Strether, Isabel Archer—struggle to create victories out of defeat. James recommended absurd creation: to Edith Wharton he wrote, " 'Only sit tight yourself *and go through the movements of life*. That keeps up our connection with life—I mean of the immediate and apparent life;

behind which, all the while, the deeper and darker and unapparent, in which things *really* happen to us, learns, under that hygiene, to stay in its place.' "[3] He saw complex connections between humor and the absurd. (For the New York Edition of *Wings of the Dove*, James twice changed the word "funny" to "absurd."[4]) In his characters' tiny, seemingly indifferent gestures, in his plots' apparently trivial incidents, crossings, and meetings, lie the enormous meanings and paradoxes that afflict us all. His is the difficult comedy of the complete ambiguity of the scene before us.

Huckleberry Finn set the example for the modern hero or non-hero in twentieth-century American humorous fiction: always open is the choice to run from an intolerable absurd situation in the hope of finding a tolerable one. As long as a protagonist lives to run, the humor of his book is never entirely bleak. Only two fliers survive Colonel Cathcart's insane manipulations of catches one through twenty-two, Yossarian and Orr. Orr, the meticulous Franklinian man, ditches his airplane in the sea (he's been practicing the maneuver throughout the book) and rows to Sweden. Yossarian, having learned that war and Cathcart cannot change, exits *Catch-22* running. To be sure, the action of running is no final solution: just behind him in hot pursuit is Nately's whore, her knife flashing. But Yossarian lives, and Yossarian will get to Sweden. Chief Bromden, liberated by the Christ-like courage of McMurphy, runs from the Cuckoo's Nest toward the mountains and rivers of his tribe's idyllic land. Kesey's rhetoric is clear: Bromden can escape The Combine's asylum, that world most inmates take to be the norm.

Some of the major novelists of this century whose characters find alternatives to despair display an absurd sense without humor or humor without an absurd sense. Steinbeck was an example of the latter. Some of his books are genuinely funny, and in *East of Eden* the sense of humor is equated with true creativity: the best character, Samuel Hamilton, is a funny and eccentric genius. But Steinbeck's books always imply a nonabsurd solution to difficulties that are absurd only in context. The Okies starve in California in the midst of plenty, and, while that is absurd, it is not presented as mankind's condition but as a function of the greed of landowners and banks. The absurdity is limited and theoretically solvable. Ernest Hemingway displayed an absurd sense without humor. Jake Barnes, Robert Jordan, Frederick Henry—all have moments when meaninglessness is a certainty. Usually Hemingway's characters defy the absurd in a way most closely resembling the futile struggle of armless Enceladus. Jordan prepares to die fighting. Catherine, helpless in the face of death, says simply, " 'I just hate it.' " Santiago is crushed by the sharks but thinks of new ways to fight when he goes fishing again.

Santiago's story, while containing little intentional humor, is a parable of absurd confidence. Santiago alone decides values in a neutral universe. He calls the sea by its feminine name, he seeks the marlin with deliberation, he chooses his adversaries and his brothers. In such ways, he gives form to the entire quest. There is one hint that Santiago is fully aware that he is creating his world in the face of annihilating forces, not accepting a pattern inherent in it. He and Manolin talk about eating rich food and catching bait even though he has nothing to eat and no net to cast. We are told that they go through this fiction every day. It is a ritual of confidence. (Compare the Colonel's remark in *Across the River and into the Trees*: "Every day is a new and fine illusion."[5]) Santiago says repeatedly that a fisherman needs confidence to catch fish. The confidence that is a theme of *The Old Man and the Sea* is not arbitrary, however. It is always tied to some concrete quality, usually a combination of physical power and native shrewdness. The old man does know how to catch great fish, and the eighty-four fishless days are the result of bad luck, not bad fishing. " 'Have faith in the Yankees, my son,' " he says; " 'Think of the great DiMaggio.' " As long as the DiMaggio has the strength to hit, the Yankees will win. This faith must abide, or the spur in the heel and the age of the fisherman will overcome the spirit as well as the life of the creative hero.

Absurd humor and an implied or overt solution to the absurd dilemma are combined in the work of several major living authors, chief among them J. D. Salinger and Saul Bellow.[6] Salinger's protagonists learn that the normal world is the absurd world, and in response they often discover some unique mode of life to counter absurdity. Seymour's resistance paradoxically takes the form of absurd acceptance. His suicide does not seem nihilistic but somehow consistent with his belief in the continuity and interconnectivity of all things in the universe. As a God-knower he can never be separate from God. Franny and Zooey learn, through their ludicrous telephone dialogue, that a solution to the frantic and hellish world outside the Glass apartment lies in a self-created image, a self-determined role as God's and man's actress and actor.

Bellow's Henderson is a con man on the run, but that does not make the book appear to have a strong motif of confidence. Rather, it is *Herzog* in which one can find an overriding transcendental resolution. Herzog is comic and absurd, totally aware of his and man's condition. On a ship lost in fog on the Gulf of Mexico, in front of an open radio microphone for all the fleet (which he can't find) to hear, Herzog utters a crystalline declaration of the absurd dilemma: " 'We're lost! Fucked!' " He is a man "longing for grace, but escaping headlong from his salvation." Finally, however, in the midst of pastoral intensity (blue, white, and green hills; birdsong), at rest, alone, Herzog experiences "—something, something, happiness . . . 'Thou movest me.' "[7] For Herzog, the answer lies within; the creation of life begins with the end of running.

2 · THE GIGGLE IN THE JUNGLE

The more startling absurd humor of modern American fiction is without declared hope. In this literature—and "grim humor" barely begins to describe it—humor offsets and emphasizes nihilism without canceling it. The last decade or two has marked the flowering of this kind of cheerful nihilism in American fiction (as well as in the cinema), and the popular lexicon includes the terms "black humor," "absurdist comedy," and "the grotesquely real." J. P. Donleavy chronicled the saddest summer of Samuel S. and thereby produced a dark comedy based on the paradox of the growth of disintegration. And Bellow, who has portrayed a Herzog capable of finding grace, also drew Joseph of *Dangling Man,* a nonhero dangling from the paradox of freedom. Joseph finds that freedom somehow cancels being since being demands definition and definition negates freedom—a humorous paradox at which no one chuckles. Thomas Pynchon's V yields a fine recurring metaphor for the busy meaningless universe: the yo-yo.[8] Donald Barthelme's well-loved Snow White waits for an American prince who will never come; all she gains in her fairy tale is the certain knowledge that hers is a story of loss. Richard Brautigan has reflected the decay of American history in a number of compact, funny books, chief among them *Trout Fishing in America* (which is and is not about trout fishing). One of his characters exits a chapter "looking for America, often only a place in the mind," and another records an all-time fishing record: 2,231 trout hooked; 2,231 trout lost, a seven-year average of 13.9 trout lost for each of 160 fishing trips.[9] The American trout (rainbow, of course) eludes the Adamic fisherman forever. And finally, as Philip Roth's Portnoy complains, laughter itself is painful, for it is always the laughter of the victim of the joke: "Doctor, *please,* I can't live any more in a world given its meaning and dimension by some vulgar nightclub clown. By some—some *black humorist!* . . . The macabre is very funny on the stage— but not to live it, thank you!"[10]

The humor of loss is the humor of our time, but it is not a new humor in America, as a study of the early frontier humorists demonstrates. One finds grim humor based on a sense of the absurd throughout other kinds of American fiction, too—a touch of it in Charles Brockden Brown or in John Neal; a lot of it in Ellen Glasgow or Nathanael West. In Poe the real and the distorted are combined in such a way that horror becomes not so much the quality of the supernatural as of the real; the modern reader of Poe wakes to find that distortion is the norm. In 1969, this equation is echoed by Joyce Carol Oates in a note accompanying review copies of *Them*: " 'Gothicism, whatever it is, is not a literary tradition so much as a fairly realistic assessment of modern life.' "[11] The humor of those who are labeled literary humorists— from George Horatio Derby and Artemus Ward through James Thurber and S. J. Perelman—is laced with a sense of peril. In Thurber we find a touchstone: "the claw of the sea-puss gets us all in the end."[12] Ours is the age of the fulfillment of what R. W. B. Lewis has called the apocalyptic mood in fiction; ours are the "Days of Wrath and Laughter."[13]

Kurt Vonnegut, Jr., is the present master of the simple and direct black joke. His ambiguities are reduced to a fundamental few; his tragedy and laughter are based on the absurd recognition that life means death. In *Cat's Cradle*, Philip Castle tells the narrator about the great plague of San Lorenzo, recalling the stacks and stacks of bodies that piled up outside and inside his father's jungle hospital:

"It was all we could do to find a live patient to treat. In bed after bed we found dead people.

"And Father started giggling," Castle continued.

"He couldn't stop. He walked out into the night with his flashlight. He was still giggling. He was making the flashlight beam dance over all the dead people stacked outside. He put his hand on my head, and do you know what that marvelous man said to me?" asked Castle.

"Nope."

" 'Son,' my father said to me, 'someday this will all be yours.' "[14]

This is an emblematic joke, one of the keenest to be found anywhere in American literature. Mankind's inheritance is a heritage of death. The capacity to giggle is not a capacity to annihilate death; it is man's echo of death. The giggle in the jungle proves to us that the cosmic joke is our own invention after all.

The subtleties and involuted ambiguities to be found in John Barth's extended investigation of the comedy of absurd creation are not to be found in Vonnegut, so that defiance in *Cat's Cradle* is as simple and direct as is the pattern of despair. Bokonon, the inventor of religious and civil tension in San Lorenzo (and thus the inventor of meaning where life is patently meaningless), recommends arbitrary action. He knows that the drama men pretend soon becomes (for better or worse) the only reality that is. The reader of *Cat's Cradle* finds himself laughing over the end of the world: a grand *ah-whoom* and all moisture is turned into ice-nine. Is there anything for the handful of doomed survivors to do? Bokonon writes as the final piece of advice in his *Books:* "If I were a younger man, I would write a history of human stupidity; and I would climb to the top of Mount McCabe and lie down on my back with my history for a pillow; and I would take from the ground some of the blue-white poison that makes statues of men; and I would make a statue of myself, lying on my back, grinning horribly, and thumbing my nose at You Know Who."[15]

That defiance is as old as art. What proves increasingly difficult —yet ever more necessary—is the act of inventing confidence in the saving grace of that horrible grin.

N O T E S

WHENEVER POSSIBLE, chapter numbers in parentheses follow the page numbers cited for quoted passages. Thus the reader may refer to any edition of the works discussed.

I · *The American Sisyphus*

1. Albert Camus, *The Myth of Sisyphus and Other Essays*, trans. Justin O'Brien (New York, 1955 [Vintage Book]), p. 90. French equivalents are given when needed from the Librairie Gallimard edition (1942).

2. Ibid., p. 2.

3. Ibid., p. 22.

4. Ibid., p. 27

5. When I wish to avoid the ambiguity, I use the term "creator of the absurd," but I generally prefer to retain the term and its ambiguity.

6. Camus, p. 41.

7. Ibid., p. 69.

8. Ibid., p. 51.

9. Ibid., pp. 69-70.

10. Ibid., p. 5.

11. Ibid., p. 6.

12. Camus, Librairie Gallimard edition, p. 74.

13. Bruce Jay Friedman, ed., *Black Humor* (New York, 1965 [Bantam Book]), pp. vii-xi.

II · *Faith and Confidence: American Solutions*

1. Michael Wigglesworth, *The Day of Doom*, ed. Kenneth B. Murdock (New York, 1966 [reissue of 1929 edition]). Stanza numbers are cited in text.

2. A concise and accurate analysis of the Great Awakening in its his-

torical context is the introduction to *The Great Awakening*, eds. Alan Heimert and Perry Miller (Indianapolis and New York, 1967).

3. Cf. Perry Miller, *The New England Mind: From Colony to Province* (Cambridge, Mass., 1953 [reissue of 1939 edition]), p. 227.

4. See Norman S. Grabo, *Edward Taylor* (New Haven, Conn., 1961), pp. 31-39.

5. The scene is included in the acting edition of the play (1954) as Act II, Scene 1. See also Miller's note to the appendix of the Bantam paperback edition (New York, 1967). Not all printings of the Bantam edition contain the appendix, which includes Miller's note and the deleted scene.

6. Quoted in Ola Elizabeth Winslow, *Jonathan Edwards* (New York, 1940), p. 139.

7. The most complete version of "Of Insects" is in the *Andover Review,* XIII (1890), 5-13, but a more often cited version is in *The Works of President Edwards*, ed. Sereno E. Dwight, I (New York, 1829), 23-28 (omitted in some later editions). A most convenient reprinting is in Ola Winslow's edition, *Jonathan Edwards: Basic Writings* (New York, 1966 [Signet Classic]) hereafter cited as *Basic Writings*; this quotation is p. 37. The first edition of Dwight is not universally available, and later editions are differently arranged. Here, page numbers refer specifically to Winslow's more available text, and general references are made to the first edition of Dwight for readers who have it available. Edwards's *Freedom of the Will* has, of course, appeared in the Yale edition.

8. Edwards, *Basic Writings*, pp. 92-93; the personal narratives are in Dwight, I, 58-62, 64-67, 98-99, 131-36.

9. Edwards, "The Soul," *Basic Writings*, pp. 44-45. Winslow's text retains manuscript spelling and is from E. C. Smyth, "Some Early Writings of Jonathan Edwards, A.D. 1714-1726," *Proceedings of the American Antiquarian Society*, N.S., X (1895), 237-47.

10. Jonathan Edwards, *Freedom of the Will*, ed. Paul Ramsey (New Haven and London, 1957), p. 333.

11. Edwards, *Basic Writings*, pp. 46-47; Winslow's source is Smyth. The title was not Edwards's but was added by later editors. Edward Davidson has demonstrated other uses of Edwards's use of the logic of absurdity but has pointed out that Edwards always accepted Scripture as irrefutable and not subject to absurd reasoning; "From Locke to Edwards," *Journal of the History of Ideas*, XXIV (July-September, 1963), 369 and n. 21.

12. Edwards, *Basic Writings*, pp. 66-67; Winslow's text is from Dwight, I, 114-15.

13. Benjamin Franklin, *Autobiography*, eds. Leonard W. Labaree, Ralph L. Ketcham, Helen C. Boatfield, and Helene H. Fineman (New Haven and London, 1964), p. 58.

14. Cotton Mather, *Essays to Do Good*, American Tract Society (Boston, 1710), pp. 86-90. These passages are discussed by Alfred Whitney Gris-

wold in an excellent analysis of the paradoxical relationship between Franklin's materialism and Mather's rationalizations in "Three Puritans on Prosperity," *The New England Quarterly*, VII (September, 1934), 475-93.

15. Franklin, *Autobiography*, p. 150.

16. Ibid., p. 159.

17. Ibid., p. 168. The controversy over Hemphill among the Philadelphia Presbyterians occurred during the years 1734-1735.

18. Ibid., p. 235. Franklin practiced the artificial construction of religious appearances many times during his career. Cf. Alfred O. Aldridge's chapter, "Religion by Hoax," in *Benjamin Franklin and Nature's God* (Durham, N.C., 1967).

19. Franklin, *Autobiography*, pp. 156-57.

20. After Francis Franklin's death, Franklin published a newspaper announcement that the boy had not been inoculated; rumors had been circulating that the boy died from inoculation; ibid., p. 170 and n. 9.

21. Ibid., pp. 87-88.

III · *From the Absurd Frontier*

1. Cf. the description of southwestern subjects in Franklin J. Meine, *Tall Tales of the Southwest* (New York, 1930), p. xxvi.

2. Many scholars of southwestern and southern humor have discussed the problem of the pseudonym, but a good summary is in Hennig Cohen and William B. Dillingham, eds., *Humor of the Old Southwest* (Boston, 1964), pp. xi-xii. Note: Cohen and Dillingham stated that contributors "rarely" included actors, artists, and army officers. Actually, the leading journal of the genre, the *Spirit of the Times*, received contributions from a large number of actors, some artists, and literally scores of army officers; see Norris W. Yates, *William T. Porter and the Spirit of the Times* (Baton Rouge, 1957), and Richard Boyd Hauck, "The Literary Content of the New York *Spirit of the Times*, 1831-1856," unpublished dissertation (Urbana, 1965).

3. *Spirit of the Times*, XXVI (March 8, 1856), 48.

4. Bernard DeVoto, *Mark Twain's America* (Cambridge, Mass., 1960 [reprint of 1932 edition]), pp. 55-57.

5. Edmund Wilson, "Poisoned," *New Yorker*, XXXI (May 7, 1955), 138-42; reprinted in *Patriotic Gore* (New York, 1962).

6. John Q. Anderson has identified "Madison Tensas" and written his biography. Included in the volume with the biography is a modern reprinting of Lewis's works, and this edition is the one hereafter cited as *Writings*; *Louisiana Swamp Doctor: The Life and Writings of Henry Clay Lewis* (Baton Rouge, 1962). Lewis died in August, 1850. His sketches

were published in the *Spirit of the Times* between 1845 and 1850 and collected as *Odd Leaves from the Life of a Louisiana Swamp Doctor* (Philadelphia, 1850).

7. Lewis, "The Curious Widow," *Writings*, pp. 116-21.

8. Lewis, *Writings*, pp. 89-91.

9. Ibid., pp. 152-53.

10. Ibid., p. 156.

11. Lewis, "The City Physician versus the Swamp Doctor," *Writings*, p. 189.

12. See Anderson in *Writings*, p. 57.

13. John S. Robb's story first appeared in the St. Louis *Reveille* of December 9, 1844, was reprinted in the *Spirit of the Times* of January 18, 1845, and was collected in William T. Porter, ed., *The Big Bear of Arkansas* (Philadelphia, 1845). Convenient reprintings are in Cohen and Dillingham, *Humor of the Old Southwest*, pp. 143-45, and an appendix to John Francis McDermott's edition of Robb's *Streaks of Squatter Life, and Far-West Scenes* (Gainesville, 1962). McDermott's is a facsimile of the story as it appears in *The Big Bear of Arkansas*. Note: AMS Press, Inc., has issued a reprint of Porter's collection (New York, 1968).

14. "The Fight" first appeared in Augustus Baldwin Longstreet's *Georgia Scenes* (Augusta, Ga., 1835); the modern edition is B. R. McElderry, Jr., ed. (New York, 1957), pp. 42-53. It is also reprinted in Cohen and Dillingham's anthology.

15. Cf. Longstreet, "The Horse-Swap" and "The Gander Pulling," *Georgia Scenes*, pp. 14-21, 97-105.

16. Jesse Bier, *The Rise and Fall of American Humor* (New York, Chicago, and San Francisco, 1968), p. 61.

17. Longstreet, *Georgia Scenes*, p. 53.

18. This yarn was collected in T. A. Burke, ed., *Polly Peablossom's Wedding* (Philadelphia, 1851). Convenient modern reprintings are in Meine, *Tall Tales;* Walter Blair, *Native American Humor* (San Francisco, 1960 [reprint of 1937 edition]); and Cohen and Dillingham, pp. 134-36. I have followed Cohen and Dillingham's text.

19. Blair, *Native American Humor*, p. 517.

20. Ibid., p. 268.

21. Ibid., pp. 272-73.

22. James Kirke Paulding's play, *The Lion of the West*, lost for a century, was discovered and edited by James N. Tidwell (Stanford, Calif., 1954). Quotations are pp. 54-55.

23. Told by DeVoto, *Mark Twain's America*, p. 149. DeVoto wrote, "Tall talk, in 'But a shotgun lets me out,' acquires the sharp edge of realism that is the West's manner."

24. The yarn is told in *A Tramp Abroad;* see Samuel Clemens, *The Writings of Mark Twain*, III (New York, 1907), pp. 15-22.

25. Thomas Bangs Thorpe's story appeared in the *Spirit of the Times*, XI (March 27, 1841), and was collected in the Porter anthology of the

same name and an anthology of Thorpe's sketches entitled *The Hive of "The Bee-Hunter"* (New York, 1854). Convenient modern reprintings are in Meine, *Tall Tales;* Blair, *Native American Humor;* and Cohen and Dillingham's anthology. I cite Blair's reprinting, which has kept the spelling of the Porter collection (especially "bar" for "bear"). My analysis of Thorpe's yarn is initially dependent upon Walter Blair's excellent reading, "The Technique of 'The Big Bear of Arkansas,'" *Southwest Review*, XXVIII (Summer, 1943), 426-35. A modern study of Thorpe is Milton Rickels's *Thomas Bangs Thorpe* (Baton Rouge, 1962).

26. Blair, *Native American Humor*, pp. 337-40.

27. Ibid., pp. 343-45.

28. Ibid., pp. 347-48. The famous story of Captain Scott and the coon is a variation of an old tale. In it, a treed raccoon scoffs at a dog who tells him that several hunters are coming to shoot him. The raccoon knows that these hunters are poor shots. Then the dog tells him that Captain Scott is also coming, and the coon, who knows of Scott's reputation as a crack shot, rolls up in a ball, falls out of the tree, and gives up to the dog in the certainty that his life is over anyway. See Yates, *Porter and the Spirit*, pp. 170-72.

29. Blair, *Native American Humor*, p. 348.

30. William P. Hawes (whose pseudonym was "J. Cypress Jr.") is a leading example of the many fine tall tale and burlesque writers working in the 1830s and 1840s who were not from the South and Southwest. Traditional research in the genre of native humor has neglected a number of such regional authors, whose work can be found in almost any issue of a northern paper such as the *Spirit of the Times*. Hawes's stories were collected by Henry William Herbert ("Frank Forester") as *Sporting Scenes and Sundry Sketches; Being the Miscellaneous Writings of J. Cypress Jr.*, 2 vols. (New York, 1842). This collection is not widely available; I have cited the original *Spirit of the Times* appearances.

31. William P. Hawes, "A Shark Story," *Spirit of the Times*, XIV (November 16, 1844), 445, credited to the *American Turf Register* of February, 1840 (the latter publication was owned and edited at that time by Porter, also). The piece was reprinted in a collection of yarns designed as a companion to *The Big Bear of Arkansas*: William T. Porter, ed., *A Quarter Race in Kentucky* (Philadelphia, 1847).

32. William P. Hawes, "A Bear Story and No Mistake!" *Spirit of the Times*, X (October 17, 1840), 391, credited to the *Turf Register*.

33. Benjamin Franklin, "To the Editor of a Newspaper," Letter of May 20, 1765, in Albert Henry Smyth, *Writings*, IV (New York, 1907), 369.

34. The story of this hoax has been aptly told and analyzed by Alfred Owen Aldridge in a chapter which bears the enlightening title, "Religion by Hoax," in *Benjamin Franklin and Nature's God* (Durham, N.C., 1967), pp. 133-43.

35. Leslie Fiedler has pointed out that Smith's literary treatment of Pocahontas, liberal as it is, is relatively cynical when compared to the

vast number of variations upon her story that have grown up during all of American history (especially during the twentieth century). Fiedler's book is, of course, devoted to showing that this kind of creative madness is what defines the West; *The Return of the Vanishing American* (New York, 1968), p. 71.

36. Constance Rourke, *American Humor* (New York, 1931), p. 5.

37. See discussions of the confidence man as rascal in Kenneth Lynn, *Mark Twain and Southwestern Humor* (Boston and Toronto, 1959), pp. 73-86; Bier, *The Rise and Fall of American Humor*, passim; and Victor M. Hoar, "The Confidence Man in American Literature," unpublished dissertation (Urbana, 1965).

38. The book is in actuality rare, too; only one copy is extant. *Life and Public Services of An Army Straggler* was first published in Macon, Georgia, 1865, and has been edited for a modern edition by Floyd C. Watkins (Athens, Ga., 1961); cited hereafter as *Straggler*.

39. Warren, *Straggler*, p. 9. Warren also compared Billy and his kind to Longstreet's Ransy Sniffle. He saw both as deadly manipulators of other men—"minute men" who were not ready to fight, but " 'ready at a minute's warning' to shove other people into the scrape." See pp. 30-31.

40. Ibid., p. x.

41. Ibid., p. 27.

42. Ibid., p. 67.

43. Ibid., pp. 89-98.

44. Johnson Jones Hooper, *Some Adventures of Captain Simon Suggs* (Philadelphia, 1846), p. 12. Most of the important chapters from Hooper's book are in Cohen and Dillingham, *Humor of the Old Southwest*. I have cited the original edition, no scholarly modern edition being available. An excellent modern study of Hooper is W. Stanley Hoole's *Alias Simon Suggs* (University, Ala., 1952).

45. Hooper, *Simon Suggs*, pp. 13-24.

46. Ibid., pp. 21-29.

47. Ibid., pp. 12-13.

48. Ibid., pp. 85-87.

49. See Walter Blair, *Horse Sense in American Humor* (Chicago, 1942), p. 103; Robert Hopkins, "Simon Suggs: A Burlesque Campaign Biography," *American Quarterly*, XV (Fall, 1953), 459-63; and Lynn, *Mark Twain and Southwestern Humor*, p. 80.

50. Hooper, *Simon Suggs*, pp. 7-10.

51. George Washington Harris's book first appeared as *Sut Lovingood. Yarns Spun by a "Nat'ral Born Durn'd Fool"* (New York, 1867). The modern edition is in M. Thomas Inge, *Sut Lovingood's Yarns* (New Haven, Conn., 1966), hereafter *Yarns*; this quotation is from "Sicily Burns's Wedding," p. 77.

52. Harris, "Sut Lovingood's Daddy, Acting Horse," *Yarns*, p. 37.

53. Harris, "Sut Lovingood's Sermon," *Yarns*, p. 138. Cf. Cohen and

Dillingham, p. 156. According to Inge, positive reactions to Sut are more common among critics than negative ones; *Yarns*, p. 12.

54. Harris, "Mrs. Yardley's Quilting," *Yarns*, pp. 114-22.

55. As tempting as the idea is, I cannot go as far as Milton Rickels, who said that, through Sut, "Harris provided his readers a source of profound, if unrecognized, release for one of his community's feelings: the unutterable longing for the death of God"; *George Washington Harris* (New York, 1965), p. 86.

IV · *The Descent to Faith: Herman Melville*

1. Herman Melville, *White Jacket* (London, 1922), p. 136 (XXVI). I use the Constable edition of this book, *Redburn,* and *Mardi;* the Hendricks House edition of *Moby-Dick, Pierre,* and *The Confidence-Man;* the Northwestern-Newberry *Typee* and *Omoo* which are the first two volumes of the new scholarly edition of Melville's works; and the University of Chicago Press edition of *Billy Budd.*

2. Herman Melville, *The Confidence-Man: His Masquerade,* ed. Elizabeth S. Foster (New York, 1954), p. 1 (I).

3. Herman Melville, *Moby-Dick,* eds. Luther S. Mansfield and Howard P. Vincent (New York, 1952), p. 162 (XXXVI).

4. Albert Camus, *The Myth of Sisyphus and Other Essays,* trans. Justin O'Brien (New York, 1955 [Vintage Book]), p. 83.

5. Edward Rosenberry has drawn some tangible parallels between Melville's humor and the rough humor of the frontier in *Melville and the Comic Spirit* (Cambridge, Mass., 1955).

6. Herman Melville, *Typee,* eds. Harrison Hayford, Hershel Parker, G. Thomas Tanselle (Evanston and Chicago, 1968), p. 234 (XXXII).

7. Ibid., pp. 231-38 (XXXII).

8. Ibid., p. 173 (XXIV).

9. Melville did at times seem theoretically to prefer primitive, basic morality and living codes. But *Typee, Omoo,* and the portrait of Winsome in *The Confidence-Man* indicate that he was skeptical about the possibility of achieving ideal simplicity on earth. Lawrance Thompson has done a splendid job of tracing Melville's reaction to the confusions inherent in Calvinism, but I am here disagreeing with his contention that Melville idealized the primitive life; *Melville's Quarrel with God* (Princeton, N.J., 1952), p. 51.

10. Herman Melville, *Omoo,* eds. Harrison Hayford, Hershel Parker, G. Thomas Tanselle (Evanston and Chicago, 1968), p. 46 (XII).

11. Ibid., pp. 116-18. (XXXI).

12. Ibid., p. 132 (XXXIV).

13. Ibid., p. 110 (XXIX).

14. *White Jacket,* pp. 98-99 (XIX); cf. Rosenberry on the puns about the white jacket, *Melville and the Comic Spirit,* p. 45.

15. *White Jacket,* p. 10 (III).
16. Ibid., p. 205 (XL).
17. Ibid., p. 27 (VI).
18. Ibid., p. 35 (VII).
19. Ibid., p. 259 (XLIX).
20. Ibid., p. 245 (XLVI).
21. Ibid., p. 333 (LXIII).
22. Ibid., p. 322 (LXIII).
23. Ibid., pp. 313-14 (LXI).
24. Ibid., pp. 147-48 (XXVIII).
25. Ibid., p. 173 (XXXIV).
26. Ibid., pp. 366-71 (LXX).
27. Ibid., pp. 230-31 (XLIV).
28. Ibid., pp. 57-58 (XII).
29. Ibid., p. 204 (XXXIX).
30. Ibid., pp. 500-504 (XCIII-XCIV).
31. Herman Melville, *Redburn* (London, 1922), p. 379 (LVIII).
32. Ibid., p. 356 (LV).
33. Ibid., p. 323 (XLIX).
34. Herman Melville, *Mardi* (London, 1922), I, 36 (IX).
35. Rosenberry thought this mixture of tone something of a fault. Melville seemed to him to be trying and failing to combine the Swiftian method of satire with the solemnly allegorical method of Bunyan; *Melville and the Comic Spirit,* p. 69.
36. *Mardi,* I, 134 (XXXV).
37. Ibid., II, 356-59 (LXXXI).
38. Ibid., I, 3 (I).
39. Ibid., I, 193 (LIV).
40. Ibid., I, 45-49 (XIII).
41. Ibid., I, 14-16 (III).
42. Ibid., I, 9-10 (II).
43. Ibid., II, 376 (LXXXIV).
44. Ibid., II, 127 (XXXI).
45. Ibid., II, 42 (XI).
46. Ibid., II, 56 (XVI).
47. Ibid., II, 379 (LXXXIV).
48. Ibid., II, 400 (XCI).
49. Ibid., I, 47 (XIII).
50. Ibid., II, 352 (LXXX).
51. Ibid., II, 299-301 (LXXI).
52. Ibid., II, 312 (LXXIII).
53. The same passage Hemingway used to set the tone for a book about *nada.*
54. *Mardi,* I, 277 (LXXVIII).
55. Ibid., II, 315 (LXXIV).
56. Ibid., II, 380 (LXXXV).

57. Lawrance Thompson suggested that Babbalanja's reason has slipped and his electing to stay in Serenia is a conversion to a ludicrous faith similar to the Calvinism that Melville had been attacking throughout the book. Actually, the contemplators of Alma's life are similar to primitive Christians, and Serenia represents what Melville thought Christianity ought to be. Babbalanja's conversion is absurd but not condemned as Thompson suggested. *Melville's Quarrel with God,* p. 65.

58. *Moby-Dick,* p. 508 (CXXIII).

59. Ibid., pp. 414-15 (XCIV).

60. Ibid., p. 564 (CXXXV).

61. Hugh W. Hetherington, *Melville's Reviewers* (Chapel Hill, N.C., 1961), pp. 202-204.

62. *Spirit of the Times,* XXI (December 6, 1851), 494; see John F. McDermott, "The *Spirit of the Times* Reviews *Moby Dick,*" *New England Quarterly,* XXX (September, 1957), 392-95; and John T. Flanagan, "The *Spirit of the Times* Reviews Melville," *Journal of English and Germanic Philology,* LXIV (January, 1965), 57-64.

63. *Moby-Dick,* p. 326 (LXXIII).

64. Ibid., p. 372 (LXXXV).

65. Ibid., pp. 393-96 (LXXXIX).

66. Ibid., pp. 466-67 (CVIII).

67. Ibid., p. 519 (CXXVII).

68. Ibid., pp. 386-87 (LXXXVII).

69. Ibid., p. 477 (CX).

70. See note 567.2, *Moby-Dick,* p. 831.

71. Herman Melville, *Pierre,* ed. Henry A. Murray (New York, 1949), p. 357 (Bk. XXII, sec. 3).

72. Ibid., p. 6 (Bk. I, sec. 2). See Jesse Bier, *The Rise and Fall of American Humor* (New York, 1968), p. 380; as Bier argues, Melville was never incidentally humorous, and he took his ironies seriously.

73. *Pierre,* p. 14 (Bk. I, sec. 4).

74. Ibid., p. 21 (Bk. I, sec. 6).

75. Ibid., pp. 363-66 (Bk. XXIII, sec. 2).

76. Rosenberry, *Melville and the Comic Spirit,* pp. 159-61.

77. *Pierre,* p. 49 (Bk III, sec 1), and p. 98 (Bk. IV, sec. 5).

78. Ibid., p. 194 (sec. 1).

79. Ibid., pp. 200-201 (Bk. IX, sec. 4).

80. Ibid., pp. 410-11 (Bk. XXVI, sec. 1).

81. Ibid., p. 341 (Bk. XXI, sec. 2); cf. Rosenberry, *Melville and the Comic Spirit,* pp. 166-67.

82. *Pierre,* p. 250 (Bk. XIV, sec. 3).

83. Ralph Waldo Emerson, *Complete Works,* VIII (Boston and New York, 1904), 157-74.

84. Cf. discussions on Melville's reading of Emerson and Thoreau in Merton M. Sealts, Jr., *Melville's Reading: A Check-List of Books Owned and Borrowed* (Cambridge, Mass., 1950); Elizabeth Foster's edition of *The*

Confidence-Man, pp. 351-54; and Egbert S. Oliver, "Melville's Picture of Emerson and Thoreau in *The Confidence-Man,*" *College English,* VIII (November, 1946), 61-72.

85. Letter to Evert Duyckinck, March 3, 1849, in *The Letters of Herman Melville,* eds. Merrell R. Davis and William H. Gilman (New Haven, Conn., 1960), pp. 78-79.

86. See Eleanor Melville Metcalf, *Herman Melville: Cycle and Epicycle* (Cambridge, Mass., 1953), p. 91; Paul Smith, "*The Confidence-Man* and the Literary World of New York," *Nineteenth-Century Fiction,* XVI (March, 1962), 330; and Foster in *The Confidence-Man,* pp. 353-54.

87. Cf. Thompson, *Melville's Quarrel with God,* p. 297.

88. Three excellent studies of the educative function of the Confidence-Man as light-bringer are Foster's discussion in the edition I am using here; H. Bruce Franklin's introduction in his edition, the Bobbs-Merrill paperback (Indianapolis and New York, 1967); and Leon F. Seltzer, "Camus's Absurd and the World of Melville's *Confidence-Man,*" *PMLA,* LXXXII (March, 1967), 14-27.

89. I am here disagreeing with Seltzer that "the whole technique" of this book "is designed to betray the futility of hope," "Camus's Absurd and the World of Melville's *Confidence-Man,*" p. 26.

90. Cf. Foster, pp. 290-91; Franklin, p. 4, n. 8.

91. *The Confidence-Man,* pp. 2-5 (I). The edition whose pages I cite is Foster's, but I am indebted to Franklin for some annotations which go beyond Foster's, and I mention those separately.

92. Ibid., pp. 9-18 (III). In response to the classic question of whether or not Black Guinea is actually the Confidence-Man, one can answer only that there is plenty of evidence on both sides. I believe that all the avatars of the Confidence-Man are the same man and that any other confidence man who appears on the scene at the same time as one of the main avatars is one of the many lesser confidence men of the world of the *Fidèle.* I also believe, however, that Melville worked very hard to force us to take this on sheer faith.

93. Ibid., p. 15 (III); see Franklin, p. 22, n. 15.

94. *The Confidence-Man,* pp. 27-30 (V).

95. Ibid., p. 53 (IX).

96. Ibid., p. 282 (XLV); see Franklin, p. 345, n. 33.

97. Counterfeit detectors were actually published by counterfeiters to match their bogus money. See Ted N. Weissbuch, "A Note on the Confidence-Man's Counterfeit Detector," *Emerson Society Quarterly,* no. 19 (1960), 16-18; Franklin, p. 342, n. 29.

98. *The Confidence-Man,* p. 77 (XIV) and n. 77.14; cf. Franklin, p. 95, n. 5.

99. *The Confidence-Man,* pp. 82-85 (XV).

100. Franklin, p. 104, n. 10.

101. *The Confidence-Man,* p. 90 (XVI).

102. Ibid., p. 89 (XVI); Franklin, p. 109, n. 12.

103. *The Confidence-Man,* p. 93 (XVI) and n. 93.34; Foster points out that this Biblical verse was a slogan of the New England Transcendentalists.

104. Ibid., p. 123 (XXI).

105. Ibid., p. 137 (XXII).

106. Ibid., p. 146 (XXII).

107. Ibid., p. 185 (XXIX) and n. 185.23.

108. Ibid., p. 210 (XXXIV).

109. Ibid., p. 211 (XXXV).

110. An additional irony here is that Winsome has quoted an Apocryphal text, Ecclesiasticus 12: 13; see Foster, n. 214.17.

111. *The Confidence-Man,* pp. 213-16 (XXXVI).

112. Ibid., p. 259 (XLII).

113. Ibid., p. 285 (XLV); Franklin, p. 349, n. 40.

114. For a summary discussion of the wry irony of the story, which has often been noted by critics, see Herman Melville, *Billy Budd, Sailor,* eds. Harrison Hayford and Merton M. Sealts, Jr. (Chicago, 1962), p. 27.

115. Ibid., pp. 124-25 (XXVI).

116. Ibid., p. 130 (XXIX).

117. Melville's selection of the *Athée* was the result of some deliberation; his original choice, *Directory,* was not transferred from notes to manuscript. See *Billy Budd,* note to leaf 336, p. 199.

v · *The Prisoner at the Window: Mark Twain*

1. Samuel Clemens, *The Writings of Mark Twain,* XVI (New York and London, c. 1911), 146 (XVIII). This is one of the twenty-five volumes of the Author's National Edition, a more readily available text than the "Definitive Edition" (37 vols., New York, 1923-1925), which is actually no more definitive. Pagination varies in different printings of the Author's National Edition; as usual, chapter numbers are included here to guide the reader using another edition.

2. Albert Bigelow Paine, *Mark Twain: A Biography* (New York, 1912), p. 1238; cf. John S. Tuckey's introduction to the story in *Mark Twain's Which Was the Dream?* (Berkeley and Los Angeles, 1967), p. 431. The *Hamlet* fragment is in *Mark Twain's Satires & Burlesques,* ed. Franklin R. Rogers (Berkeley and Los Angeles, 1967), pp. 49-87.

3. An excellent recent book on the seriousness of Twain's humor is James M. Cox, *Mark Twain: The Fate of Humor* (Princeton, 1966).

4. *A Connecticut Yankee,* p. 151 (XVIII).

5. Samuel Clemens, *My Dear Bro., A Letter from Samuel Clemens to His Brother Orion,* ed. Frederick Anderson (Berkeley, 1961), p. 6; cf. Cox, *Mark Twain: The Fate of Humor,* p. 33.

6. Cox, *Mark Twain: The Fate of Humor,* pp. 23-24; cf. Justin Kaplan, *Mr. Clemens and Mark Twain* (New York, 1966).

7. Clemens, *Writings*, I, xxxvii; hereafter volume numbers indicate the volume numbering of *Innocents Abroad* only, not *Writings*.

8. *Innocents Abroad*, I, 183 (XIV).

9. Ibid., I, 206-207 (XVI).

10. Ibid., I, 337 (XXV).

11. Ibid., II, 153 (XII).

12. *Roughing It* occupies Volumes VII and VIII of Clemens, *Writings;* hereafter volume numbers indicate the volume numbering of *Roughing It.* The mosquito yarn is in *Roughing It*, I, 22 (II), and Mrs. Wagner's take-apart body is described in II, 122-23 (XII).

13. *Roughing It*, I, 297 (XXXVIII).

14. Volume IX of Clemens, *Writings*, 69 (VII).

15. *Life on the Mississippi*, pp. 71-72 (VIII).

16. Ibid., pp. 116-18 (XIV).

17. Volume XIII of Clemens, *Writings*, 32 (III).

18. *Huckleberry Finn*, p. 53 (VII).

19. I am indebted to W. R. Moses's ingenious comparison of Dante's *Inferno* and *Huckleberry Finn*, "The Pattern of Evil in *Adventures of Huckleberry Finn*," *The Georgia Review*, XIII (Summer, 1959), 161-66.

20. *Huckleberry Finn*, p. 287 (XXXII).

21. Ibid., pp. 129-30 (XVI).

22. Ibid., p. 160 (XVIII).

23. Ibid., p. 163 (XIX).

24. *A Connecticut Yankee*, p. 14.

25. Ibid, p. 25 (II).

26. Ibid., pp. 162-66 (XX).

27. Ibid., pp. 143-44 (XVIII).

28. Cf. Henry Nash Smith, *Mark Twain's Fable of Progress* (New Brunswick, N.J., 1964), pp. 107-108. Smith concludes that Twain's proclamation of a doctrine of fallibility through a protagonist with whom he identified "reveals an absolute despair." He also pointed out that *A Connecticut Yankee* was but one effort of many after *Huckleberry Finn* to demonstrate "that, as the dying Yankee believed, the world is too absurd to be anything but a dream." I find this an impeccable judgment.

29. Tuckey, *Which Was the Dream?* pp. 1-2, and *Letters from the Earth*, ed. Bernard DeVoto (New York, 1962), pp. 284-86.

30. Quoted by Tuckey, *Which Was the Dream?* p. 17.

31. Quoted from the Mark Twain Papers, University of California, Berkeley, by Tuckey, *Which Was the Dream?* p. 2.

32. Kaplan, *Mr. Clemens and Mark Twain*, pp. 340-41.

33. Samuel Clemens, *The Love Letters of Mark Twain*, ed. Dixon Wecter (New York, 1949), p. 312; cf. Tuckey in *Which Was the Dream?* p. 5.

34. Clemens, *Which Was the Dream?* p. 57.

35. Samuel Clemens and William Dean Howells, *Letters*, eds. Henry Nash Smith and William M. Gibson (Cambridge, Mass., 1960), pp. 675-76; cited by Tuckey, *Which Was the Dream?* p. 16.

36. The date is March 19, the birthday of the older girl, Jessie, who is eight. Mark Twain's daughter Susy was born March 19, 1872. See Tuckey, *Which Was the Dream?* p. 102, n. 9.

37. Clemens, "The Great Dark," *Which Was the Dream?* p. 104.

38. Ibid., pp. 122-23.

39. DeVoto in *Letters*, pp. 284-86, and Tuckey in *Which Was the Dream?* pp. 18-19.

40. Clemens, "The Great Dark," *Which Was the Dream?* p. 150.

41. William M. Gibson, ed., *Mark Twain's Mysterious Stranger Manuscripts* (Berkeley and Los Angeles, 1969), p. 1. Tuckey traced the complicated evolution of the book in *Mark Twain and Little Satan* (West Lafayette, Ind., 1963).

42. Quoted by Gibson in *Mysterious Stranger Manuscripts*, p. 30; cf. Tuckey, *Which Was the Dream?* p. 24.

43. Clemens, *Mysterious Stranger Manuscripts*, pp. 404-405; see note 403.17. Cf. Tuckey, *Mark Twain and Little Satan*, p. 74.

44. Tuckey, *Mark Twain and Little Satan*, p. 81.

45. Clemens, "Three Thousand Years Among the Microbes," *Which Was the Dream?* p. 437.

46. Ibid., p. 447.

47. Ibid., p. 446.

VI · *The Prime Maniacal Risibility: William Faulkner*

1. *Faulkner in the University*, eds. Frederick L. Gwynn and Joseph L. Blotner (Charlottesville, Va., 1959), p. 39.

2. The uninitiated among my students invariably seem to respond first in horror to *As I Lay Dying*, then develop a sense of the humor of the book after a brave classmate has said something like "I may be crazy, but I think this book is funny." Some students are embarrassed to admit they laughed.

3. *Lion in the Garden*, eds. James B. Meriwether and Michael Millgate (New York, 1968), p. 253.

4. William Faulkner, *Light in August* (New York, 1950 [Modern Library reprint of 1932 edition]), p. 405 (XIX).

5. William Faulkner, *Sartoris* (New York, 1929), p. 380 (Part V, sec. 3).

6. Cf. Warren Beck's treatment of the Snopes trilogy, *Man in Motion* (Madison, Wisc., 1961). Beck has shown that Faulkner's conceptual power expresses life as motion which evokes values. A similar thesis is extended to all of Faulkner's major fiction by Richard P. Adams in *Faulkner: Myth and Motion* (Princeton, 1968).

7. Frederick J. Hoffman wrote that the rhetoric of this passage in the Nobel Prize speech is effective but entirely unclear as an instrument of understanding literature. I believe the statement is clear: the artist's

talking generates values. See *Faulkner: Three Decades of Criticism*, eds. Hoffman and Olga W. Vickery (East Lansing, Mich., 1960), p. 30.

8. Meriwether and Millgate, *Lion in the Garden*, p. 280.

9. Ibid., pp. 70-71.

10. Gwynn and Blotner, *Faulkner in the University*, p. 5.

11. Meriwether and Millgate, *Lion in the Garden*, p. 73.

12. Gwynn and Blotner, *Faulkner in the University*, p. 26.

13. Faulkner was emphatically not the "naturalistic monster" his earliest and severest critics thought him to be. For a review of this early misjudgment, see Hoffman's introduction to *Three Decades of Criticism*.

14. Meriwether and Millgate, *Lion in the Garden*, p. 223.

15. Ibid., p. 255.

16. Ibid., p. 71.

17. William Faulkner, "Delta Autumn," *Go Down, Moses* (New York, 1942), p. 350.

18. William Faulkner, "The Old People," *Go Down, Moses*, p. 184 (II).

19. Gywnn and Blotner, *Faulkner in the University*, p. 27.

20. Hoffman reviews serious, cynical, and satirical critical responses to the vague Christ symbolism in Faulkner in *Three Decades of Criticism*, pp. 32-38. Edwin M. Moseley is one of the few scholars who has tentatively guessed that the imitation of Christ in Joe Christmas is some kind of colossal Faulknerian joke; see *Pseudonyms of Christ in the Modern Novel* (Pittsburgh, 1962), p. 138. See also Richard B. Hauck, "The Comic Christ and the Modern Reader," *College English*, XXXI (Feb., 1970), 498-506.

21. Gwynn and Blotner, *Faulkner in the University*, p. 85.

22. I cannot agree with Jesse Bier that *The Reivers* is Faulkner's *The Tempest* or that the mudhole scene compares to Huck Finn's smallpox trick. There is an essential difference: no genuine problem of survival and morality is involved in *The Reivers*. See *The Rise and Fall of American Humor* (New York, 1968), pp. 347-53.

23. William Faulkner, *Sartoris*, pp. 234-35 (Part IV, sec. 4).

24. Gwynn and Blotner, *Faulkner in the University*, p. 61.

25. William Faulkner, *The Town* (New York, 1957), p. 1 (I).

26. Gwynn and Blotner, *Faulkner in the University*, p. 2.

27. Faulkner's idea of motion as meaning was not unambivalent: "At times it seemed that [the mule, John Henry, and Bayard] were traveling backward, that they would crawl terrifically past the same tree or telephone pole time after time; and it seemed to [Bayard] that the three of them and the rattling wagon and the two beasts were caught in a senseless treadmill: a motion without progress, forever and to no escape." *Sartoris*, p. 212 (Part III, sec. 4).

28. Gwynn and Blotner, *Faulkner in the University*, p. 29.

29. William Faulkner, *The Hamlet* (New York, 1940), pp. 3-6 (Bk. I, ch. 1).

30. Olga Vickery, *The Novels of William Faulkner* (Baton Rouge, 1964), p. 168.

31. *The Hamlet,* p. 19 (Bk. I, ch. 1).

32. Ibid., pp. 23-24 (Bk. I, ch. 1).

33. Ibid., pp. 29-44 (Bk. I, ch. 2).

34. *The Town,* p. 3 (I).

35. *The Hamlet,* p. 372 (Bk. IV, ch. 2).

36. Ibid, p. 280 (Bk. IV, ch. 1).

37. Ibid., p. 83 (Bk. I, ch. 3).

38. Ibid., p. 191 (Bk. III, ch. 1).

39. Ibid., p. 166 (Bk. III, ch. 1).

40. Ibid., p. 167 (Bk. III, ch. 1).

41. *The Town,* p. 146 (VIII).

42. Ibid., pp. 315-18 (XX).

43. Ibid., p. 102 (VI).

44. Ibid., p. 70 (III).

45. Ibid., pp. 358-59 (XXIV).

46. William Faulkner, *Intruder in the Dust* (New York, 1948), p. 201 (IX).

47. Ibid., p. 247 (XI).

48. Gwynn and Blotner, *Faulkner in the University,* p. 33.

49. William Faulkner, *The Mansion* (New York, 1959), p. 39 (Bk. I, ch. 1).

50. Ibid., p. 6 (Bk. I, ch. 1).

51. Ibid., p. 86 (Bk. I, ch. 4).

52. Ibid., p. 101 (Bk. I, ch. 5).

53. Ibid., pp. 435-36 (Bk. III, ch. 18).

54. *The Hamlet,* p. 52 (Bk. I, ch. 3).

55. William Faulkner, *As I Lay Dying* (New York, 1964), p. 74 (the chapters are not numbered).

56. Meriwether and Millgate, *Lion in the Garden,* p. 254.

57. *As I Lay Dying,* p. 250.

58. Ibid., p. 228.

59. Ibid., pp. 204-205.

60. Ibid., pp. 243-44. James E. Miller, Jr., has also described Darl's "insanity" as the ability to perceive real absurdities; furthermore, "When last seen, Darl has become double, and can even see the absurdity of his own incarceration." See *Quests Surd and Absurd* (Chicago, 1967), pp. 57-58.

VII · *These Fruitful Fruitless Odysseys: John Barth*

1. John Enck, "John Barth: An Interview," *Wisconsin Studies in Contemporary Literature,* VI (Winter-Spring, 1965), 12.

2. Ibid., p. 4.

3. Ibid., p. 8.

4. Ibid., p. 11.

5. John Barth, *Lost in the Funhouse* (Garden City, 1968), p. 140.

6. Ibid., p. 153.

7. Ibid., p. 130.

8. Ibid., pp. 3-6.

9. Ibid., p. 12. This story shows some startling resemblances to Twain's "The Great Dark" and "Three Thousand Years Among the Microbes." The night-sea journey was discussed extensively by Jung, who saw it as part of a cycle of quest myths, all of which reflect the longing to attain rebirth through a return to the womb.

10. Ibid., p. 73.

11. Ibid., p. 89.

12. Ibid., p. 95. One of the writers Barth admires most is Jorge Luis Borges, one of whose works is titled *Labyrinths*. Speaking of this book, Barth said, "That brings us to his favorite image of all, the labyrinth. . . . A labyrinth, after all, is a place in which, ideally, all the possibilities of choice (of direction, in this case) are embodied, and . . . must be exhausted before one reaches the heart. Where, mind, the Minotaur waits with two final possibilities: defeat and death, or victory and freedom." See "The Literature of Exhaustion," *The Atlantic*, CCXX (August, 1967), 29-34.

13. *Lost in the Funhouse*, p. 105.

14. Ibid., pp. 111-13.

15. John Barth, "Anonymiad," *Lost in the Funhouse*, p. 199.

16. Ibid., p. 183.

17. *Lost in the Funhouse*, p. 97.

18. John Barth, *The Floating Opera* (Garden City, New York, 1967), p. 1 (I).

19. Ibid., p. 176 (XX).

20. Ibid., p. 7 (I).

21. Ibid., p. 100 (X).

22. Ibid., p. 168 (XVIII).

23. Ibid., p. 51 (V).

24. Ibid., pp. 109-10 (XI).

25. Ibid., p. 124 (XIII).

26. Ibid., p. 130 (XIV).

27. Ibid., p. 171 (XIX).

28. Ibid., pp. 199-203 (XXII).

29. Ibid., pp. 223, 228 (XXV).

30. *The Floating Opera* (1956), Chapters XXVIII and XXIX.

31. *The Floating Opera* (1967), pp. 246-50 (XXVIII).

32. John Barth, *The End of the Road* (New York, 1967), p. 94 (VII).

33. Ibid., pp. 65-66 (V).

34. Ibid., pp. 122-23 (X).

35. Ibid., p. 69 (VI).

36. Ibid., pp. 76-84 (VI).

37. Ibid., p. 188 (XII).

38. For a detailed account of the differences between Barth's "history"

and the "real" history, see Alan Holder, " 'What Marvelous Plot . . . Was Afoot?' History in Barth's *The Sot-Weed Factor,*" *American Quarterly,* XX (Fall, 1968), 596-604. Holder points out that, while Barth's political characters all fluctuate from villain to hero, the archives themselves are ambiguous as to the morality of their various activities. The one thing I do not agree with in Holder's excellent article is his assertion that Burlingame believes Maryland's lack of history allows him to subordinate goals to action. Burlingame's absurd philosophy allows him to argue that there are no goals and that meaning lies only in action.

39. See Lawrence C. Wroth, "The Maryland Muse by Ebenezer Cooke," *Proceedings of the American Antiquarian Society,* XLIV, pt. 2 n.s. (October, 1934), 267-335; includes a facsimile of the poem.

40. John Barth, *The Sot-Weed Factor* (Garden City, 1960), p. 164 (Part II, ch. 7).

41. Ibid., p. 330 (Part II, ch. 22).

42. Ibid., p. 25 (Part I, ch. 3).

43. Ibid., p. 146 (Part II, ch. 5).

44. Ibid., p. 345 (Part II, ch. 23).

45. Ibid., pp. 455-66 (Part II, ch. 32).

46. Ibid., pp. 128-29 (Part II, ch. 3).

47. John Barth, *Giles Goat-Boy* (Garden City, 1966), p. 383 (Vol. I, Third Reel, ch. 7).

48. Robert Scholes, *The Fabulators* (New York, 1967), p. 135.

49. *Giles Goat-Boy,* p. 7 (Vol. I, First Reel, ch. 1).

50. Ibid., p. 313 (Vol. I, Third Reel, ch. 4).

51. Ibid., p. 708 (Posttape).

52. Ibid., p. 650 (Vol. II, Third Reel, ch. 1).

53. Ibid., p. 679 (Vol. II, Third Reel, ch. 5).

VIII · *A Heritage of Corpses*

1. James E. Miller, Jr., uses this quotation (from *Moby-Dick,* Chapter XLIX) as a touchstone to set the tone for *Quests Surd and Absurd* (Chicago, 1967).

2. Ellen Douglass Leyburn, *Strange Alloy* (Chapel Hill, 1968).

3. Ibid., p. 171.

4. Ibid., p. 148.

5. See Bickford Sylvester, " 'They Went through this Fiction Every Day': Informed Illusion in *The Old Man and the Sea,*" *Modern Fiction Studies,* XII (Winter, 1966-1967), 473-77, and Carlos Baker, *Hemingway: The Writer as Artist* (Princeton, 1963 [3d ed.]), p. 273.

6. Professor Miller listed as modern American writers having absurd potential of one kind or another James Jones, Norman Mailer, Carson McCullers, Truman Capote, Jack Kerouac, James Baldwin, James Purdy, John

Hawkes, Terry Southern, William Burroughs, Ralph Ellison, William Styron, Bernard Malamud, Salinger, Flannery O'Connor, Bellow, Wright Morris, John Updike, Reynold Price, Philip Roth, J. P. Donleavy, John Barth, Joseph Heller, Ken Kesey, and Thomas Pynchon. David D. Galloway studied Updike, Styron, Bellow, and Salinger in *The Absurd Hero* (Austin, Texas, 1966). Jonathan Baumback discussed R. P. Warren and Edward Lewis Wallant in *The Landscape of Nightmare* (New York, 1965), a book which demonstrates the literary reflection of the modern feeling that "madness daily passes for sanity" in this world. Joseph J. Waldmeir, however, felt that only two American novelists since the war had seriously tried to write an absurd novel; see "Two Novelists of the Absurd: Heller and Kesey," *Wisconsin Studies in Contemporary Literature*, V (Autumn, 1964), 192-204.

7. Saul Bellow, *Herzog* (New York, 1961), pp. 160, 184, 340.

8. Cf. Don Hausdorff, "Thomas Pynchon's Multiple Absurdities," *Wisconsin Studies in Contemporary Literature*, VII (Autumn, 1966), 258-69.

9. Richard Brautigan, *Trout Fishing in America* (San Francisco, 1967), pp. 72, 85.

10. Philip Roth, *Portnoy's Complaint* (New York, 1969), p. 112.

11. Quoted by Geoffrey Wolff in "Gothic City" (review of *Them*), *Newsweek*, September 29, 1969, p. 121C.

12. See Stephen A. Black, "The Claw of the Sea-Puss: James Thurber's Sense of Experience," *Wisconsin Studies in Contemporary Literature*, V (Autumn, 1964), 222-36.

13. R. W. B. Lewis, *Trials of the Word* (New Haven, 1965).

14. Kurt Vonnegut, Jr., *Cat's Cradle* (New York, 1963), p. 135.

15. Ibid., p. 231.

INDEX

absurd, the, Camus' essay on meaninglessness and, xi, 3-14; cheerful nihilism as reaction to, xi, 3-14, 237-42; in comic fiction of the frontier, 40-76; conscious and unconscious, 15-21; creation as a counter to, xi, 3-14, 237-42; defined, 4; humor of, in American fiction, xi-xiii, 8-13; and Puritan perplexity, 21-25; *see also* American absurdists

Adam, 5, 17-18

Adams, Henry, 152

Adventures of Huckleberry Finn, The, 12, 66, 145-51, 240

ambiguity, Barth's, 203; Henry James as master of, 239-40; in Melville, 77-79, 238

"Ambrose His Mark," 207-8

American absurdists, and American humor, xi-xiii, 8-14, 237-45; Barth's complexities, 201-36; cheerful nihilism of, xi-xiii, 8-13, 237; contemporary as without hope or confidence, 242-45; Edwards and the solution of being, 25-35; faith and confidence in, 15-39; Faulkner's maniacal risibility, 167-200; Franklin's confidence, 32-39; historical summary of, 237-42; living authors, 241-45; Melville's ambiguities and ambivalences, 77-132; native writers of the frontier, 40-76; Puritans, 21-25; Twain's nihilism, 133-66

Aristotle, 124

As I Lay Dying, 168, 176-78, 195-200

authors of absurd fiction. *See* American absurdists

Barth, John, 201-36; absurdity of, 9; ambiguities of, 244; "cheerful nihilism" phrase coined by, 8; *The End of the Road,* 217-22; *The Floating Opera,* 210-16; fun derived from creating the absurd, 201-9; *Giles Goat-Boy,* 230-36; *Lost in the Funhouse,* 203-9; mentioned, xii, 13; mythotherapy, 219-22; and Reality, 202-3; *The Sot-Weed Factor,* 222-30; sperm-narrator of "Night-Sea Journey," 204-7

Barthelme, Donald, 243

Beatty, Charles, 35

being, Jonathan Edwards on, 25-32

Bellow, Saul, 241-42

"Big Bear of Arkansas, The," 56-60

Billy Budd, 130-32, 238

"Birthmark, The," 239

"black humor," 242

Blithedale Romance, The, 239

"Blue-Jay Yarn," 54-56

Bouvard, Loïc, 172

Brautigan, Richard, 243

Brown, Charles Brockden, 243

Calvinistic theory, 16-18

Camus, Albert, Barth's comment on, 201; Faulkner compared with, 172; meaninglessness and the absurd in Sisyphus essay, xi, 3-14; on *Moby-Dick,* 78-79, 104

Catch-22, 12, 240

Cat's Cradle, 244

cheerful nihilism, of American humorists, xi, 3-14, 237-45; derivation of phrase, 8

Chesterton, G. K., xiii

Christ, Franklin's imitation of, 33-34; symbolism in Faulkner, 176-77

(265

Index